Work Changes Gender

Results of the Research Project
Work Changes Gender –
New Forms of Work, New Orientations for Men's Lives,
Opportunities for Gender Equality
Funded by the Fifth Framework Programme (FP5) of the European Union

Research partners
Dissens e.V., Berlin – Germany (Coordination)
Bar Ilan University, Ramat Gan – Israel
Catholic University for Applied Sciences Berlin (KHSB) – Germany
Männerberatung (Men's Counseling Center), Graz – Austria
Universitat Autonoma de Barcelona – Spain
University of National and World Economy, Sofia – Bulgaria
Work Research Institute, Oslo – Norway

Project management
Coordination:
Ralf Puchert, Stephan Höyng and Marc Gärtner, Berlin
Management of the economic surveys:
Jacques Silber and Shoshana Neumann, Ramat Gan
Management of the organisational research survey:
Øystein Gullvåg Holter, Oslo
Management of the socio-psychological survey:
Christian Scambor, Graz

Co-funding and support
Austrian Federal Ministry for Education, Research and Culture
Styrian Governmental Department for Economy, Finances and
Telecommunication
Styrian Governmental Department for Science and Research
Bulgarian Ministry of Labour and Social Policy
Institute for Trade Union and Social Research, Sofia
The Research Council of Norway
Catholic University of Applied Sciences Berlin
German Federal Ministry for Education and Research: Das dieser Ver-
öffentlichung zugrundeliegende Vorhaben wurde mit Mitteln des Bundes-
ministeriums für Bildung und Forschung unter dem Förderkennzeichen
01 FP 0140 gefördert.

Editorial coordination
Marc Gärtner
With Klaus Schwerma, Brian Frank, Mart Busche and Xavier Ramos

Ralf Puchert
Marc Gärtner
Stephan Höyng (eds.)

Work Changes Gender

Men and Equality in the Transition
of Labour Forms

Preface by Michael Kimmel

Authors:
Paco Abril, Marc Gärtner, Sigtona Halrynjo,
Øystein Gullvåg Holter, Stephan Höyng, Ralf Puchert,
Vera Riesenfeld, Christian Scambor, Elli Scambor,
Klaus Schwerma

With:
Yair Amichai-Hamburger, Margarita Atanassova,
Margareta Kreimer, Selma Therese Lyng, Shoshana Neumann,
Xavier Ramos, Jacques Silber, Violeta Velkova

Barbara Budrich Publishers, Opladen 2005

A CIP catalogue record for this book is available from
Die Deutsche Bibliothek (The German Library)

© 2005 by Barbara Budrich Publishers, Opladen
       www.barbara-budrich.net

ISBN 3-938094-13-3   **paperback**
ISBN 3-938094-14-1   hardcover

Das Werk einschließlich aller seiner Teile ist urheberrechtlich geschützt. Jede Verwertung außerhalb der engen Grenzen des Urheberrechtsgesetzes ist ohne Zustimmung des Verlages unzulässig und strafbar. Das gilt insbesondere für Vervielfältigungen, Übersetzungen, Mikroverfilmungen und die Einspeicherung und Verarbeitung in elektronischen Systemen.

Die Deutsche Bibliothek – CIP-Einheitsaufnahme
Ein Titeldatensatz für die Publikation ist bei Der Deutschen Bibliothek erhältlich.

Verlag Barbara Budrich Barbara Budrich Publishers
Stauffenbergstr. 7. D-51379 Leverkusen Opladen, Germany

2963 London Wall. Bloomfield Hills. MI 48304. USA
www.barbara-budrich.net

Jacket illustration by disegno, Wuppertal, Germany – www.disenjo.de
Printed in Europe on acid-free paper by
DruckPartner Rübelmann, Hemsbach

Contents

Preface by Michael Kimmel 7

Editors' Preface 11

1.   Introduction 15
1.1   Basic Ideas and Objectives 15
1.2   Current State of Research on Masculinities 17
1.3   Structure of the Project 19

2.   Labour Market Changes and Gender 21
2.1   Trends in European Labour Markets 21
2.2   Labour Market Participation: Non-active Population and
      Unemployment 25
2.3   Changes in Forms of Employment 38
2.4   Gender Segregation 54
2.5   Working Biographies 64
2.6   Conclusions 67

3.   "We don't have anything like that here!" – Organisations,
      Men and Gender Equality 73
3.1   Gender and Organisations 73
3.2   Design and Method 75
3.3   Results: An Overview 78
3.4   Organisational Change 87
3.5   The Status of Domestic Work 100
3.6   The Costs of Equality 101
3.7   Concluding Remarks 103

4.   Male Job and Life Patterns: A Correspondence Analysis 105
4.1   Profile 105
4.2   The Contexts of Work Reduction 108
4.3   Four Adaptations 110

5.	Towards a New Positioning of Men	117
5.1	Introduction	117
5.2	Theories and Concepts	118
5.3	The Study: Overview	122
5.4	Models of Change	132
5.5	Diversity	134
5.6	Men and Caring: The Misplacement Model	142
5.7	General Models of Self-concept Change: SEMO and PROMO	160
5.8	Men and Changes	167
6.	Men are Gendered, not Standard: Scientific and Political Implications of the Results	175
6.1	Ways to Changes	176
6.2	Equality in Gender Relations and Masculinity Models	182
6.3	Closing Remarks	191
References		193

Preface

Michael Kimmel

"No man on his deathbed ever said he wished he'd spent less time with his family." It's a cliché, of course, but one that reveals an important insight. For decades, we've listened to men – and women! – complain that men work too hard, too long, and spend too little time with their families. Men say they want to spend more time with their families, if only they could. But it's hard to find the time. And who can afford the loss of income?

What is interesting these days is the increasing number of men who are "walking their talk," who are actually doing something different in their working lives to better accommodate their family lives.

A recent survey published in *Newsweek* found that while 21% of American men would sacrifice family time for a more exciting job opportunity and higher pay, more than three times as many (72%) said they would sacrifice those exciting job opportunities and higher pay for more time with their family. By far the single most common way for men to spend free time was hanging out with their family – more than hanging out with friends, working around the house, and playing golf combined. And another recent survey found that younger fathers are spending far more time with their families than in earlier generations and are increasingly opting for "Daddy Track" jobs.

While these and other data are encouraging, they provide only the broadest of outlines. The significant questions are not whether or not men are changing, but how they are changing? Which groups of men are changing, and in what directions? What are the variations among men in the scope of these changes? What is the relationship of these behavioural changes to attitudinal changes among men, especially in their relationships with women? And why would men be changing in the first place?

If men's family lives are changing so significantly, what relationship does that have with men's working lives – and, indeed, with the structure of the workplace? What is the impact on the workplace of these changes in men's family lives? And what is the impact on men's family lives of significant changes in the workplace?

The present volume is significant in many ways. It deepens studies carried out by the network CROME,[1] sponsored by the European Union, taking the reader inside the broad trends noted by that initial study. Like the CROME project, this report gathers a veritable "dream team" of empirical researchers from several different European countries who have begun to disentangle the strands of change in men's lives, examining the mutually reinforcing, or contradictory, strands of attitudes, behaviours, relationships and working situations. They offer the most comprehensive and sophisticated assessment to date of the ways contemporary European men are struggling to balance work and family commitments, and the consequent stresses and satisfaction that such a struggle inevitably brings.

A core insight in this project is that the changes in individual life patterns among men are as much a response to changing working conditions as they are the result of some shift in ideology about involved fatherhood. These workplace shifts – shorter working hours, less secure employment, more sporadic work biographies, and part-time working lives, and the like – are constraining to men's aspirations, but they also potentially free men up to spend more time with their families. As a result, the project engages in a difficult but illuminating dialectic: the impact of changing workplaces on masculinity, and the impact of a changing masculinity on the workplace.

Among some of the key empirical findings are:

- Men are becoming more receptive to women working, but that receptivity is greater in principle than in reality. Men continue to be ambivalent about women working.
- Men's concerns about work-family balance are driven at least as much by structural and institutional forces as they are by new attitudinal or ideological commitments.
- Part-time work among men is not a solution to the problem of men balancing work and family; indeed, it may be part of the problem of workplace inflexibility. The greater participation in part-time work does not necessarily lead to greater participation in child care. While part-time work may yield more flexibility, it requires active state policies to really enable healthy and satisfying work-life balance.
- "Men change when women change." It is largely the changing experiences and expectations of women that are the prime mover in changes among men. At the same time, there is some movement among men on their own, in response to their changing work environments, in addition to their relationships.
- "Men's caring relationships form the centres of change." Often children are central, but it may be other family members or partners. Men are

1   Critical Research on Men in Europe: The Social Problem and Societal Problematisation of Men and Masculinities. Research Network funded by the European Union Framework V.

more embedded in family and intimate life than we initially may have thought.
- Despite this, the "new man" model of masculinity fails to resonate for a sizeable majority of men. They are looking for flexibility, not transformation. They are looking for/developing "strategies to shape their own lives."
- There are "hidden structures" preventing equality by a male-bound work culture. Even if all the men in Europe awoke suddenly to find themselves fully committed to gender equality, egalitarian family lives and better balance between work and family, the structure of working life – its institutions, norms, cultures – would make such a transition particularly difficult.
- One of the chief problems with workplace culture is the centrality of overwork. There is widespread corporate/organisational rigidity laced with ever-expanding demands.
- Changes among men in this direction are not institutionally supported anywhere. The problem of change is individualised. If that is true, this is almost sure to stymie it. Individuation is a primary force to resist change, and it cleverly masquerades as exactly what change-seekers want: individual freedom, choices, flexibility.
- There are fairly easily discerned stages of institutional transformation. In the first stage, individual change (such as taking parental leave) is risky for male workers; in a second phase, increased numbers of men do so; and finally, the institution may begin to transform itself to even expect this behaviour.

Predictably, there are variations between different countries, among different economic sectors, and among men in different class locations. While predictable, some are revealing of the ways in which class, sector or national origin may over-determine individual efforts by men for social transformation.

However, two major findings stand out:

First, all the time-use studies suggest a convergence between women and men's wage work and family work patterns. There is far less gender division either in paid work or family work than at any previous time. This is critical. Not only does it disprove the notion that women and men are from different planets, but it also illustrates how women and men are actually capable of being allies in the struggles to find a coherent balance between work and family.

Second, this convergence is as likely to be because "work changes gender" as because "gender changes work." That is, despite the initiative of the study to observe how work changes gender, it is just as often the case that gender changes work.

This is, in part, a reflection of the inflexibility of workplaces, but it also suggests the partial success of the gender transformation signalled by the women's movement. Women have changed dramatically, in both attitudes and behaviours; and a "new woman" has been around so long that she is hardly even "new" anymore. But not only has the "new man" not emerged – he continues to lag behind women in the efforts to fully be transformed by new structural opportunities offered by the gender revolution among women (increased opportunities for part-time work, flexible hours, parental leave).

Structural workplace inflexibility is matched by an ideological inflexibility. Men who do seek to better balance work and family are still re-imagined as more "feminine" – weaker, less manly. They are accorded less respect, fewer opportunities, and lower status.

Yet there is hope. This research offers important evidence about how change can be achieved – indeed, it suggests that there are seams in an edifice that is already undergoing important changes. Family-friendly workplace policies need to be specifically designed to include men (like the "Daddy Days" of Nordic parental leave schemes). Where state actors and bureaucracies are disinclined to change, many private sector organisations have jumped into the breach.

Change in our working lives will not come easily or quickly. But if men truly want to live the lives they say they want to live – lives animated by close and intimate family experiences, with close relationships to their partners and their children – then they will continue to push up against the structural limits of workplace culture. Perhaps, when enough of us push, the door will begin to open a little wider.

New York, December 2004

Editors' Preface

Ralf Puchert, Marc Gärtner and Stephan Höyng

"Crisis can be a productive state. One has only to take the smack of catastrophe from it."

Max Frisch

Labour has become increasingly differentiated. In every European country, employment patterns have become very different from the traditional, normal labour conditions. In fact, less than 50% of the workforce in Europe now have a full-time, long-term job with a traditional employment contract: patterns of employment vary widely across Europe, but the same trends are visible everywhere. It is noteworthy that this development has, to a large extent, resulted in changes in the characteristics of the male labour force. Up to now it has clearly been more common for men than for women to work under traditional, standard conditions of employment. But in recent years, the number of men facing discontinuities in their working career or working part-time is constantly increasing, as does the number of women working full time.

Labour is a core part of masculinity and therefore changes in masculinities are connected to or dependent upon changes in working life. This link itself is in a period of transition and is possibly becoming less direct than before. In fact, two social processes are at work here: a dynamic of working life and a process of change in terms of inter-gender arrangements.

The guiding idea of this research was that in a process where economic structures and values are changing, one can also expect a modification of the relations between the genders. This should, sooner or later, lead to a redefinition of the position of men in society as well as of the perceptions men have of themselves. These developments offer an opportunity for improving the quality of life for both men and women. The "smack of catastrophe", however, can only be taken away, if insecurities and risks are not simply individualised, but embedded in a new social debate about equality and solidarity.

Gender studies and gender research have been going on now for about thirty years, yet the history of men's studies is even shorter. The social analysis of men and masculinities tends to be rather idealist if not morally coloured when the conditions of working life are not taken into account. To treat all of the mentioned connections, this research project combines economic, sociological and psychological approaches. The empirical analysis focuses on the individual and institutional conditions under which men are dealing with these new trends.

In some way, the initiative for carrying out this project was inspired by a survey conducted in the early 1990s, in which Dissens Institute analysed men's reactions to equality measures in Berlin public administration, asking under which conditions men put up with or even supported equality measures. One of the answers was that men who do not work full-time contribute structurally and individually to gender equality (Höyng et al. 1995, Höyng and Puchert 1998). Thus, part-time employment and non-standard contracts, which have increased in the past 20 years, assumed significant meaning for us, especially from the perspective of promoting gender equality.

"A life-enhancing time-culture" (*Lebensvolle Zeitkultur*) became the working title of the proposal that later turned into "Work Changes Gender." We wanted to clarify which conditions give rise to a situation where men could benefit from working less. We regarded the shift away from professional work as an equality-oriented step, which also offered personal opportunities. Furthermore, this shift was accompanied by the possibility of men assuming more non-professional responsibility.

We first looked outside the employment sphere for the resources in this increasing precariousness, namely at the expansion of the lifeworld (Lebenswelt) and personal opportunities of men. But we also had to recognise the increasing flexibility of working conditions for men mainly as a process of increasing uncertainty and an increasing reduction of social security. In the operating process in our international consortium it turned out, however, that in an international context there are also chances and opportunities for individuals amidst the risks of deregulation and neo-liberal cut-backs. Although risks are distributed to different degrees according to social positions, there are also new opportunities for self-determination arising from new forms of employment. Without ignoring the risks men face, this report aims to convey the structural and individual preconditions that facilitate good practise changes in gender-work relations.

Our study explores the area of Europe, which due to its cultural-historical differences, is economically and socially rather heterogeneous. The research consortium was constructed in full view of these social and gender-related differences in (and beyond) Europe:

– Norway, as a Scandinavian welfare state with a very high level of corporate structure and a comparatively rich tradition of gender equality, is an example of a trend in the material where new gender relations have a more independent impact both on working life and on men's personal relations. At The Work Research Institute in Oslo, Øystein G. Holter, Sigtona Halrynjo and Selma Therese Lyng focused on new results from organisation development and research, and especially on work partnership/domestic partnership reconciliation.

– Austria and Germany both show a high level of corporatist labour agreements and, with the exception of the former GDR, a tradition of male breadwinner family arrangements. Christian Scambor (Männerberatung/ Men's

Counselling Centre, Graz) and Klaus Schwerma (Dissens, Berlin) carried out the socio-psychological study, while Elli Scambor (Männerberatung) and Vera Riesenfeld (Dissens) focussed on organisational research, and Margareta Kreimer (University of Graz) on gender and economy. Stephan Höyng (Catholic University of Applied Sciences, Berlin); Ralf Puchert and Marc Gärtner (Dissens) coordinated different areas of the project.

–   Spain has a deep Roman-Catholic background, relatively late industrialisation and ongoing Mediterranean traditional family arrangements. The former south-western periphery has been taking big steps forward toward modernisation in the last decades and features some "booming" regions, the most advanced of which is perhaps Catalonian Barcelona. Research for Spain was carried out at the Universitat Autonoma de Barcelona, Xavier Ramos Morilla conducting the economic part, and Paco Abril Morales, the sociological part.

–   Eastern European transformation out of centralised socialism was undertaken by the University of National and World Economy, Sofia (Bulgaria), specifically by Margarita Atanassova (economy), and Violeta Velkova (sociology). Here we find a tension between huge economic problems, a socialist gender equality tradition in terms of labour and a very low discursive support of gender issues.

–   Israel, lying outside of Europe but closely linked to it, is a bridge between the West and the Middle East. The Jewish culture within Israel is also very differentiated. From Bar Ilan University, Ramat Gan, Shoshana Neumann and Jacques Silber contributed to the economic research. Yair Amichai-Hamburger did the socio-psychological part of the research.

This composition has turned out to be a good starting point for studying differences and the homogeneity/continuity of gender arrangements and models of masculinity between different cultures, as well as policies either aimed at or affecting gender relations.

In addition to being international, the consortium was also interdisciplinary, representing at least three focuses: economic (first stage), sociological (second stage) and psychological (third stage). These three ways of "looking at the world" were dealt with in regular joint meetings, because only such an interdisciplinary approach might allow the authors of this study to grasp the essence of the fundamental changes. The qualitative approach allows an access to the world of the attitudes, habitudes and feelings of men.

As coordinators, we strongly believe in the positive effect of this diversity. Competencies and resources from very different cultural, economic and academic backgrounds flowed together into a cooperation and synergy on the level of work structure and discussion.

Acknowledgements

The collaboration in the research consortium was determined by a highly collective process of planning, data collection and analysis. Thus, the texts finally written by the authors would not have been possible without the cooperation of all partners. In this respect, we had to strike a balance between the pragmatic, academic standard of personalised editor- and authorship and the rendition of collectivity and cooperation.

The editing work was carried out mainly by members of the coordinating team of Dissens Institute, Berlin, with the valuable editorial assistance and translations of Brian Frank.

The study was built on contributions, encouragement and support of many helping hands, friends and institutions.

The Fifth Research Framework Program of the EU funded the project. Virginia Vitorino brought very positive and reliable supervision skills to the project in her capacity as a scientific officer. The project was co-funded by the German Federal Ministry for Education and Research, the Austrian Federal Ministry for Education, Research and Culture, the Styrian Governmental Department for Economy, Finances and Telecommunication and the Styrian Governmental Department for Science and Research. Catholic University of Applied Sciences, Berlin, supported the project with personnel and material resources. Director Andreas Lob-Hüdepohl was a reliable and helpful cooperation partner.

Adrian Ziderman, Ramat Gan and Lalko Dulevski (Sofia) were valuable dialog partners and contributors.

Dissens Institute provided a relaxed work atmosphere for the coordination group, including discussions on many practical components of gender and masculinity topics. Ludger Jungnitz was a vital contributor to the writing of the research proposal, and without the support of Andrea von Marschall, many of our jobs would not have received co-funding. Wladimir Boger, Andreas Sander, Rachel Herweg, Mart Busche, Dag Schölper and Dirk Stöckigt were engaged in various important aspects of the project.

We would also like to thank many contributors for their invaluable help with interviews, translation, conference and other work: Galina Georgieva, Alfons Romero Diaz, Daniel Leal González, Pere Compte, Lola Gacía Sandoval, Oliver Geden, Fritz Reinbacher, Bernhard Könnecke, Fonka Grba, Christoph Paschedag, Jörg Meyer, Micha Scheunemann, Joachim Voitle, Christian Stiplosek, Gerhard Löffler, Maria Rock, Ina Mastnak-Winkler and Elisabeth Müller.

Most of all, we thank the men and the experts who participated in the interviews and were interested in our study. Considering that our topics were often new, sometimes surprising, one project finding stands out: the great interest and openness shown by those we contacted.

Berlin, December 2004

14

1. Introduction

Marc Gärtner and Stephan Höyng

> "In times of rapid change, men are hit in their Achilles heel: The central definition of a male life loses its basis when labour is more and more socially devalued or vanishes all together. The social cleavage between winners and losers of this process intensifies."
> Hans-Joachim Lenz (2001: 384, translated by the editors)

1.1 Basic Ideas and Objectives

The rapidity of change and its unpredictability are among the most important characteristics of contemporary production systems. As a consequence, the forms of employment in Europe are also experiencing radical changes. Current European work regimes are characterised, on the one hand, by a richer variety of lifestyles and by economically and socially beneficial developments; but on the other hand, there is growing insecurity, inconsistency and the risk of increased social marginalisation. Economically active individuals experience adverse pressures and uncertain outcomes. This has been accompanied by many changes in private life and gender relations. Therefore in working life as well as in the private sphere, men face demands which are more complex and less foreseeable than some years ago.

This research project explored the main features of the changes that are taking place at work in order to see the different ways male and female workers are affected and hence how these changes will ultimately have an impact on equality between the genders.

Standard Work is no Longer Normal

Labour is becoming increasingly heterogeneous, and types of employment, more and more diversified. There is a profound modification in the way individuals – in particular men – live.

Up to now, it has definitely been more common for men than for women to work under traditional conditions of employment: the standard employee has been male, had an unlimited labour contract, social security and worked full time. But in recent decades, two main developments have taken place that challenge this model: the end of Fordist regime of industrial economy and women's claims for economic and political power. The traditional patriarchal model of masculinity was thus confronted by the same crisis affecting the predominant model of work. (cf. Holter 2003a, Höyng and Puchert 1998).

15

As a consequence, the number of men facing discontinuities in their careers (or working part-time) is constantly increasing, while the number of women working full time is increasing. The inactivity rate of men and women is converging, as will be shown in the following chapter, and a large number of European males who are fit to work are now active in short term, fixed term, reduced or precarious forms of labour – or have no jobs at all. The male self-concept used to be based on labour ("the capacity to fill the breadwinner role was the key to masculinity") (Holter 2003a: 79), but a growing number of working biographies of men show discontinuity, insecurity, parallel jobs and unemployment. A good illustration is the city of Berlin, which in this respect, may lead the way in the Federal Republic of Germany: here one can notice a 15.1% decrease in the number of men in standard work between 1991 and 1998. Only 40.3% males fit for work[2] aged 15 to 65 in Berlin are now employed in standard jobs. The corresponding percentage for women in Berlin is 31.4%, with a decrease of 7.4% in the same period (cf. Oschmiansky and Schmid 2000: 20ff).

Changes in Work-life Balance

Men's working lives cannot be adequately understood unless the job/home-relationship is addressed, with changes in the sphere of reproduction having a separate impact on working life. Analyses must relate changes in households of choice[3] and utilisation of domestic time and family "time culture" to new ways of adapting to working life. In Western Europe, women's participation in wage labour increased from a low level, but their rising share of the household income and the general societal and cultural impact of feminism and equal status policies have changed many men's views. The co-habitation/marriage sphere, like the sphere of wage labour, is in transition, and some changes have arguably occurred more rapidly here than in wage labour. New institutional patterns are emerging, containing more diverse forms of masculinity.[4] This is associated with increasing equality in private life which affects couples of either sexual orientation, parental duties, and rights following divorce. There is a growing emphasis on gender equality among men, especially in the area of caring and relational competence. These developments suggest that men are developing a new culture in dealing with work and private life.

---

2   We prefer this calculation base, because it – in contrast to other studies – does not only assume the male work force, but also includes unemployed men or students. This more comprehensive approach shows that the concept of the full-time working breadwinner does not represent the whole social reality.

3   The term is used as an alternative to "family" or the heterosexual norm of partnership. It takes the multitude and diversity of partnership and household models or lifestyles into account, which have become more visible in the last three decades (cf. Adam 2004).

4   Cf. Connell (1995), who conceptualises masculinities as alternatives that construct the masculine gender.

In terms of gender equality, these developments involve risks but they may also open the way for an improved quality of life. There is a need for change among men in many areas of society, yet it is mainly practical behaviour where this change has so far been most evident: the increased amount of time fathers spend caring for their children. The lack of men in caring roles, while less evident in the home and family sphere, has not changed much in working life, and today this is the primary reason for the continued segregation of working life in some parts of Europe.

Although new forms of work may seem to have beneficial economic and social repercussions, one cannot ignore the fact that at the same time there is a growing risk of social marginalisation and insecurity. Thus, if economic forces result in new patterns of behaviour, one has to be aware of the fact that not all these changes are welcome by individuals in general, men in particular. There is likely to be a conflict between novelty and traditional stereotypes, whether they refer to the position of men at work or their role at home.

Male Change Patterns

One may expect to observe a modification of the relations between the genders and this should, sooner or later, lead to "new types of masculinity," i.e., to a redefinition of the position of men in society as well as of the image they have of themselves. These developments include many risks for a social polarisation in terms of their participation in the work sphere, but there is also the opportunity for improving the quality of life for both men and women.

Masculinities are based on gender relations, in particular the gendered division of labour (cf. Connell 1995). With respect to men, the pre-eminent ideological role within gender relations has been the role of "men as breadwinners." What is the concept of masculinity men have themselves? The "ability to deal with disequilibria" is more and more considered by economists as the essence of human capital in the modern world. We ask whether all men are able to take an active attitude towards pervasive change or whether some, if not many of them, are content to passively react to pressures. And if different types of responses exist, what are the determinants of this variety of reactions and what should be done to promote such an "ability to deal with disequilibria?" How do changing labour markets affect the self image of males?

1.2 Current State of Research on Masculinities

Gender is on the verge of becoming a mainstream focus in the humanities and social sciences. It is a category describing social inequality and is thus similar to ethnicity/race and class. It is a vitally important organising phenomenon in the logic and structures of society and culture (Kroll 2002: V). Masculinity in the sense of gender is not a biological destiny, but refers to an identity lived out within complex social relations. Research on masculinity nowadays is part of an open, relational gender research. It is less a discipline than a cross sectional task, which reflects the seemingly gender neutral assumptions in every science. Thus, it offers a part of the picture of gendered social relations.

The following theoretical approaches and studies strongly influenced our project – at least the background of discussions and main focus, but sometimes also in detail. Since the single subprojects of this volume address the topic of work and masculinity from different angles and with methodological variety, theoretical frameworks are introduced in the respective chapters.

Internationally, the most striking and perhaps ground-breaking approach has been that of Australian sociologist Robert W. Connell (1995). Looking for the connection between gender, power and action, he identifies a two-pronged strategy of male oppression: power over women and competing masculinities, which are various.[5] Anthropologists and ethnologists have contributed to this approach by describing the variety of masculinities in comparing different cultures (Völger and Welck 1990, Gilmore 1990).

Building on Bourdieu's habitus concept,[6] the German social scientist Michael Meuser (1998) has investigated the cultural patterns of masculinity as they are interpreted by men themselves. Male gender habitus refers to a premodern kind of identity, which seems to be non-reflexive and non-reflectable. Meuser discerns the highest potential for gender equality practice in the milieu of skilled workers.

In a church-funded representative survey in Germany, Paul Zulehner and Rainer Volz (1998) compared the attitudes of a large number of men. They distinguish between four types of men: 19% traditional, 37% insecure, 25% pragmatic, and 20% new men (who differ from traditional patterns, are open to gender equality in their attitudes and practice).

The first European representative surveys on men and gender equality appeared in Scandinavia: Jalmert (1984) in Sweden and Holter (1989) in Norway explored such topics as male friendships, work, family and social life. British researchers on masculinity in the tradition of the Anglo-American "(new) men's studies" have produced organisational studies (Witz and Savage 1992, Hearn 1998, Cockburn 1991). In Germany, Ralf Puchert and

---

5   Further important inputs for research on masculinity arose from queer theory and the deconstructionist debate (see Butler 1990, Maihofer 1995). One consequence was the subjection of both the dualistic gender order and the monolithic understanding of each of the genders to close scrutiny. Indisputable attributions to men and women now seem antiquated and are more and more replaced by a focus on gender diversity.

6   Pierre Bourdieu's (e.g., 2000) concept of habitus tries to describe the interrelations between a power-related social framework and the social sense of the subject, his or her actions and long-lasting habits. Gender and power relations play a central role here.

18

Stephan Höyng (1998) followed this direction with research on men's reaction to the process of equality in working life and discovered that it is seldom the attitudes, but rather the informal behaviour of men within a male-encoded labour culture, which prevents women from achieving equal opportunities.

Strong impulses and trends come from Anglo-American and Scandinavian countries, but also from the Netherlands, where research on masculinities has traditionally been connected with effective equality-bolstering policies, particularly in terms of family and the labour market. Regarding Scandinavia, Øystein Holter (2003a) has recently discussed a change of male role models based on new work-life relations and a new caregiving-model.

Since the concept of gender mainstreaming is established in the European Union, an increasing number of socio-economic surveys about the labour market are published from a gender specific perspective. The first international European research project on men, CROME, did explorative international research exchange on men and masculinity, emphasising the topics home and work, social exclusion, violence and health.

In the area of European labour market research, gender specific differentiations are relatively usual, but the focus here lies on women, while men are used as the standard. Although feminist labour researchers show established networks, a deeper analysis of male behaviour and strategies seldom appears.

1.3 Structure of the Project

By carrying out research on men in the context of changes in their working conditions, this study attempts to determine the main features of the new forms of work. We try to show to what extent discontinuities have become central in contemporary labour markets and whether they refer to part-time employment or temporary job contracts. This study examines the implications of such innovations for all aspects of men's individual life, including the images men have of themselves. On the basis of such an investigation, recommendations will be made concerning "best practices," that is the ways that seem best to cope with such transformations and foster an improved quality of life.

The project's examination of male work and life conditions was divided into three sub-projects:

- Subproject 1 constitutes an examination on an socio-economic level. Data from panel surveys, European and national labour market and household statistics on gender aspects of labour markets and men's work life have been analysed.

  Here, main tasks concerned the labour force participation rates of men and women, the distribution between part-time and full-time work, between temporary and permanent work-contracts.

Longitudinal surveys, stressing the impact of changes on occupational segregation and wage discrimination or working patterns among young workers, have been taken into account but are presented in more detail in a different publication.[7] This part is presented in chapter 2.

- Subproject 2 presents the *organisational research*, which was carried out in ten companies, and offers interesting conclusions that contrast with different aspects of our initial questions and assumptions. These researchers conducted expert interviews on different levels of the organisations as well as in-depth interviews with employees in non-standard job arrangements. Gender equality has become an important issue in organisations and enterprises and is no longer the domain of equality representatives or labour legislation. Even personnel managers and human resources representatives have begun to discuss the topics of equality and diversity from the company's perspective.

  But how are men perceived in this respect? And if the "male breadwinner" model is challenged by structural changes, is it changing in the organisations? Chapter 3 tries to answer these questions. As a link to the following step, a correspondence analysis maps and compares different types of male work-life patterns (chapter 4).

- Subproject 3 deals with the *socio-psychological investigation*. The analysis focuses on the ways men cope with pervasive change in general, growing discontinuities in their employment career in particular. The subproject discusses the repercussions that such transformations have on men's self-images, and more generally on their self-concept. Particular emphasis is given to men in caring situations. Good ways of "coping with changes" and "dealing with disequilibria" are shown in light of this investigation, which is described in chapter 5, followed by a concluding summary with policy recommendations in chapter 6. Policy recommendations as to what could be implemented as "good practice," that is as good ways of "coping with change" and "dealing with disequilibria" are made in light of this investigation.

The change of work requirements all over the world is not to stop by political institutions, even by European politics. But instead of promoting flexibility only of working people, the political institutions could foster security of the employees within flexible working situations – a policy often called "flexicurity." Examples, how this can correspond to interests of a lot of workers as well as employers we will show in the following chapters.

---

7   International Journal of Manpower, 2005, Vol. 26, no. 3, Emerald Group Publishing Limited.

2. Labour Market Changes and Gender

Stephan Höyng, Ralf Puchert and Øystein Gullvåg Holter

2.1 Trends in European Labour Markets

Compared to other economic regions like the US or Russia, European development has been characterised by relative egalitarianism. Although increasing globalisation and (in some cases) a weakening of the welfare state have led to some increase in social stratification in Europe from 1980 to 2000, the difference between these regions is still quite large. According to the Gini Index, a standard measure of income inequality, Europe remains considerably more egalitarian than the US or Russia. For example, Germany had a Gini Index value of 0.252 in 2000, compared to 0.368 in the US and 0.424 in Russia (LIS 2004). Relative social equality can be seen as a potential source for developing competitive diversity.

On the other hand, neo-liberal policies of labour market de-regulations have decreased the level of security and equality, even in former welfare states. Altvater and Mahnkopf (2002) call recent developments the "Globalisation of Insecurity" and mention informal work and the grey economy as a consequence deriving from global markets (ibid.: 13-17).

Men face changes relating to women's increasing education and labour market participation, changes due to the changing orientation of work (towards more complex services), changes due to increased diversity and globalisation, and other major trends. In this wider context, we see men facing the trend away from the "standard occupation."

In this labour market overview, we have also included non-wage domestic work. This enables us to see the strong relations existing between the two spheres and simultaneously allows us to bring into sharp focus the main dilemma of many men – combining career and care. At first, we will outline some general trends in European labour markets, which form the background of our study. Later, we will provide more detail, strengthen connections and explore difficulties.

2.1.1 Rise of Women's Participation in the Labour Market

The increase in participation of women in the workplace constitutes a main long-term trend.

The "male breadwinner" model is in fact a modern concept, which developed with the advent of middle class society and the emergence of the industrial system: "As industry was normalised, it also became masculinised." (Holter 2003a: 77)[8] Women were gradually excluded from industrial labour and increasingly recruited for more "feminine" jobs instead. Throughout most of the 20th century, the institutions and traditions of the market were built into a culture of masculine hegemony and gender segregation.

In this context, Peuckert (1996) emphasises the development of the middle class family ideal and a "normative orientation" (ibid.: 23) to it that extended to all levels of middle class society in the 20th century.

Nowadays, the middle class traditions of breadwinner and housewife are being challenged. This is partly connected to the rise of service work and, we argue, to part-time work. The increase in participation of women in the labour market is a multi-facetted process, characterised not only by a numerical increase, but also in competence levels and decision-making authority. In Europe, this has been a gradual process, where setbacks have been observed (e.g., Eastern Germany). Yet it has profound effects on the family and the household sphere as well as on society and culture in general.

2.1.2 Differentiation of the Gender Wage Gap

In the US, "(t)he narrowing of the gender wage gap by approximately one percentage point a year since 1980 is particularly significant, since during the 1980s and '90s the overall wage level rose little and the wage inequality between skilled and unskilled workers grew. Without enhanced skills, women's wages would have likely fallen further behind men's. However, market pressures have helped to generate corrective mechanisms, and as the costs of

---

8   The connection between masculinity and labour has an arguably long history (cf. Dörr 1997). But the essential element of this process was the gender-related division of spheres – private for women, public for men – and labour (as well as the claim of their "naturalness," cf. Honnegger 1991). The completely new formation of the production spheres in this time period was accompanied by an increasing masculinisation of the core proletariat, which previously had still been comprised, to a significant extent, of women and children (Holter 2003a: 67): On the basis of a socio-historical investigation by Ute Frevert, Meuser and Behnke (1998) outline the development of the model of middle class masculinity in the 19th century and conclude: "Commitment to one's job, social success, and a solid, materialistic orientation characterised the middle class man as a worthy representative of his class." (Ibid: 19, translation by S.H. et al.). This social pattern, however, seems to be valid for the middle classes (and some regions), but less (and less gender-exclusive) for the working class, where women have to contribute to the household income.

denying employment to women mounted, prejudices were set aside."
(Venable 2002: 2)

In Europe, this development has not been observed on a comprehensive level. According to the data published by EUROSTAT (which is based on the household panel of the European Community (ECHP), the gender-specific difference in wages without adjustments remained the same between 1994 and 2003. The average hourly wage (gross) of women has stagnated at a level 16% lower than that of men (EUROSTAT 2005). The general picture seems to be that the wage gap remains large in Europe even though women are moving upwards and men downwards in terms of contracts and occupational positions. This is due to a persistent and sometimes even increasing gender segregation (horizontal wage gap) in different sectors and lines of business.

In terms of gender equality, this is the case even in the advanced areas of Europe. Gender equality in terms of wages has not advanced much in Norway or the other Nordic countries over the last twenty years, because there has been renewed segregation (horizontal wage discrimination). It is worth noting here that the gender wage gap has remained constant in the 1990s, although women's education and qualifications have increased markedly.

Wage research also indicates that gender-traditional forces are stronger upwards in the Norwegian social structure, not downwards. The wage gap increases with increasing education and income. The gap is less for lower-paid jobs than for well-paid jobs (Aftenposten 16.5.03). This is contrary to the ideology of "the enlightened upper classes," which is often displayed more in word than deed with regard to gender matters.

In the long run, the increased education participation among women may have effects in the labour market. In the majority of European countries, more young women than men go on to higher education, and in more than three quarters of all countries in the region, the majority of degrees at university level are awarded to women. In many countries, women account for more than 60% of graduates.

2.1.3 Increase of Service Work

In the past decades, the economy and labour market center shifted from industrial sector to services. The European Comission remarked:

The largest changes in the labour market over the past decades concern service work. We see a long-term increase in services (both production-related and reproduction-related or social services) and a decrease in other forms of work. A hundred years ago, the vast majority of wage workers produced physical things; today, they produce services. This change has affected the current generation in particular. In general, the economies with the largest gross domestic product also show the highest proportion of service jobs. This is linked to an increase in education and more information-based jobs. It is generally held to be true that education and competence are the main productivity factors in Europe. (EC 2003)

2.1.4   Differentiation of Employment Patterns

Globalisation and deregulation have led to a differentiation of employment forms all over Europe. The traditional Fordist form of standard work and life patterns have decreased. In some regions and agglomerations (like Berlin, cf. Oschmianski and Schmidt 2000), less than 50% of the workforce has a full-time, long-term job employment contract. Patterns of employment vary widely across Europe, but the same trends are visible everywhere.

Two main assumptions are crucial to our analysis:

– There has been a reduction in standard work
– This reduction affects men in particular

However, in detail this trend is uneven, and we found two different reasons for this development. In some regions (e.g., the Nordic region), male employees are increasingly demanding work-family balance and gender equality. In addition to an increasing service orientation, education and gender equality have been more noticeable than the dissolution of standard work contracts. In these contexts, gender equality reforms can make transitions among men easier and function as 'buffers' in the labour market (like men's parental leave).

In other regions, increasing job insecurity and the dissolution of standard contracts (something not desired by employees) often precede gender equality changes, having different and more negative implications for men as well as women.

2.1.5   New Patterns of Time Use

The economic relations constituting the labour market – recruitments and exits, formal or informal contracts – are associated with many social and cultural factors, including people's conceptions of free time and work. If young fathers and mothers are not given sufficient opportunity to balance production (mostly wage work) and reproduction (partly non-wage work), both production and non wage work will suffer. Historically, this conflict was first identified in England in the mid-19th century, when early industry required an excess of labour from workers, leading to long workdays and poor working conditions. The result was the necessity for the state and the enlightened bourgeoisie to agree on a limit to working hours or a "normal work day." In the 20th century, the average work week in the labour market gradually fell to around 37-40 hours.

Although some have interpreted gender equality as an issue for women only and assert that it is treated with hostility or ambivalence by men, research from the last decade has shown that men's practices have developed too. Domestic work and other tasks are more equally shared between men and women, and the gender gap in time-use has been reduced (Gershuny 2003). In some European countries, reforms have been introduced to deal with these new trends, e.g., by offering a part of the parental leave time for fathers. Considering that these reforms rearrange 'core' gender relations, it is especially interesting that the new role is taken up by a majority of men (Holter 2003a). Evidence from Northern Europe demonstrates in particular that men will take advantage of gender-equality reforms if the latter are clearly designed for men as well as women and include a fair level of wage compensation, e.g., for parental leave.

Seen from this perspective, it is not an anomaly that the labour market has become relatively gender-conservative in comparison to changes elsewhere in society. Perhaps "gender equality pays" and leads to increased profits, as is shown by some new studies (Nutek 1999). Yet such new arrangements can remain marginalised and fail to become an effective norm. Work life has a lot of structural and institutional inertia that is not necessarily driven by direct gender discrimination in the workplace, but rather is an effect of how the market has developed over time in its institutional environments.

In the following, we take a detailed look at some developments in the European labour market, paying close attention to gender relations.

After taking a brief look at employment activity rates, we will turn to the tendencies in new forms of employment as seen through a comparison of the results from the participating countries in this project. Here, examples are shown to discuss gender segregation in professional and household work. Finally, some indications will be given that deal with non-standard working biographies. The focus here will be on men, even though the basic statistical information refers to women and men.

2.2 Labour Market Participation: Non-active Population and Unemployment

There are two aspects that will be stressed in this perspective on European labour market participation and unemployment. First, it is not "normal" to have a work contract and even less so to have a long-term full-time contract. This applies for women and men. Second, the European labour market is characterised by diversity as well as inequality. The enormous variation in labour market conditions reveals a background of different national power relations, politics and challenges constituting obstacles in the creation of competitive diversity, more equal standards, and improved social cohesion.

2.2.1 Europe

Non-active Population

Statistics are frequently based only on the economically active portion of the population. The following statistics are based on the population of all persons over the age of 15 in order to make clear how large the population of professionally non-active women and men is. Included are students, handicapped persons, retired persons and prisoners. The inclusion of persons over 65 is defensible, because a portion of this group still pursues paid work in some countries and thus needs to be considered for the entirety of their lives.

Fig. 1:   Economically Inactive Population – EU 15 (not officially unemployed) in % of the population over 15 years old of each sex

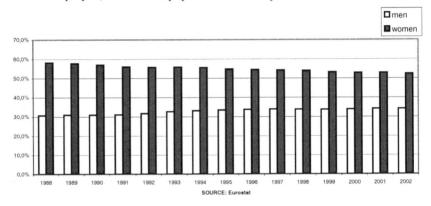

SOURCE: Eurostat

The diagram shows important changes for men and women over a relatively short period of time. The inactivity rate for women is continually decreasing, while the rate for men continually rises. The gap has shrunken by almost a half – from 28% to 18% over 14 years.

There are some factors "outside" of the labour market that are important for interpreting these changes. The increase in life expectancy and the rise in the number of individuals going to school both contribute to the increase in the inactivity rate of men and women. The higher rate for women is in large part attributable to career interruptions due to child raising and a higher life expectancy. In Israel, time spent in the military is an important factor increasing the inactivity rate for men.

Unemployment

The unemployment rate in Europe follows the cycles of economic activity but seems to be shrinking in general. Here too, the gender gap is clearly diminishing: in the 14 years documented by the study, it dropped from 4.6% to 1.7%. There seems to be an assimilation tendency in Europe, but there are still enormous differences existing between European countries. The global process of changes in production affects countries at different levels (social system, gender distribution of labour, etc.), which sometimes seems to mark progress, and other times, backlash.

Fig. 2:   Unemployment – EU15 in % of the labour force for each sex

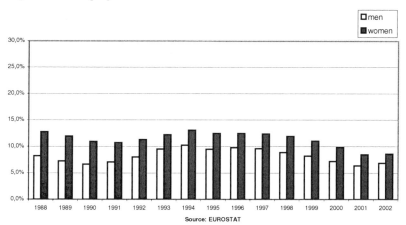

In many countries, a distinction is no longer seen in the unemployment rate when it is measured in terms of the activity rate according to sex. A clear exception is Spain, where the unemployment rate for women is much higher than for men. Viewed as a whole, unemployment rates vary greatly from country to country.

In the following, the variety inside Europe is documented by a view on the participating countries.

2.2.2   Austria

Austria seems to be an example of a well executed modernisation of a welfare state.

The overall employment rate in Austria is higher than the average employment rate in the European Community. Major processes in the labour market in Austria affect men and women in very different ways. The female labour force

27

participation rate has increased in past decades, caused by a steep rise in the number of service sector jobs and the increase in 'atypical' employment.

Fig. 3: Economically Inactive Population – Austria (not officially unemployed) in % of the population over 15 years old,both sexes included

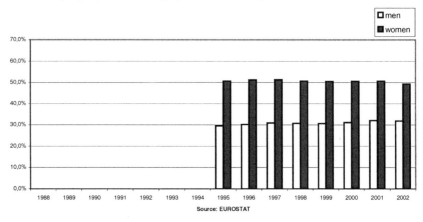

Source: EUROSTAT

One of the main developments in the Austrian labour market over the past 30 years is the slight increase in the male activity rate (from 54.6% in the year 1971 to 56.3% in 2000) and a strong increase in the female activity rate (from 30.4% in 1971 to 40.7% in 2000).

Fig. 4: Unemployment – Austria in % of the labour force for each sex

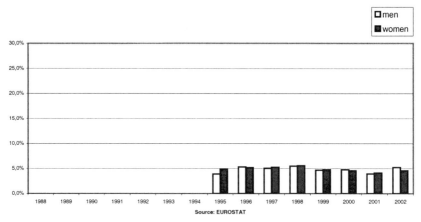

Source: EUROSTAT

The results of a survey on the Austrian National Action Plan for Employment in 2000 refer to this development. The male participation rate was highest for men between 25 and 50 (age range of main participation in the labour market), while the female participation rate was 20 % lower. Nevertheless, the increase in female employment is caused by participation of women with children. (Kreimer et al. 2003: 1f)

The unemployment rate in Austria is one of the lowest in the EU. In contrast to the EU, the male unemployment rate has been somewhat higher than the female unemployment rate over the past few years.

2.2.3 Bulgaria

Bulgaria, a future member of the European Union, has in the last 15 years undergone the most significant changes in our sample, including the end of the socialist economy and the implementation of a market economy.

Table 1: Size and Dynamics of Bulgaria's Workforce During the Period 1990-1999

					Indices			
Year	Workforce		People employed		People employed in the public sector		People employed in the private sector	
	Number	%	Number	%	Number	%	Number	%
1990	4,145,247	100.0	4,096,848	100.0	3,855,134	100.0	241,714	100.0
1995	3,716,810	89.7	3,282,138	80.1	1,949,404	50.6	1,332,779	551.4
1999	3,614,888	87.2	3,087,830	75.3	1,085,162	28.1	2,000,668	828.5

The period 1990-2000 in Bulgaria was characterised by institutionalisation and the formation of the labour market as well as the building of its infrastructure. It is characterised by several basic tendencies:

–   During the period 1993-1999, the coefficient of employment and the coefficient of economic activity of the population have been constantly decreasing and have reached their lowest levels.
–   A dramatic decrease in the country's workforce in the 1990s by 17.9%: The decrease in employment in Bulgaria during that period marks one of the most sudden drops among all of the economies of Eastern and Central Europe.
–   The sharp and continual decrease of public sector employment and the rapid increase in employment in the private sector of the economy: which means that by 1999 the public sector had shrunk by 71.9% in 9 years. During the same period, the number of people employed in the private sector increased by more than 8 times.

29

– The relatively high number of people that have left their workplace in the period 1990-1999 compared to the people that have been hired on a labour code basis. During the ten years in question, 4,7 million people in total have been hired on a labour code basis, and 7,2 million people have left their jobs, including people that lost their positions due to closure of factories or reductions in production. (cf. Atanassova and Dulevski 2003: 1f)

Fig. 5: Economically Inactive Population – Bulgaria (not officially unemployed) in % of the population over 15 years old, both sexes included

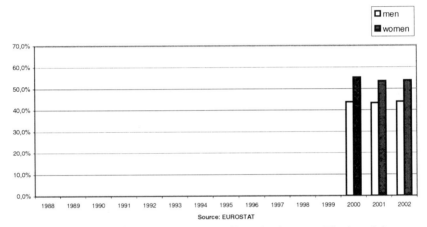

Source: EUROSTAT

The employment crisis described above affects both sexes. The inactivity rate in Bulgaria is the highest of all the countries investigated in our study. The difference between the sexes is, however, the slightest.

Unemployment rose from 2% in 1991 to 18% in 1999. Bulgaria's unemployment level in the late 1990s and early 2000s was about twice that of the EU, although some EU countries (like Spain with 15.2% in 1997) also had high levels. The gap is probably even larger, however, if we also include in the unemployed category the people who were discouraged people in October 1999 (according to the data of the National Statistical Institute 357,300 thousand people). In this case the total number of unemployed people would be 967,800 and the real unemployment rate, 28.6%. In Bulgaria, the gender gap in unemployment seems to be disadvantageous for men.

30

Fig. 6: Unemployment – Bulgaria in % of the labour force for each sex

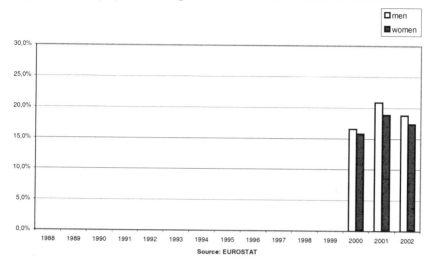

2.2.4 Germany

Fig. 7: Economically Inactive Population – Germany (not officially unemployed) in % of the population over 15 years, both sexes included

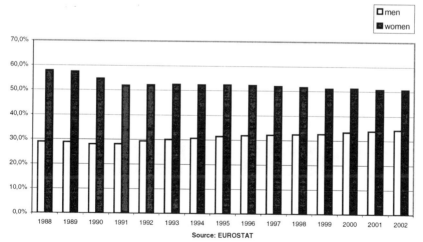

In comparison with most economies in the west, the German labour system
and economy have been in a deep-rooted process of restructuring since the

31

1970s. This process implied different processes of increasing flexibility and deregulation in structures of production, as well as the privatisation of public structures (Bischoff and Detje 1989). The structural unemployment is caused by a decoupling of economic growth and employment (Höyng and Gärtner 2003: 1).

The inactivity rate in Germany is very similar to the average in Europe. In comparison with West European economies, there is a convergence of rates for men and women in Germany. Because the west of Germany is four times larger than the east, the inactivity rate numbers for the whole country tend to be more of a reflection of the west. In this case, east-west differences have to be looked at to gain a clearer picture of what is happening. Given that the country has been united since 1991, it is remarkable that these different economic backgrounds are still very prominent.

In particular, different labour participation rates in east and west are crucial. In spite of a tight labour market, women's participation in the west has remained stable. The employment quota – employed women's share of the resident population between 15 and 65 – was 55.3% (compared to the 1998 figure for men: 72.3%, Allafi 1999). The employment orientation of females in the west turns out to be largely immune to cyclical fluctuations. Increasing female education as well as growing part-time availability leads to a reduction in work interruptions (cf. Engelbrech 1998). While men's employment quota in the east and west have converged, females in the east are more employment-oriented than their counterparts in the west (Arbeitsamt 2000: 1ff).

Fig. 8:   Unemployment – Germany in % of the labour force for each sex

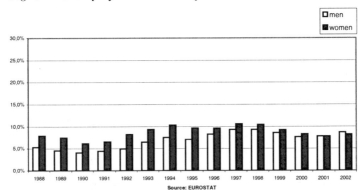

Source: EUROSTAT

The convergence of male and female unemployment mirrors trends in Europe. Changing labour patterns and a shift in job sectors may explain this. Male dominated jobs are more and differently affected by labour cut-backs. While significantly more women today are working in the western service sector (ibid.), strong convulsions in the manufacturing trade (including the building

32

trade) lead to a cut-back of 1.3 million male and 0.5 million female jobs (ibid.).

2.2.5 Norway

Of all the countries participating in our study, Norway has by far the lowest non-activity rate and the smallest gender gap. The Nordic welfare states show a relative level of equality. The reasons for this may be historical and attributable to the unusual path of Norwegian industrialisation. First, the process of industrialisation in Norway developed relatively late. As in the rural culture, men, like women, worked the land for their sustenance, the bourgeoisie (an important contributor in the formation of modern European gender ideology) could not get that strength in Norway. Large-scale industry emerged for the most part between 1890-1900 and later. From the very start, the structure of Norwegian industry was dominated by two agendas: cheap energy (especially water power) and raw materials (e.g., minerals). In the 20th century, industrial production remained less developed than, for instance, in neighbouring Sweden.[9]

Fig. 9: Economically Inactive Population – Norway (not officially unemployed) in % of the population over 15 years old, including both sexes

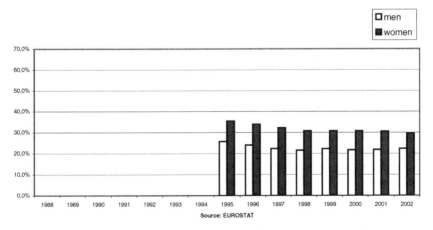

Source: EUROSTAT

From the 1970s onwards, the oil industry in the Norwegian sector of the North Sea has given the country an economic and technological boost. In the

---

9   For example, the attempt to produce cars in the 1950s (the Troll car), only resulted in a few models before the firm went bankrupt.

1970s and 1980s, expansion in education, health and social services contributed to a "women's revolution" in the labour market. The proportion of women doing wage work grew rapidly. One significant factor contributing to the lower non-activity rate of women is the necessity of caring for small children on a full-time basis.

Despite the high rate of employment activity for men and women (fig. 9), the unemployment rate is very small and the difference between rates for men and women is extremely slight.

Fig. 10: Unemployment – Norway in % of the labour force for each sex

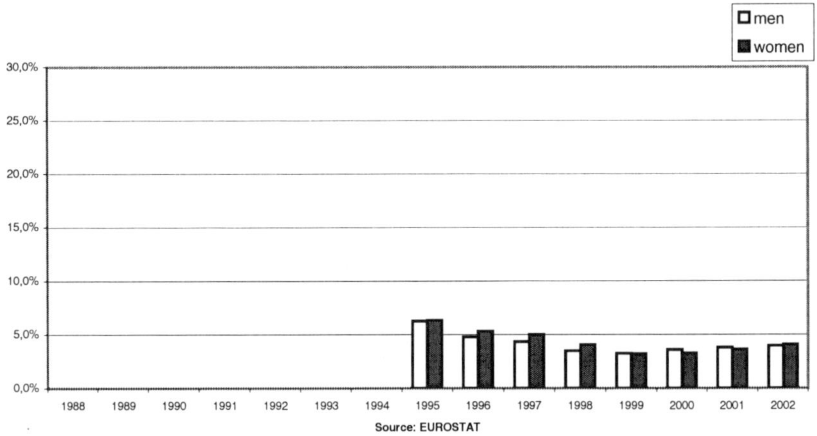

Source: EUROSTAT

2.2.6 Spain

Since its entry into the EU, the Spanish economy has been characterised by growth and gender equality. The Spanish labour market has improved the imbalance in labour activity and closed the gap with the European Union. Nevertheless, there are still important differences. A large disparity in comparison with the EU is found in the non-activity rate, which is around 5 points higher.

Spain's activity-rate disparities with Europe are very high for women and slight for men (fig. 11). In fact, labour-market associated problems are increasingly affecting women. In terms of non-activity rates, Spain has the largest gender gap among European countries.

The Spanish unemployment rate is decreasing, but still high. The gender gap in unemployment rates is higher than in all other countries. People under 30 constitute the age group with the highest incidence of unemployment.

One in four is unemployed (women in this age group: one in three). This ratio is nine points higher than the EU average. Moreover, discrimination against women is clearly evident among young people in Spain in comparison with their counterparts around the rest of the EU. While the unemployment rate among young men is only 2% higher than that of men in the EU (17.3% versus 15.0%), the unemployment rate among young women in Spain is 13% higher than that of men (32.4% versus 19.7%). (cf. Abril 2002)

Fig. 11: Economically Inactive Population – Spain (not officially unemployed) in % of the population over 15 years old of each sex

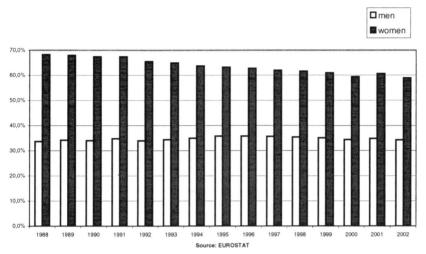

Source: EUROSTAT

Fig. 12: Unemployment – Spain in % of the labour force for each sex

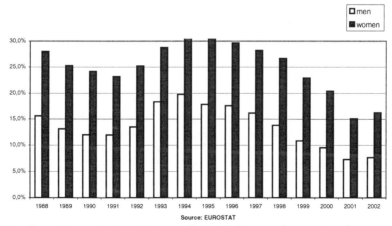

Source: EUROSTAT

Spain's disparities with the EU regarding activity, employment and unemployment rates are much greater among women than among men. The dispari-

35

ties among men are very small. In fact, the problems of the labour market are taking on a more feminine character. Dealing with these problems is necessary for meeting the challenge of incorporating women into professional and wage labour activities.

2.2.7   Israel

Israel seems to have relatively high standards of equality. The difference between women and men in activity rates and unemployment exists, but is smaller than in the most countries of the EU.

Fig. 13:   The Civilian Labour Force among Men and Woman Age 15+
1955-2001 (Percent)

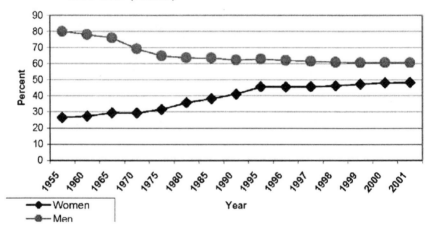

(Kraus 2002)

Women's participation rate in the civilian labour force among the overall population of women age 15+ has increased continuously since the mid-1950s. This trend can be attributed to women's increased education, the declining number of children per family, and changes in norms pertaining to working women. Almost half the women in Israel in 2001 worked outside the home; nevertheless, their share remains lower than that of employed men.

Compared to women's increased participation in the labour force, men's participation is continuously declining due to their late entry into and early exit from the workforce. The reasons for this decline include men's expanded participation in higher education, men's military service, and governmental

36

support and allowances, which make up a large portion of the family's income.

The Israeli economy has to integrate a huge number of immigrants with a large variety of cultures. Table 2 views the labour market situation from a somewhat different vantage point, showing the comparative rates of participation among the Jewish population (natives), immigrants and the ultra-orthodox. The first two groups have very similar patterns, but among the ultra-orthodox the participation rate is very low. There are comparatively fewer women in the workforce and extremely fewer men. It is also interesting to note that there was a major decline in the number of employed ultra-orthodox men from 1980 to 1997.

Table 2: Participation in Israeli Workforce, Ages 25-54, 1980, 1997

	1980 (%)			1997 (%)		
	Men	Women	Ratio	Men	Women	Ratio
Jewish Population	88.5	54.5	0.62	84.9	74.3	0.88
Immigrants	85.8	63.7	0.74	88.4	74.8	0.85
Ultra-Orthodox	37.0	NA	NA	20.8	56.2	2.70

The employment situation of ultra-orthodox men in Israel is comparatively unique. None of the other countries involved in the project contained a group of men with such a low rate of labour market participation. This indicates a form of masculinity that does not focus on wage work and thus is legitimated in terms of "masculinity standards" that are totally different from those found in other cultures. Masculinity in this case seems to be strongly based on religiousness. Since ultra-orthodox gender arrangements are modelled on traditional patriarchal structures, this example demonstrates that a deviation from wage-work based masculinity does not necessarily lead to gender equality.

Fig. 14: Unemployed Men and Women in the Civilian Labour Force, 1955-2001 (Percent)

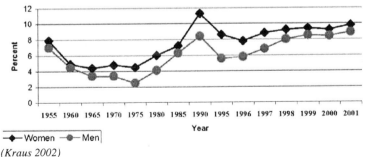

(Kraus 2002)

37

The proportion of unemployed women in the civilian labour force remained stable between 1998 and 2000, while the proportion of unemployed men changed. However, 2001 data indicate a rise in the unemployment rate of both men and women – an increase related to the economic situation in Israel. The unemployment rate was stable from the 1960s through the beginning of the 1980s. We can see that unemployment increased from the beginning of the 1980s and reached its peak at the beginning of the 1990's. The rate dropped through the mid-1990s, but then began to rise once again. One data figure remains constant: a continuous gap between unemployed men and women, but it is a small one in relation to a lot of European countries.

2.2.8 Summary

In all participating countries, the inactivity rate for women and men is converging. Only in Bulgaria the data base is too small for a reliable analysis. A regional exception is Eastern Germany, where the difference in the inactivity rate is growing. In most of the participating countries, the unemployment rate for women and men is converging and currently about the same. Only in Spain there is a large gender gap.

2.3 Changes in Forms of Employment

The standard form of work is defined as wage-based, non-temporary, full-time work. The following table 3 gives an overview of differing forms of employment:

Table 3: Employment forms

Standard employment	Emerging forms
Employed	Phases of non-employment Unemployed Sabbatical Parental leave Vocational training
Full- time	Part-time E.g. reduction of working hours Three weeks on, one week off
Permanent	Temporary, e.g. seasonal work Project related employees Subcontractors
Dependent – with wage or salaries	Self-employed Freelancers Informal work/moonlighting

38

The non-standard forms of work listed above hardly reflect all the changes in the labour market. "The introduction of new work-time models such as annualised hours or work-time accounts, as well as flexible employment contracts such as temporary employment or work-on-call indicate just a few illustrations of the changes that are likely to modify employment patterns." (Buchmann, Kriesi, Sacchi 2004: 166) To concentrate on one symptomatic change, in the following, we look mainly at part-time work, but also focus briefly on temporary work and self-employment.

In the EU, a part-time worker is defined as "an employee whose normal hours of work, calculated on a weekly basis or on average over a period of employment of up to one year, are less than those of comparable full-time workers." (Corral and Isusi 2004) Since this is not easy to compare, we have used the definition provided by Eurostat, which states that every work schedule containing less than 35 hours a week (this is the full-time threshold in Europe), is part-time.

2.3.1   Part-time

Comparative Overview

In western countries, about 29% of all employed women work part-time, compared to an average of 7.4% of all employed men (UN Statistics Division: 2002). These numbers are close to the averages of part-time employment in the EU-15.

Fig. 15:   Part Time EU – 15 in % of total employment for each sex

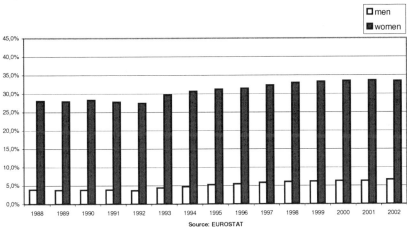

Source: EUROSTAT

In the time period covered by this study (and beyond it), the incidence of part-time employment has increased. Part-time employment is clearly a women's domain. The rise of women's participation in part-time is probably a medium-term trend, but not a long-term trend. "The jury is still out," but the main trend seems to be longer hours and more full time. This is also where there is political pressure.

Beginning from a lower level of incidence, the number of men working part-time is increasing more rapidly than it is for women. In the 14 years investigated, the number of men working part-time has doubled. Part-time work thus deserves closer attention, despite the fact that this form of employment also has the largest gender gap of all forms of employment.

Looking closer at the European countries, we discern extreme differences between them: In 2000, the proportion of women employed part-time in Western Europe varied between 17% (Spain) and 41% (UK). It was as high as 55% in the Netherlands, a special case, which also had a higher rate among men. It was much lower in parts of Eastern Europe (e.g., 1% in Bulgaria).

Although increasing slightly among men, part-time employment continues to account for only a very small proportion of men's employment, between 3% and 9% in Western Europe (12% in the Netherlands). Men's part-time employment has risen in Central Europe in particular (Germany, Austria), but at a low rate (e.g., from 2% to 5% in Germany), a phenomenon attributable to the overall expansion of part-time employment across the country (Holter et al. 2003).

What is striking about men is also the distribution by age: 17.1% in the cohort below 24 work part-time, 3.9% in the cohort 25-49, 6.7% age 50-64, and 45.2% over 65. Thus, the start and end of the professional life stand out clearly (European Foundation for the Improvement of Living and Working Conditions 2003).

A fact which can be seen across all of Europe is that part-time employment is most frequently found in the service sector, and thus the increase in the number of service jobs has in part led to the increase of part-time positions (cf. Abril 2002, Höyng and Gärtner 2003, Holter 2003b, Kreimer et al. 2003). This means the distribution of part-time is unequal between gender, ages and countries; it differs as well between sectors and occupations (Corral and Isusi 2003). Here we limit ourselves to focussing on the specific situations of the six countries participating in the research project and representing northern, western, eastern and southern parts of Europe. The multitude of distributions of part-time and full-time work show that the previously assumed (yet not questioned) normality of full-time in some western and eastern countries is in fact a protean form. Upon closer examination of the six countries, two aspects stand out: one is the proportion of part-time working women and men; the second – which interests us more here – is the number of part-time working men.

The Average: Austria and Germany

The overview of the countries investigated focuses on their specific situations, different reasons for and the perspectives of part time work. It begins with Austria and Germany, which reveal average data.

Fig. 16: Part-Time – Austria in % of total employment for each sex

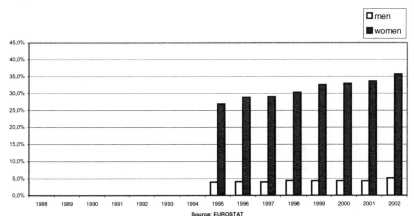

Source: EUROSTAT

In 2002, about 16% of all the employees in Austria worked part-time (below the EU average, Kreimer et al. 2003). The percentage of persons working part-time has increased continuously over the past decades, and this trend is going to continue in the future. Part-time work in Austria is a female domain. In 1999, an average of nearly 9 out of 10 part-time workers in Austria were female. Male part-time workers still play a marginal role in Austria. Nevertheless, their participation rate has grown in the past 25 years from 0.9% to 3.0%. The increase in female participation in the labour market is a result of the increase in part-time work in Austria. Female part-time employment has almost doubled in the past 25 years.

Especially in the trade sectors, full-time work has been supplanted by part-time work. Part-time work is more common in the service sector than in industry (ibid.).

The German situation is rather similar to the Austrian. The number of working women increased, while the number of working men shrunk (Allafi 1999), but the increase in the women's quota did not lead to a proportional increase in the volume of work. The total number of jobs requiring less working hours climbed (Engelbrech and Reinberg 1997). The part-time quota of women rose to 40% by 1998, the men's to 5%. Women work part-time mostly in the public administration, the public and private service sector and in the trade, hotel and restaurant industry. Apart from the male-female difference,

41

the east-west gap is striking: "Unlike in west Germany, full-time work is more significant for East German females." (Arbeitsamt 2000) While part-time contracts for females in the east in 2001 was 26.1 % (west: 45.1 %), for men in the east it was only 4.8 % (west 5.5 %). (Wagner and Lehndorff 2003).

Fig. 17: Part-Time – Germany in % of total employment for each sex

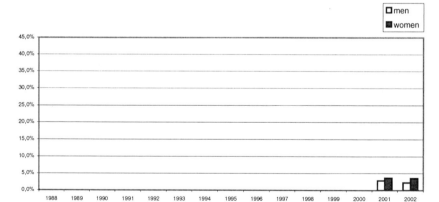

Source: EUROSTAT

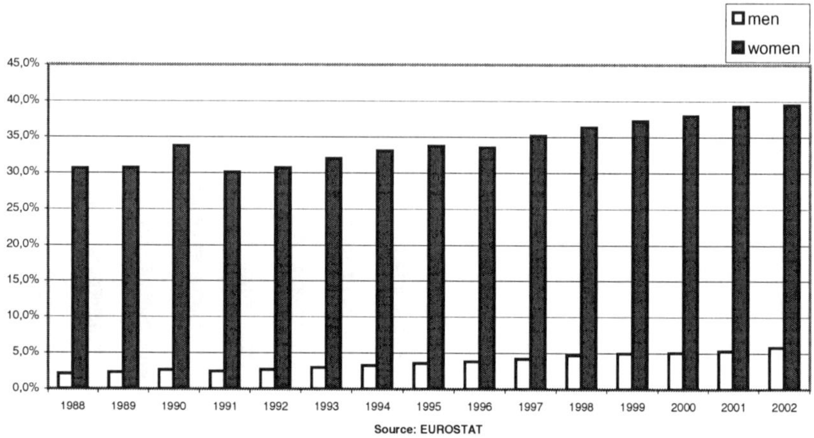

Small Number of Men Working Part-time: Different Backgrounds in Bulgaria and Spain

Fig. 18: Part-Time – Bulgaria in % of total employment for each sex

Source: EUROSTAT

Bulgaria has the smallest percentage of part-time working men in our sample of countries, but since the number of women working part-time is nearly as low, the distribution of part-time work amongst men and women most nearly approaches equality in comparison with the other countries in the sample. Like East Germany (but with even greater significance), Bulgaria shows a "full-time for women and men" labour pattern.

As mentioned above, part-time work in Bulgaria does not betray any significant gender aspects. In 2000, 5.6% of the employed men and 8.3% of the employed women work part-time. The vast majority, 75.2% of the employed men and 78.9% of the women, work 40 to 49 hours a week, and women are even fairly well represented in the 50+ category of those who work more than the standard number of working hours (3.4 % of the women employees are found here, 5.1% of the men, Atanassova and Dulevski 2003).

The situation is different in Spain: there is also a small number of part-time working men (2.6 %) but part-time working women make up about 17 % of the employed women. So, on a lower level, the gender gap is as strong as in the European average.

Fig. 19:   Part-Time – Spain in % of total employment for each sex

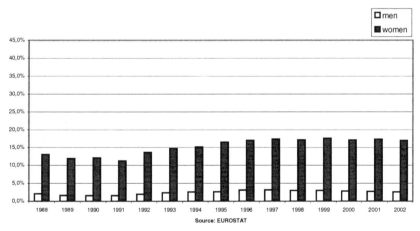

Source: EUROSTAT

The percentage of people working part-time in Spain (8%) is 10 points below the European average (18 %). There is no specific regulation of part-time employment that could explain this difference. Even though participation in part-time work is fairly low in Spain compared to Central and Northern Europe, the proportion has increased. Part-time employment grew after the labour market reform of 1994, which facilitated the extension of this form of employment. This increase in part-time work largely involved women. The

43

growth of part-time employment in Spain in the 1990s (at an average annual rate of 7.5% between 1992 and 1999), was basically due to the increase in part-time employment in service sector work such as large-scale retailing, telemarketing and other forms of home shopping such as those related to fast food; caring services as well as more traditional activities such as cleaning or domestic service and hotels and catering also increased.

The figure also indicates that part-time employment as a proportion of total employment has ceased to increase (a slowdown after 1996, with no increase from 1999 to 2000). This stagnation was particularly apparent in 2000: 37,100 part-time jobs (the vast majority for women) were created in the second quarter of 2000, compared with 60,200 in the first quarter of 2000 and 85,000 in the second quarter of 1999. This distinguishes the current Spanish situation from that of other European Union countries.

High Percentages of Male Part-time Work – More Equality in Norway and Israel?

In Norway and Israel, the difference between the part-time rates of men and women are smaller than the EU-average, but the high rate of participation of men working part-time in both countries is noteworthy.

Fig. 20: Part-Time – Norway in % of total employment for each sex

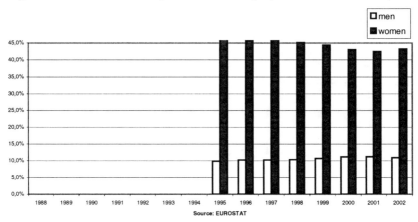

Source: EUROSTAT

In Norway, 10% of the men and over 40% of the women work part-time. This indicates an enormous total amount of part-timers in, and one of the highest part-time rates of men in the countries investigated in our study. With a growing labour market and a high level of participation, Norway is slowly integrat-

44

ing part-time employed women into full-time. One clue here was the decrease in part- time employment during the years of economic expansion.

Although Norway has a high proportion of women in the labour force, it is also near the top amongst European countries in the number of women who are employed part-time. This has many implications: for example, it reinforces domestic sphere inequality in terms of money and time. The unequal distribution of jobs and the element of *gender segregation* – which are thereby strengthened – stand in contrast to more gender-equal developments in Norwegian politics, culture, social life, family, etc. The proportion of part-time work among men is, relative to women, still low and shows only small indices of increase.

The structure of the Israeli economy forces both parents to work. Therefore, more than 35% of the working women in Israel are employed in part-time jobs and more than 15% of the working men.

The diagram reveals that in all the years surveyed, the share of part-time workers among employed women is higher than that among men. Additionally, due to the economic situation, the share of part-time employees among both men and women increased from 2000 to 2001.

Fig. 21: Israel Part-Time Workers in the Civilian Labour Force Among Men and Women, 1955-2001 (Percent)

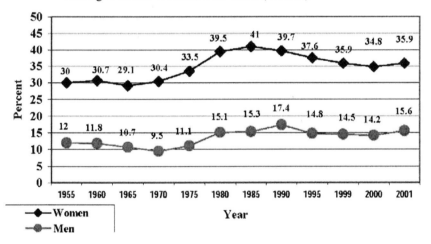

(Figure: Kraus 2002)

A slight increase is evident in the share of part-time workers among both sexes since 1955, climaxing in the 1980's, and followed by a decline since the beginning of the 1990's. In 2001, 35.9% of employed women filled part-time positions, compared to 15.6% of all employed men. Lack of uniformity is found in a comparison with part-time employees in other Western countries. Compared with the other countries in the sample, there is the highest proportion of men working part time: more than 15%. Remarkable: In contrast to the changes in Western Europe, the Israeli part-time rate has been high for over fifty years and reveals a stable gender difference.

Reasons and Motives for Part-time

Men are still rarely found in part-time positions. When they do work part-time, the reason given for this tends to be that these men are preparing for their next career move (e.g., freeing up time to re-train) and not that they do so in order to fulfil obligations to their families. To gain a deeper understanding of what is actually happening here, it is necessary to consider the different reasons for working part-time. These reasons are also important for the assessment of perspectives in this form of labour.

European conditions seem quite similar to those of the US, where an study concluded that

in 2000 one-quarter of all women employees worked part-time, compared to less than 10% of men. Nearly 85% of those who worked part-time did so for non-economic reasons, e.g., to spend more time with the family or to further their education. In general, married women prefer part-time work at a rate of 5 to 1 over married men. (Venable 2002)

We can see very different reasons for working part time between men and women. Nearly a quarter of the men cite "education and training" reasons, while only 7.6% of the women do. Furthermore, only 4.2% of the men cite "care" as a reason, but nearly a third of the women do so. The gender difference is not that large concerning involuntary part-time, and very small for all other reasons. It becomes evident that the largest group (larger than those who give care or have other reasons) is the group that does not want to work full time (nearly a third of men and women). These men and women need to be considered more carefully.

Table 4: Main Reasons for Working on a Part-Time Basis by Gender, EU15 2002

Main reason	Men	Women	Total men and women
Impossible to find a full-time-job	19.0	12.8	14.1
Do not want to work full time	31.0	32.2	31.9
Involvement in education or training activities	23.6	7.6	10.9
Sickness or disability	5.9	2.4	3.1
Child and adult care	4.2	31.5	25.8
Other reasons	11.8	11.7	11.7
No reasons	4.5	2.0	2.5
Total	100.0	100.0	100.0

Source: Eurostat Labour Force Survey, 2002
(European Foundation for the Improvement of Living and Working Conditions 2003b)

Correspondingly, in Austria reconciling family and labour seems to be a major reason for part-time, because in this country it is most positions are filled by women. According to a labour force survey on reasons for part-time work in Austria, men and women stated different reasons for doing part-time work. While women regard part-time work as a useful means of reconciling family work and professional work, men stated that they "could not find a full-time job" or chose atypical employment in the years preceding their retirement or to allow them to continue their education. Only 14.4% of the men stated "family duties" as a reason for part-time work.

This gender pattern is confirmed in Norway, where a recent study of fathers shows that only 5% of the fathers worked part-time, and most of these men had not actively chosen part-time work (Kvande and Brandth 2003). Overtime work is much more typical than part-time work in this group. So in Norway, part-time seems to be a step toward full time for women, and a new time-culture for men.

These gender patterns break at the border of the former socialist countries, e.g., in the states of the former GDR, females working part-time have longer working hours than part-time working females in the west. "Moreover, according to Microcensus figures, more than half of the part-time working women in the east only work part-time because of a lack of full-time jobs." (Arbeitsamt 2000, translation by Höyng et al.)

Like the formerly socialist part of Germany, in Bulgaria full-time work has had a high value for both men and women since the socialist era. The lack of job offers and demand could be interpreted as an absence of an ideology of gender roles, which is strongly associated with a bourgeois context, and points to a pragmatic tradition of combining work and the rest of life. The lack of demand could also be interpreted by a current situation that has a low official labour market participation, where jobs are too valuable to be divided up voluntarily, and where private networks regulate problems of care.

In spite of a strong gender gap, the reasons that lead people to accept a part-time job in Spain are seldom seen as being motivated by personal choice, the main reason given in the rest of the EU. Instead, Spanish part-timers claim that their employment status is due to the type of activity involved, or that they could not find another job. This is the same in Greece, Italy, Portugal and Finland, indicating that it is typical for Southern European countries. In Spain, the reason for the low part-time rate is the high precariousness of the employment when employers are allowed to cover part-time activities through temporary employment in full-time work. This reflects another specifically Spanish characteristic: the high rate of temporary employment among part-time workers – 57.8% of part-time workers had temporary contracts in 1999. Women do not choose the precarious part-time positions because of reconciliation reasons, but are trying to gain a foothold in the labour market. This leads to the conclusion that the much higher part-time rate of women is a consequence resulting from the discrimination on the part of those who offer work. (cf. Abril 2002)

The part-time participation of Israeli men is higher than in all European countries. We may find a explanation for this by looking at the reasons for choosing part time.

Table 5: Israeli Men and Women Employed: Part-Time by Usual Employment Scope and Part-Time Employment; Reasons, 1999-2001 (Percent)

Part-time employment reasons	1999		2000		2001	
	Women	Men	Women	Men	Women	Men
Considered full-time position	21.9	18.8	23.5	21.4	21.9	21.1
Did not find full-time employment	19.7	17.6	19.8	19.0	20.0	19.2
Disease or disability	3.4	9.6	3.6	8.2	3.8	8.9
Retirement	4.3	12.2	4.4	11.3	4.4	10.8
Housewife	20.2	0	18.5	0	17.5	0
Studies	14.1	33	14.5	32.7	15.6	30.7
Not interested in full-time employment	12.8	4.2	13.4	5.0	13.7	6.1
Other	1.8	2.7	2.4	2.1	3.1	3.0

(Kraus 2002)

Men's reasons differ from women in some respects: fewer men are not interested in full time, or housewife (what kind of question...) men choose part-time more often as a form of early retirement and because of disease. As with women, a major reason for men seems to be that they have failed acquire full-time employment. Thus, part-time seems to be chosen as a means of getting or keeping a job in difficult circumstances. And this solution is not only typical for women – as in Spain – but for men too. In Israel, half of both men and women use part-time to transition into fulltime; the other half do so because of personal reasons.

European studies (Corral and Isusi 2003) reveal the advantages and disadvantages accompanying part-time work: disadvantages are a weaker job tenure, lower salary levels, less access to supplemental payment, and social protection. The advantages of working part-time include the possibility of achieving a positive work-life balance and experiencing less job-related health problems. Sociological approaches to the topic of part-time usually stress one of those consequences: the advantages or the disadvantages.

Part-time as a Transition to Full Time

In the theory of economy, part-time employment is often seen as an intermediate level in transition from non-participation (school, domestic work) to full-time work.

The partial progress of women in the labour market is attributed to part-time work and functions as an intermediate position filled by women who may be thought of as today's 'reserve army.' This is supported by the fact that countries with the highest female employment rate also have the highest proportion of women in the part-time workforce, e.g., Norway and the Netherlands. The decline in the proportion of women in part-time positions since the early 1990s in the countries with the highest female employment rates, e.g., Sweden, Norway, is due to a transition from part-time to full-time work. Continuing labour market participation of women increasingly leads them from part-time to full-time.

In some countries such as Germany, the proportion of women working part-time increased in the 1990s. Yet the main long-term trend is an increase in both long-term part-time and full-time employment among women. The rise in the number of women employed part-time (in Germany, for example) has been attributed to the overall increase in the number of women employed and to the increased convergence of female and male employment rates.

Finally, this approach is supported by the fact that young people are more often in part-time. Part-time working people continue to face disadvantages. In the USA, an study stated that

(w)hile part-time work usually increases flexibility, the part-time worker loses out on promotions and pay increases. Part-time work also tends to mean lower hourly pay. Shorter labour stints and part-time work contribute to the probability of working for the minimum wage. Nearly two-thirds of minimum wage earners are women. (Venable 2002)

In Europe, the wage penalty incurred by those working part-time is higher in countries with a high proportion of women working part-time, than in countries with a low proportion. Part-time employment is disadvantageous to one's professional career. Promotion is hardly achievable for part-time workers. It is more likely in fact that one will be demoted or relegated to a lower wage bracket. Furthermore, the risk of being dismissed and becoming unemployed is higher. In many European countries, part-timers have less access to supplemental payment and social protection (Hipp 2004).

The "transition" approach is based on the assumption that people prefer full-time jobs. This seems to apply to Spanish women, Norwegian men, and both Israeli men and women. It does not seem to apply to the majority of part-timers who voluntarily reduce working time. This leads to the second approach, which is based on the assumption that people, if they can afford it, will pursue interests outside of work (ibid.).

Part-time as an Expression of a New Balance of Labour and Private Life

In some sociological literature, one can find a very positive approach to the phenomena of part-time as an indication of a new time-culture:

> To a greater degree than is commonly assumed, it (part-time work, especially in the service sector) is an expression of the general attitude towards work that places more emphasis on reconciliation of family and working life, education and volunteering activities. Accordingly, part-time employment in Germany might be considered as an evolving and developing form of employment that is mainly based on the voluntary decisions of those who are employed. (Hagenkort 2003: 22).

The Netherlands – with the highest level of part-time employment in Europe – can be regarded as an advanced illustration of this trend. The small rise in male part-time employment in Europe may support this approach as well. In the focus are the benefits and chances of part-time work for people and society.

Among non-standard forms of work, part-time employment is particularly interesting because it usually guarantees much more social security than other forms of non-standard work. Furthermore, it can contribute to a more egalitarian-arranged private life and work life for men and women. With regard to men working part-time, it is thus possible for wage and non-wage work to be evenly distributed, particularly within the partnership. Even if we limit our focus to work life, it can be demonstrated that men who work part-time thereby contribute to the equality of the sexes. Such men also represent a model of masculinity that is an alternative to the one requiring that men always be prepared to work. If working part-time was not simply the preferred form of work for mothers juggling a family and a job, then part-time work would most likely be highly looked upon.

Today, the benefits of part-time employment are more evident outside the workplace than in it. A higher life quality can be attained, as is pointed out in many studies that show, e.g., that

> (p)eople who work part-time are more healthy (less job-related health problems). These analyses also indicate that part timers – in spite of bearing responsibility for both care and

> labour work, which is undertaken by many part-timers – are more satisfied and feel they have a better balance between life and work. (Corral and Isusi 2003: 8)

This could be brushed aside as a middle class argument justifying a hedonistic lifestyle, and is thus not applicable to people with low incomes. But this does not explain the majority of the cases where part-time is chosen.

2.3.2 Temporary Work

The frequency of temporary work largely depends on national labour market regulations, especially on dismissal protection. A permanent contract in Great Britain can involve uncertainties resembling those of a temporary contract in Spain.

Fig. 22: Temporary Work – EU 15 in % of total employment for each sex

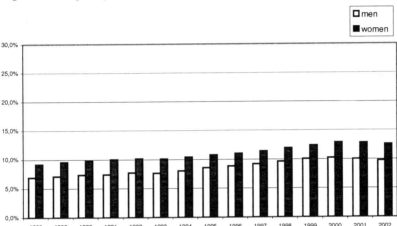

Source: EUROSTAT

On a European level, perhaps the first thing to take note of is that there are many differences regarding both the legal structure and the usage of temporary contracts across member states (Ramos 2002). For instance, temporary contracts represent only 3% of total dependent employment in Luxembourg and as much as 33% (eleven times higher) in Spain, while the EU zone average is 13%. The evolution of temporary employment has also tended to differ state by state. Temporary employment increased very rapidly in France and Spain from 1985 to 1998 but it has remained rather stable in most other countries. In terms of gender, the proportion of women in temporary employment is usually higher than that of men in all EU countries. However, the male to female proportion of temporary work in total dependent employment has been converging since 1985.

Data taken from two countries with different concepts of temporary employment – Britain and Spain – offer a better understanding of temporary jobs and temporary workers (ibid.). Relative to other EU countries, Britain has the least restrictive labour laws and a rather small and stable share of temporary employment (around 7%), whereas Spain has much stricter labour laws and a larger and growing proportion of temporary employment.

51

Temporary and permanent employment differ in aspects other than the flexibility they provide to employers, the level of employment protection, or their shorter average duration. Evidence gathered in Britain shows that temporary jobs account for a large proportion of part-time employment, reveal a greater dispersion of normal hours worked per week, and pay lower wages. Furthermore, temporary workers are more likely to be less satisfied with certain aspects of their work than are permanent workers. All and all, this evidence indicates that temporary employment is worse than permanent employment.

This would not be that bad if temp jobs led to better jobs and good careers. Is that so? The empirical evidence is not at all conclusive here. For Britain, Booth et al. (2002) find evidence that temporary jobs are a stepping stone to permanent work for both men and women. However, Böheim and Taylor (2000b) find significant evidence among unemployed individuals who state that the termination of a temporary job was the reason for separation. For Spain, the evidence suggests the existence of a trap between temporary work and short unemployment spells. As far as future earnings are concerned, temporary work seems to be a handicap for men but not for women.

The amount of temporary jobs available in the labour market seems to be determined by demand-side factors – such as pressures to lower labour costs or to gain more flexibility – while supply-side factors are likely to determine the composition of temporary jobs. British evidence indicates that (1) they are held mostly by the young and the old; (2) there are important gender differences across employment sectors; (3) some women seem to hold fixed-term professional jobs on a career basis; (4) education exerts a positive effect on the probability of being in temporary work for women; and (5) only school-age children increase the probability of that one will have a temporary contract.

A chief, fundamental imbalance in the labour activity in Spain is its excessive temporality combined with the lack of employment for young people and women. In Spain, one of every third working person has a temporary job. The Spanish temporary job rate (32%) is currently almost 19 points higher than the rate for Europe as a whole.

This difference cannot be attributed exclusively to the increasing specialisation of the Spanish production structure in areas dominated by temporary labour (agriculture and tourism). Indeed, the temporary rate remains very high for an annual period of three months even in areas with significant seasonal variation. In this case (and in comparison with Europe), the difference is similar even if we eliminate the areas of tourism and agriculture.

2.3.3　Self-employment

Data evaluation of the six countries investigated suggests that the frequency of self-employment depends on the prosperity of the nation: the higher the level, the less the number of self employed. Even if a Swiss survey suggests that self employed are more satisfied (Falter 2002), labour market participants seem to choose a safe job if possible.

Fig. 23: Self Employment – EU 15 in % of total employment for each sex

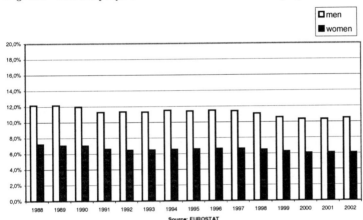

With the exception of some individual countries, the rate of self-employment in Europe as a whole is decreasing. This trend is clearly evident in male domains of employment. The proportion of self-employed men is almost double that of women. No other form of employment bears such marked differences from country to country. Significant differences exist even in the general frequency of incidence, in the proportion of men and women, and in temporal development. The most striking feature here is the lack of uniformity. The poorest countries have the highest rate of self-employment (Spain, then Bulgaria). In Germany, the figure increases slightly. Although self-employed workers earn less on average, their level of satisfaction with their work is higher than that of those who are dependently employed workers. This is due to more favourable working conditions (Falter 2002).

2.4 Gender Segregation[10]

The labour market is still quite markedly gender-segregated in Europe, although there has been a decrease in segregation that is associated with women's upward mobility, e.g., in formerly masculine occupations and middle class jobs. Some countries with a high level of female employment also have a high level of segregation (e.g., Norway).

Gender segregation is a major problem in the European labour market. Studies of occupational segregation show that segregation is often higher at the micro (workplace) level than appears in statistical data, and that the "long lines" of gender segregation are remarkably persistent.

Feminisation of services and masculinisation of industry can be seen as two very broad indicators of the main form of gender segregation in working life. Long-term historical analysis of employment statistics from the industrial revolution (1830s in England) onwards indicates that the proportion of women (and children) in manufacturing was high at the beginning of this period (especially in early, textile-led industrialisation). The female proportion stagnated in the early 20th century and then decreased gradually in the period from 1920 to 1980 in all or almost all industrialised countries. In the service sector on the other hand, the female proportion generally increased as women appeared in these jobs from the 1880s onwards, slowly rising as a gradual tendency in the first part of the 20th century, and increasing more markedly once again in the 1970s and 80s.

Current labour market segregation is to a large extent connected with these long-term patterns. Indicators show a general tendency in industrial society that technically oriented work became more purely masculine, and socially oriented work more purely feminine. Although gender differences in rank were diminished, differences in work orientation increased.

But are these two long-term processes still active? It seems that the reduction in the proportion of technical positions held by women has more or less come to a halt, albeit women account for an insignificant number of workers in the tech sector. In Spain, the masculinisation of industry decreased slightly between 1995 to 2002, while it remained stable in Germany. The feminisation of services is noteworthy, if quite gradual in some countries (Germany, for example).

Gender-specific segregation patterns are present in occupations and lines of business (horizontal segregation) as well as on different hierarchical levels in the labour market (vertical segregation).

Horizontal segregation is frequently indicated by the fact that areas of work are labelled with recourse to gender dominance: men's professions, women's professions, integrated professions, etc.

---

10   The introduction and conclusion of this section on segregation is based on Kreimer 2003.

Gender-specific differences in income levels as well as differences in career paths (when the level of qualification is the same) are indicators of vertical segregation. Empirical analysis demonstrates little movement here in the way of a reduction in segregation. Men's higher level of income appears to remain constant and continues to be unaffected, even in the face of women who are clearly more qualified. (Gregoritsch et al. 2000). The increasing flexibility in the labour market has led to an increase in "atypical" forms of work and – although this change has affected women more than men until recently – there has been an overproportionate increase in the number of men affected. Because these more flexible forms of work almost always coincide with lower wages and/or higher risks, this form of segregation in relation to forms of employment makes a new contribution to vertical differentiation (Kreimer 1998, Tálos 1999, Mühlberger 1998).

The horizontal division of the labour market into women and men's areas does not necessarily imply negative consequences for the labour market opportunities of men and women. It can rather fully express individual preferences. Moreover, female and male occupations can represent niches in which women and men do not have to compete with one another. Admittedly, horizontal segregation is almost always connected with hierarchal differentiation and thus with vertical segregation, and is to the advantage of men. The essential cause of this is the prevention or concealment of the comparison of possibilities. The concentration in women's professions or lines of work makes it easier to arrive at a "women-specific" definition and evaluation of activities (e.g., fewer assessments), problematises proof of unfair treatment, and reduces the possibilities of deviation (Finder and Blaschke 1999). Horizontal segregation yields gains for men, which is expressed by the income and position discrimination against women. Labour market segregation is thus an essential cause for the continual discrimination against women in the labour market (Kreimer 1999, Heintz et al. 1997, Kleber 1988).

One of the most remarkable aspects of the labour market segregation of the sexes is its persistence despite all of the changes in the participation of women, their increased level of qualification, and their professional orientation (Kapeller et al. 1999). Women have penetrated formerly male areas of work and are able to achieve new hierarchal positions. Yet at the same time, new forms of segregation arise. The forms of segregation change but they persist nonetheless.

2.4.1 The Emergence and Development of Segregated Labour Markets

Original Segregation and the "Doctrine of Separate Spheres"

The gender-specific division of work is a phenomenon of human development. Historically however, the separation of familial and professional spheres was something new, emerging with the development of market systems (Kreckel 1993). The lifeworlds of men and women were separated and a genderised division of labour in the sense of an "original segregation" (Maier 1991) was established. Reskin and Padavic (1994) speak of the *doctrine of separated spheres*, in which women were relegated to the household and men situated in professional employment, a development that occurred against the backdrop of the bourgeois ideal of the upper middle class. The *male breadwinner - female homemaker* model became the societal norm. A complete implementation never took place though, because it was not possible to do without women in the labour market, nor was it possible at this time for there to be an unlimited provision for families on the sole basis of male incomes. Women in the labour market were thus always a reality during industrialisation and, furthermore, they accounted for a not insignificant proportion of workers (for Austria see Münz and Neyer 1986).

Establishment of the Segregated Labour Market

The situation arose then, in which women and men had to increasingly perform the same work in the presence of one another. The more that women could prove that they "could do what their men did," the greater the need was to legitimate the differing assessment of male and female work spheres. Although there was no dearth of justifications derived from the study of work, biology and ideology concerning the "female's working abilities,"[11] it was hardly possible on the level of generally valid societal norms to treat men and women differently when they worked side by side in the same contexts and carried out the same duties. The "solution" to this dilemma was to prevent women and men from working side by side and to conceal the fact that they were doing the "same" thing. In other words, a segregated labour market was established.

This segregated integration of women enabled both the unfair treatment of equals and avoided placing men and women in direct competition with one

---

11   Historical research on women reveals substantial evidence concerning the attempts to prove the "naturalness" of women and men's professions and has brought to light the social construction of the sexes (see Hausen 1993). The role of institutions (churches, parties, unions) as well as economists has already been analysed in detail (see Münz and Neyer 1986, Pujol 1992).

another. The latter was essential to the extent that it offered the male work force a source of resistance against working women (Rubery 1978). First, the increase in the availability of work decreased the negotiation potential of the workforce and lowered wages. Second, the inclusion of women as workers on equal terms would have seriously cast doubts upon the *breadwinner* model.

Around the turn of the 20th century, married (male) workers in many parts of Europe were faced with the paradoxical situation that an increasing number of children was leading to a growing reliance on the "additional income" of the wife on the one hand, while the low cost female workforce was increasingly becoming a source of competition. This trend took on more significance as women assumed more and more male occupations. Women who worked in education, secretarial work, as well as in the heavy labour positions of the war industry earned on average about less than half the men's wages (Münz and Neyer 1986). In the end, the efforts to reduce the participation of women in the labour market after both world wars were just as unsuccessful. The possibility of blocking women's access to men's professions and work spheres was, by contrast, a successful strategy for the preservation of the male-female hierarchal structure of professional employment.

Stabilisation of the Segregated Labour Market

The mechanisms by which labour market segregation is concretely implemented and stabilised are manifold. Through direct *exclusion processes,* attempts were made to legitimise the blocking of women's access to professions requiring high levels of qualification (for medicine, see Wetterer 1993). Barring married women from certain professions, so-called *marriage bars*, excluded women completely from the labour market (see Goldin 1990). Protective labour laws always had an exclusionary effect in addition to protective measures (see Münz and Neyer 1986). It is precisely the discussion of the contradictions within protective labour measures for women that demonstrates the close connection to the *male breadwinner*-model. As long as caring for children falls to women within the framework of this familial model, specific laws protecting women and mothers are necessary, and this specificity functions simultaneously as an exclusionary mechanism within certain labour spheres. Extending the application of these laws to men, as in the case of parental leave time for fathers, does not change anything if the societal distribution of labour is not altered by political means.

As women increasingly penetrated male domains, exclusionary strategies ceased functioning; when this occurred, *demarcation* became the dominant strategy. Internal labour markets and the discrimination processes in companies associated with them, the definition and legitimisation of female labour spheres or work assessment systems are examples of demarcation strategies (Rabe-Kleberg 1987, Kreimer 1999). The definition of "normal" forms of work plays a very significant role here. The pattern of women's work as an additional source of income deviates from that of the man in terms of work schedules and continuity.

By exploiting the possibilities of familial, tax and social policies, the welfare state can either substantiate or weaken the gender-specific distribution of labour in societies where the *breadwinner* model dominates. Unions, parties and lobbies also play a roll in the construction of the *breadwinner* model and the norms of forms of work. A change in the thinking and attitude among the former may lead to a change in the latter.

2.4.2 Current European Data about Horizontal Professional Segregation

A new study should shed light on the current segregation of the sexes. A crucial aspect persists: Horizontal segregation is present on an international level and is particularly pronounced in the traditional domains of the labour market.

One of the first attempts to make an international comparison of occupational segregation based on compatible occupational definitions was carried out by Deutsch and Silber (2003). Occupational classification often varies from one country to another. The Luxembourg Income Study Project, a pioneering effort in compiling data sets on income distribution that can be compared internationally, started in recent years to also gather data on employment, one result of which is that international comparisons of segregation by gender can be conducted with much greater certainty.

The data for this empirical investigation was made available by the Luxembourg Employment Study (LES) Project.[12] Compatible data was available for ten countries: Switzerland (1997), Finland (1990), France (1997), Hungary (1993), Luxembourg (1992), Norway (1990), Poland (1994), Spain (1993), Sweden (1990) and the United Kingdom (1989).

The study assumes that an occupation is considered an essentially "male occupation" if more than 90% of its workers are males. Similarly, an occupation is defined as an essentially "female occupation" if more than 90% of its workers are female. Although the cross section of data that was available does not cover the same year, they all refer to the same decade, that which covers the period from 1989 to 1997. (For the purposes of the study, this decade was simply referred to as the 1990s.) It was assumed that as far as occupational segregation is concerned, changes occur slowly over time so that an interna-

---

12 The classification of occupations that was used was the two-digit International Standard Classification of Occupations that is the one adopted by LES for making international comparisons.

tional comparison of results was still possible. Naturally, any firm conclusion should be drawn with care.

When the whole labour force, including employees and the self-employed, is taken into account, there are four occupations that appear to be male occupations in the majority of the countries for which data was available. These are the armed forces, listed in six countries as a "male occupation," extraction and building trade occupations, listed in all countries as "male occupation," metal, machinery and related trade occupations, listed in eight countries as "male occupations," and finally drivers and mobile plant operators listed in nine countries as "male occupations." No occupation is listed in at least five countries as a "female occupation." Thus, women are still excluded from some fields, while there is no "female occupation" within the general European context.

This picture changes a bit if the labour force is not taken as a whole and the focus changes to workers in part time.

If one takes a look at part-time employees only, it appears that there is no occupation in which most of the part-timers are men. There are however three occupations in which most of the part timers are women. These are life science and health associated professionals, listed in seven countries, customer service clerks, listed in six countries, and personnel and protective service workers, listed in five countries.

The investigation of gender segregation in occupational groups in ten EU countries arrived at the conclusion that there are four occupational groups that are mostly dominated by men in most of the countries investigated, but no occupational groups dominated by women. Thus, there are male-designated occupations across Europe, but the defining element of a women's profession remains culturally dependent. One needs to keep in mind here that the limit employed to define the gender of an occupation was high (90%), and that the incidence of women in professional employment is lower. The result is that a high concentration of relatively few women in certain professions does not necessarily lead to women dominance.

Male occupational groups are all situated in the production and military sectors, areas that reflect traditional masculinity. European employment in production is continually declining because of outsourcing and automation. Employment in the service sector – which is not segregated to the same extent – is, by contrast, continually increasing. It is no surprise then that the unemployment rate of men has grown at an over-proportionate rate. The military occupies a unique position here, because the original form of direct exclusion discussed above continues to function. In many countries, women cannot pursue an occupation in the military because of legal obstacles. This applies at the very least to positions in combat units.

There are female-dominated professions in almost every country but these constitute the same professions across borders in less than five countries. Female-connoted work thus appears to be less fixed than that of men. One can draw the conclusion then that the masculine is understood as the area serving as the source of this definition and categorisation. This is in line with the thesis that women are viewed as a reserve army for industry. Men occupy the permanent and hierarchal positions in the labour market, and women fill in the gaps, which change according to economic and technological developments.

Traditional masculinity is constructed upon the categorisation of male-and female-designated occupations; gendered occupations in turn produce masculinity and femininity. This appears to be changing, especially in new employment sectors. In areas of employment that are growing, less division has been evinced. The decisive question is whether this will continue over the long term. Historical investigations reveal that new occupations are initially characterised by a less marked segregation of genders, but that segregation in those fields grows over time. Cynthia Cockburn (1985) demonstrates, for instance, that vertical and horizontal segregation have crept their way into the new computer fields. On the other hand, it can be rightly assumed that global capital is less and less prepared to pay attention to gender segregation. If women are not positioned according to their talent and performance, the result is lower output per employee and thus there is a rise in additional costs.

In the new EU member states, the possibility exists that there will be a process of increased segregation within the framework of assimilation. Thus, the choice of profession for young women in the eastern part of Germany has shrunk from a relatively broad palate over the past ten years, falling into line with the five most typical occupational choices of young women in West Germany.

Viewed as a whole, segregation between and within the sexes appears to be becoming more differentiated. In the advanced industrial countries, womens' participation rates are rising, and women are more likely to have careers. Having said that, the precarious work previously reserved for women is increasingly performed by migrant women.

If vertical segregation is included, the final constant is horizontal. This means that women are more likely to be employed in precarious and/or hierarchically low positions or to face the so-called glass ceiling phenomenon.

2.4.3   Professional and Household Work

Even in highly industrialised countries, paid labour accounts for only a small portion of the total amount of work. The total amount of work in Europe appears to be distributed in a relatively equal way. The distribution of paid and unpaid work is however starkly defined along gender-specific lines. Thus, the workload is distributed in a relatively equal fashion. But in European societies, the opportunities in life as well as the social security of women and men are significantly dependent on participation in the labour market. As long as the distribution of professional employment is unequal, one cannot assume the existence of social equality. To take an example, males in Germany above the age of 10 spend on average 15 hours per week doing unpaid work and 13 hours doing paid work. In this situation, the total workload is almost equal. On average, females and males work 28 hours per week. Paid and unpaid work is however distributed in a highly unequal way between the sexes. Females work 18 hours per week doing unpaid work and 10 hours doing paid work. For males, the situation is the inverse: 16 hours per week are dedicated to professional employment and training (or career-furthering education) and 12 hours to unpaid work.

Fig. 24: Work Division of Couples in Germany

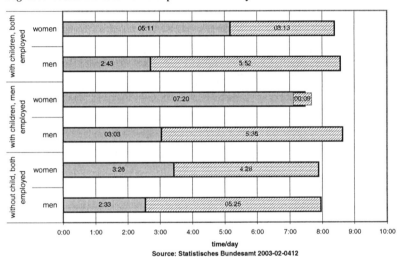

Source: Statistisches Bundesamt 2003-02-0412

Data on Europe is not differentiated in relation to the portion of household work performed by men. The following table is the result of various individual studies.[13]

---

13   Austria: Fassmann 1995: 45ff (Figures for employed men and women). Denmark: Laustsen & Sjørup 2003. Finland: Niemi & Paakkonen 2002: 59. France: Aliaga & Winquist 2003. Germany: Gesoep 1991 and 2000 (approximate figures for housework). Netherland: Time Use Survey 1980-2000 (Calculation based on SCP internet information http://www.scp.nl/onderzoek/tbo/english/tabellen/default.asp). Norway: based on Odd Frank Vaage 2002: Til alle døgnets tider, tabell 3.1, SSB Oslo/Kongsvinger (Norwegian Statistics Bureau). Sweden: based on Rydenstam 2003: Ta_resultat.pdf, p 6 (Statistics Sweden - approximate numbers). UK: Aliaga & Winquist 2003. US: based on University of Michigan Institute for Social Research (ISR) 2002: http://www.umich.edu/~newsinfo/Releases/2002/Mar02/r031202a.html. (Approximate figures). Note that the country levels are not strictly comparable due to differences in age selection, category, definition, etc.

Fig. 25: Men's Share of Domestic Work in Selected Countries 1979-2001 (percent)

	1979-1984	1985-1994	1995-2001
Austria		28,5	
Denmark		35	41
Finland	33,3	36	36
France			35
Germany east		42	33
Germany west		39	41
Netherland	24,4	28,2	32
Norway	32,8	37,3	41
Sweden		38	40
UK			36
USA		34	37

The increase in men's portion of domestic work is an important, gradual trend that has occurred over the past decades. If the trend continues, for example in Norway, equal sharing of household work will be achieved by around 2030. However, recidivism is visible in the table as well, notably in East Germany. Most of the increase in men's share in the last decade is due to women reducing their amount of domestic work, which in turn is related to women's increased labour market participation. There was only a slight increase in men's work, measured in hours and minutes.

A differentiated study of the distribution of housework between the sexes in Britain allows us to provide some important results. [14]

Ramos (2003) provides new evidence about gender differentials in domestic work time, market work time, and total work time, which update the evidence provided by Jenkins and O'Leary (1997) and Layte (1999) by using UK time-budget surveys.

The picture that emerges from the BHPS (British Household Panel) data is a rather 'traditional' and well-known one. On average, women (be they married or single) work more at home and less in the labour market than men. As a result, men and women end up doing almost the same amount of total work hours. However these average figures conceal a much richer reality that points to a less gender-equal division of total work time. For instance, depending on labour market status, average total work time is greater for women than for men.

Moreover, our results cohere with some basic findings predicted by economic theory and are well documented in the existing empirical literature (e.g., a negative relation between housework and paid work time, more housework done by women, but more market work done by men, lesser contribu-

---

14   In this case, Great Britain was not chosen because of considerations of content, but rather because the British Household Panel provides a particularly good data base.

tion to housework by younger women); and these clearly suggest that Britain is still distant from a gender equality situation. The positive side of this pessimistic conclusion is that the trends in domestic and paid work time over the nineties show a narrowing in the gender differentials, thanks mainly to the changing behaviour of women and not of men. We find that for men housework hours and paid work time remained rather constant through the nineties. For women however, total work time decreased monotonically over this period, reflecting a reduction in housework hours that outweighs an increase in paid work time.

An important message that seems to emerge (even from a simple first glance at the data) is that women are far more flexible than men. That is, men hardly react or change their behaviour in the face of (certain) situations that clearly affect women's time allocation decisions. For instance, the time women devote to housework increases when children are present in the household, whereas the impact of children on the husband's time is negligible. In much the same way, younger wives do much less housework than their older counterparts. Younger men, however, by and large spend the same amount of time on housework as their father's generation.

All and all then, the time husbands dedicate to housework depends mainly on their own amount of time spent in the labour market, the paid work time done by their wives, and their relative contribution to total labour income.

Given this situation, who are the men who show a higher contribution to housework time relative to their wives? Our results suggest that we should be looking for a rather peculiar profile: young (born after 1951), highly educated, blue collar employees holding non-permanent contracts, whose labour market time and income shares are relatively low and whose wives also posses high education levels.

In other words, we have found out that certain characteristics increase the probability of being a man who contributes more to doing housework. As one would expect, labour market time and income shares are important determining factors. In particular, both shares stand in a negative relation to the probability of being such a man. Education is another important factor which, in this case, increases the likelihood of such an identity. The education level of the husband, however, is not as important as that of the wife. This is because better-educated wives spend less time doing housework, and not because their husbands spend more time doing chores. We have also shown that men belonging to younger birth cohorts contribute more at home in relative terms, which suggests the existence of some generational effect. Finally, there are two job-related characteristics that also help to explain the probability. The most important one for this research project is the type of work contract held by the husband. We have found that non-standard contracts, that is, fixed-term or seasonal contracts, have a positive effect on probability. Thus, new forms of work may help foster greater gender equality.

2.5 Working Biographies

The traditional working life in Europe is changing. It is becoming less common for men to work 40 or more years, often with only one employer. The phases of learning, employment and paid retirement are no longer characterised by strict demarcation and clear succession.

Although women previously shared with men distinct periods of education and retirement, their working biographies were very different: long or complete exits from the labour market to do care and household work and continuous or discontinuous part-time work was the norm. Unlike now, permanent full-time work for women was atypical, and women retired earlier.

The structural changes in employment have a significant influence on emerging patterns in the working biographies of women and men. Owing to the destandardisation of the traditional course of life, the activity phases of men and women are slowly converging (Berger 1996, Bosch 2001). The standard male working-life pattern is being eroded by phases of unemployment and additional phases of vocational training, as well as by early retirement. In some countries such as those in Scandinavia, there is an observable alignment of female with male life-courses, as men increasingly request temporary reductions in their full-time work or take more leisure time in the course of their working life – or towards its end. The increasing significance of 'normal working life-courses' for young women, which has been noticeable since the 1970s and has its origin in their growing income orientation, is accompanied by a parallel increase in the numbers of discontinuous cycles comparable with those of men (cf. European Foundation 2003b: 72f).

There has also been increasing diversification of employment patterns in families with small children. In the Netherlands, a '1½ model' prevails among 50% of families, meaning one partner works full time and the other part time; Portugal has a 1 + 1 model in 61% of cases, meaning both partners work full time. The other extreme is Spain, where the dominant pattern is 1 + 0, indicating the dominance of the male breadwinner model and the prominence of a traditional female career biography (cf. European Foundation 2003b: 5f).

Based on the current changes in male and female life courses, some observers predict a closing of the gap for the following reasons: more women are in paid continuous full-time employment; the number of years spent in employment for women is now closer to that of men (in Germany it is down from a difference of 16 years to an average difference of nine years); younger women outperform older women in terms of employment rates; and the educational achievements of women are surpassing those of their male counterparts. The trend for men, on the other hand, seems to be moving in the opposite direction: more men find themselves in discontinuous employment because of unemployment or higher professional mobility; men remain longer in education and retire earlier.

Consequentially, a small number of men have what was previously an exclusively female 'patchwork' biography. In spite of this trend, the patterns of discontinuity and of combination biographies are marked by a significant gender difference. Female discontinuity is more based on choice (especially related to care, although there are many important exceptions). By contrast, men's 'patchwork' and shorter working biographies stem from unemployment, disability and (market-driven) compulsory early retirement. Working time options supporting a combination biography are also less available to men than women.

2.5.1   Start of Working Life

The transition from school to working life is an important part of the working biography and is a difficult shift to effect in many European countries. This is evinced by the high rates of unemployment for young people, rates that are becoming increasing alike for men and women.

A French empirical investigation (Hanchane 2002)[15] showed that even though educational levels and job experience have, as expected, an important effect on the probability of having a given job status in the labour market, there are important gender differences in the impact on the transition from school to work and the efforts made to balance family constraints with a professional career. Approximately 60% of the young males lived mainly in their parents' home during the first years of their active life. The corresponding figure for females was only 38%. This gap between the genders becomes smaller as the level of education increases.

This survey also shows that 27% of the young females but only 12% of the young males lived as a "couple" before or immediately upon entering the labour market.

It appears that the unobserved individual heterogeneity is higher among females in both cases (fixed duration contracts and contracts of undetermined duration). This difference between the genders had been previously observed in studies of the insertion of individuals in the labour force. One of the reasons could well be that when comparing males and females with a given diploma, there is a greater diversity of behaviour among women concerning their labour force supply, depending on the importance they give to "living as a couple" and to the education of their children.

Leaving the parent's home is a factor that increases the probability of getting a job, but does so in a very different way for women and men. As far as

---

15   The authors looked at the professional and family history of young people who left school in 1998 and were surveyed three years later, in 2001. Using original data from a survey called "Generation 98" and conducted by the French Ministry of Education and Labour, a longitudinal database was built to estimate the probability of getting a job (short term contract or unlimited duration contract) at three points in time, separately for each gender.

the relationship between the individual and her family is concerned, one observes that those women who are the most "disconnected" from the parental home are those who have the highest probability of getting a fixed duration contracts or a contract of undetermined duration.

In any case, some recent studies (cf. Battagliola 1999) indicate that leaving the parents' home before getting a job is essentially a female form of behaviour, especially if this is related to the decision to "live as a couple."

It also turns out that there are gender specific impacts on labour market outcomes when children come into play. For young men raising up to three children, it does not seem to have an effect on their commitment to professional life. For young women however, maternity seems to be an impediment to professional achievement, since it lowers the probability of getting an unlimited duration contract and even sometimes a short-term contract.

In summary, it can be maintained that young men live longer in their parents' homes after graduating than do young women. Young men who remain at home acquire permanent positions relatively faster than young women. Young women are more likely to leave home, and those who do so are more likely to acquire a permanent position than those who remain at home. The masculine answer to flexibility, unemployment and globalisation appears to be "Hotel Mama."

2.5.2 Discontinuity

A study based on Israeli insurance data (Neuman and Ziderman 2003) compared the work history patterns of men and women.[16]

It appears that among those working, only 19.4% of the men and only 10.5% of the women worked continuously throughout this 12-year period. Among those who experienced work interruptions, 14.2% of the men and 9.6% of the women had only one interruption. Similarly 6.1% of the men and 6.0% of the women had only two interruptions. The total duration of these work interruptions is relatively small but note that 42.4% of the men and 53.4% of the women had more than two interruptions.

Among the individuals not currently working, 22.8% of the men and 31.3% of the women have never worked. It appears that 77.3% of the men and 68.6% of the women not currently working have experienced work interruptions in their lifetime.

---

16 This study is based on a matching of the individual records of two censuses, those of 1983 and 1995, this data set being merged later on with data on the working profile and the wages of these individuals (data that was gathered monthly by the National Insurance Institute). Such a unique combination of data sources allows one to take a very close look at the different types of work interruption, since there are differences in the timing of these interruptions, in their length and numbers.

Taken as a whole, a clear gender distinction can be made here. Admittedly, in Israel the traditional working biography only applies to a minority of men. The vast majority must live with discontinuities and interruptions.

2.6 Conclusions

The forms of occupation are changing in the European labour market. The traditional 'standard job' – a full-time, permanent and fairly secure job – is less predominant than before. Since this type of job has mainly been a male domain, this process influences men more than women. With women's increasing labour market participation and the decrease in the incidence of standard jobs among men, the occupational relations of men and women in Europe are becoming more similar. Although part-time work is still dominated by women, the proportion of part-time employment among men has gradually increased. Gender segregation is still marked in the labour markets included in this study, but there are significant changes below the surface, some of them with a particular impact on men.

Domestic work is still unequally distributed between men and women, but younger and more educated couples are sharing domestic chores more equally. Some statistical factors increase the probability of men doing more chores, e.g., more balance between the man and the woman's income, and non-standard contracts and blue-collar jobs among men.

Studies of typical sector balances and employment forms in Europe show considerable variation, exemplified by four main socio-geographical types of service-oriented economies, including work/family relations.

The structural changes in male employment have a significant influence on the emerging new patterns of the work biographies of men. The trend for men seems to be moving in this direction: more men are in discontinuous employment through unemployment or higher professional mobility; men are working more in part time and temporary work, and men remain longer in education and retire earlier. As a result, some men have what was previously considered an exclusively female 'patchwork' biography.

2.6.1   Gender Geography of Europe

Although Europe as a whole, as mentioned, has a higher level of economic equality than USA and Russia, there are large regional differences within Europe in terms of diversity and inequality. A main divide runs east-west. The economic level (GDP per capita) is around three times higher in the west than the east. A second, weaker divide runs north-south, with the level around one and a half times higher in the north than the south. Likewise, levels of unemployment vary markedly, from around 20 % in Bulgaria to around 4 % in Austria and Norway (in 2002).

The 'gender geography of Europe' consists of the economic, political and cultural balance between men and women. It is easy to see how this varies especially along a north-south dimension, with the general rule that gender equality is further developed in the north.

However, the picture is more complex, with distinct regional labour/gender configurations and welfare/family developments, e.g., a Central European configuration and a western Mediterranean configuration. Further complexity comes in regarding the east-west dimension, since women's high economic participation in the east has been combined with a rather low social position in other terms (e.g. politics).

In the former Eastern Bloc occupational segregation was considerable, women were poorly represented among party leaders, the gender distribution of power in the family remained one-sided, and many women faced a double burden of job and home work with longer total hours per week than women in the west (Monee 1999: viii).

Studies of typical sector balances and employment forms in Europe show considerable variation, filling in the picture outlined above. A recent study of the European service sector found four main socio-geographical types of service-oriented economies, including work/family relations (Bosch and Wagner 2003: 487ff). These were

(1) a southern type with a traditional industrial sector with a small service proportion and limited demand for production oriented services, plus a traditional family structure and weak welfare systems;
(2) a northern type with a technically innovative industrial sector with high proportion services and large demand for production oriented services, plus a modern household structure (women employed) combined with high welfare system development;
(3) a continental type with a modern industrial structure with high production oriented services proportion, but a partially traditional family structure that keeps social services on a level below the Nordic level, and
(4) an Anglosaxon type with a high level of specialised production oriented services, especially in finance. Despite a traditional household structure, consumer services reached a mid level.

2.6.2   A New Culture of Work Time?

The long-term trend towards a convergence of men's and women's work and time-use patterns need not mean full-time employment for everyone. Today, however, part-time continues to be a socially sensitive labour market category with a pronounced gender link. For example, the Netherlands with its high level of part-time employment is also one of the countries with the highest gender gap in wages in the EU, although it is not as high as Germany and the UK (EC 2003: 111).

At the other end of the spectrum, parts of the labour market are characterised by overwork – especially among men. Official statistics are often poor measures of the actual total amount of work being done. A typical finding in qualitative studies of men reveals that more work is done than is officially reported, e.g., in temporary jobs and career jobs (Holter and Aarseth 1993). Our research confirms this and illuminates some of the conditions of masculine overtime culture (cf. Höyng and Puchert 1998).

Part-time employment can facilitate the transition of women and men to labour. This is inhibited by two factors: the structure and culture of organisations, and governmental regulations. Despite lower wages for part-time work, lower tax rates may make it attractive to remain under this income threshold. And EU labour laws support the equal treatment of full-time and part-time workers.

But fostering only part time leaves a hierarchy of over-performers over part timers. A consequent policy would foster as well a low general working time (Spitzley 1999, 2004), depending of the working craft potential of a country. This would divide paid work to all those, who are interested, and it would minimise the hierarchy. To foster a low general working time would divide the social secured labour to more people, which could be helpful in any country with high unemployment and inactivity rates. In Bulgaria as well as in Spain and Germany, it could lead to more gender equality as well. It could be a chance for more family work of fathers as well and could weaken the culture of overwork.

Reducing segregation by changing the division of labour

The starting point for a change in the entire societal division of work is present on two different levels. First, breaking down the gender hierarchy can be pursued through a change in the personal division of labour, one which moves toward a more balanced distribution of professional and familial work by the sexes. Second, there should be an attempt to break down the functional hierarchy abiding between professional and familial work by bringing both areas closer together. Both levels together produce a matrix of possible objectives instead of one-dimensional strategies for breaking down the segregation of the labour market.

Table 6: Matrix of Possibilities for Changing the Gender-Specific Division of Labour

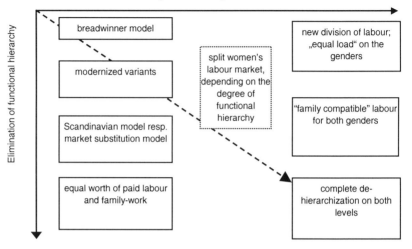

The goal of the vertical dimension is the equal appreciation of professional and familial work and thus the de-hierarchisation of the "original segregation," the minimisation and eventual elimination of the power asymmetry between production and reproduction. This requires a discussion about the concept of work and a change in the way work is evaluated. A final step is for it to become necessary for labour areas themselves, because it is not only the gender-specific wage gap that supports the hierarchy independent of qualifications and performance. In particular however, it is necessary for there to be a new regulation of the forms of paid and unpaid work, for instance how they are discussed in the context of a "basic form of social protection for everyone."

Pursuing a new way of dividing labour among the sexes enters in a relatively radical way into the lives of men. By taking on professional work and maintaining responsibility for familial work, women have managed to demonstrate an enormous potential for adaptation, indicating the possibility of changing what has been until now relatively untouched contexts of living.

Historical experience allows one to assume that breaking down the gender hierarchy without breaking down the functional hierarchy will not have a sustainable impact. From an economic point of view, it is totally conceivable that men will not willingly give up their relatively privileged status in relation to women, nor will they submit to the "burden" of familial work. Strategies that promise success and strive for a change in the division of labour must, therefore, also include a breaking down of the hierarchy present in both areas of work, so that men are not forced to take this on.

Table 7: Scenarios of elimination of segregation

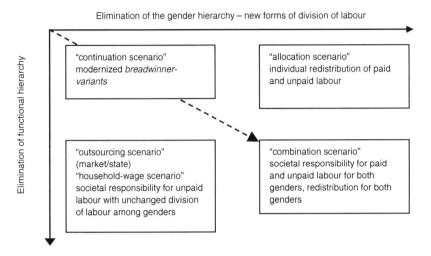

Elimination of the gender hierarchy – new forms of division of labour

"continuation scenario"
modernized *breadwinner-variants*

"allocation scenario"
individual redistribution of paid and unpaid labour

"outsourcing scenario"
(market/state)
"household-wage scenario"
societal responsibility for unpaid labour with unchanged division of labour among genders

"combination scenario"
societal responsibility for paid and unpaid labour for both genders, redistribution for both genders

Thus, a restructuring on both levels requires a comparatively large degree of work reorganisation. A concrete reduction in professional work for men is required, as is leaving behind the model of the (masculine) full-time work biography, and (at least) an increase in the amount of professional employment for women[17] in conjunction with a simultaneous shifting of a portion of unpaid work into paid work. This is required in order for both areas to achieve the same mass and so both sexes can take on the same portion of responsibility.

The key points of such a scenario would be:

Reduced work schedule functioning as a new standard for normal work situations

Elimination of the present breadwinner elements from the social security system

Integration of caring and child raising as normal components of the social security system, having an appeal for both sexes

Substantial provision and/or subsidising of qualitatively good social service facilities (see also Brouwer and Wierda 1998, Bruyn-Hundt 1996)[18]

---

17   Whether a higher participation rate of women in the labour market in this scenario is to be pursued depends on the current degree of participation and the quota of part-timers.

18   This proposal stems in large part from the Dutch model for the integration of caring work into the economy. (Brouwer & Wierda 1998). The measures and instruments need to be

The segregation of the sexes was and is an extremely persistent reality in the labour market. As has been demonstrated, segregation is subject to definite changes and can be influenced. Thus, it can also be constructed along the lines of egalitarian gender policies.

---

more precisely defined and adapted to the respective national systems. It should also be noted that many questions still remain: How will single parents get along in this model? How can the quality of outsourced caring work and caring work jobs be assured? How can it be assured that men reduce the amount of paid work hours they put in? Would the *wage gap* automatically disappear or does it require additional, specific measures?

3. "We don't have anything like that here!" – Organisations, Men and Gender Equality

Øystein Gullvåg Holter, Vera Riesenfeld and Elli Scambor

3.1 Gender and Organisations

In capitalist societies, the integration of the population into both the professional and private spheres is universal.[19] Thus, the labour market and its organisations constitute the most important social locations where the social inequality of the sexes is produced and reproduced. Claudia Honegger (1991) has made the striking observation that the formation of modern industrial societies has simultaneously brought with it the separation of both these areas and has generated "modern" gender relations with their specifically allocated competences and attributes. In the preceding chapter, we gave a more detailed analysis of the social changes in the labour market and the effects on gender relations. At this juncture, we would like to turn our attention to what occurs at the company level.

Companies mark the location where goods and services are produced and distributed. Like all the organisations of "occidental capitalism" (Weber 1980: 31ff), companies follow the advanced principle of profit maximisation on account of their integration into the stabilisation and development of capitalist means of production. Using Weber's model of bureaucracy, the continuation of the research on organisations holds two assumptions as pivotal for explaining how companies function.

According to the principle of rationality, "one best way" of managing a company is sought and this way is then implemented with objectivity, clear calculation, and high efficiency. Using this as a basis, Taylor developed the model of "scientific management." (Taylor 1913)

The principle of the abstraction from the subject is applied in the distribution of functions and competences among company employees. That means that positions are filled by those who are best suited to them and who possess the relevant abilities. The hierarchic order as well as the procedures for evaluation and promotion also follow the protocols of formality and neutrality for the person in question and do so from an objective point of view. Sex, age or ethnic background should not therefore play any role in this process.

---

19 This also includes that section of the population not currently unemployed but that is either in a pre- or post-employment phase (school, retirement), that lives on state support (which again is connected to the employment system) or is financially supported by a family member who is employed.

If this organisational sociological approach is pursued, then companies can be described as "rationally designed systems, which are defined by the relation of goals and means...(and) whose function consists in the achievement of a given goal through the use of the most optimal set of means possible" (Wilz 2002: 21).

However, both Weber and mainstream organisational research neglect an interpretation of the genderisation of social processes and the organisations in which those processes are integrated.

The way in which an organisation functions is always integrated into cultural and institutional conditions. This means that the functioning of an organisation should be viewed as a complex changing relationship between these conditions and the goals of the organisation in question. As in Pfau-Effinger (1998), different levels can be observed here. At the cultural level, every society has

> dominant models guiding the distribution of labour in the family and along gender-specific lines... which indicate the areas of social labour that are regarded as appropriate for men and women, what kind of dependence or autonomy should exist in gender relations, and what obligations exist in relations between generations. (ibid.: 183)

The second level is defined by the institutions of the labour market such as those of the welfare state, companies, and by relations between industries. These institutions

> are in a specific changing relation with cultural models; the actions in and by institutions refer to existing models and contribute to the their reproduction or change. (ibid.: 184)

The third level refers to the action of social actors. Pfau-Effinger speaks here of a gender arrangement that is manufactured by social actors with their particular interests represented in the process of negotiation:

> I speak here of an 'arrangement' because I assume that negotiation processes between social actors provide a crucial basis on which specific gender/cultural models and specific welfare-state policies are socially dominated. (ibid.)

Rational decisions by companies should therefore always be thought of as existing in this changing relation. The social organisation of labour as well as predominant gender models predetermine the realms of possibility through their "objective" structures. Rational decisions can thus also include those which are viewed as primarily irrational at the commercial level but make sense in terms of society as a whole. One example is the unequal pay rates for men and women. Men are more expensive employees but, according to the dominant model, they "bring" a wife with them, who does reproduction work at no cost. In this way, companies can have recourse to two employees.

After describing the first level in the chapter before, in the following we will provide a more detailed account of the latter two levels. Based on the companies we have studied, we will also show to what extent cultural models of gender are marked by change and to what extent they are characterised by a reproduction of dominant models.

3.2 Design and Method

3.2.1 Goals and Design

The operative challenge of this subproject was to find and describe the best practices in the area of men's new forms of work, gender equality and increased quality of life. The research was to look at new chances and possibilities but also keep a perspective on risks and social costs. Organisational factors were to be identified in particular and related to personal and family patterns on the one hand and institutional patterns on the other hand.

For this purpose, the research was focused on organisations, with a strategic sample design. Companies and organisations were to be selected through expert interviews. After a first round of interviews, each national team in the project was supposed to select four or five organisations, and then, through more interviews, the two most interesting cases. The experts were to include the most knowledgeable actors in our area, for example, leaders of gender equality initiatives among the social partners (employers, trade unions, the state) as well as organisational experts and leaders, e.g., personnel managers with family reconciliation experience.

Reports on a national level have been carried out containing the most important results from interviews with gender and labour experts. Beyond that, a comparative company matrix listed most interesting sample criteria: On a general level, business lines, sectors (private, public, non-profit), organisational structure (like company group, subsidiary company or else), regional location, size (number of employees), numeral staff development (increased, stable, cyclic (up and down), reduced), with special respect to male employees, gender ratio and company hierarchy by gender have been specified. In a second step, work contracts by gender with respect to non-standard forms were listed. Also, the structure of employees' representation was itemised: staff council, works council, equality representative, diversity representative, women's representative, or else. A more condensed part of the country report was derived from the interviews with company experts as well as with employees. This part is more narratively related to the meanings of "work", "changes" and "gender". The aim was to be able to report on institutional as well as organisational change. Therefore, the discussion part should include institutional frameworks and changes where these are relevant. Those reports have been evaluated on central partner meetings.

3.2.2 Finding Best Practices

We mainly succeeded in finding and interviewing an appropriate sample of experts. However, the further project design could not be strictly followed, mainly for gender-related cultural and political reasons. The experts often failed to identify good practice organisations in our (admittedly quite demanding) terms. When they did identify organisations combining innovative work forms and gender equality practices, it often turned out that gender equality included women only, with little or no reference to men. A further complication was that best practices regarding new work forms and gender equality were not always overlapping, although this problem was less serious than the women-only barrier.

In an explorative project like this, researchers have to find a balance between the project goals and the actual circumstances disclosed by the preliminary research. In this case, the sample design was rearranged as to be more flexible. It was more important to find interesting information than to ensure strict comparability between the participating countries. The original project design was successful in two of the six countries (Austria, Spain), where two advanced organisations were found. In three other countries (Germany, Israel, Norway), potential organisations were found, but most of them are better characterised as average than advanced. Since the expert interviews often failed to point the way forward, we sometimes had to include companies on the basis of pragmatic considerations and use companies where we could get access. In Norway for example, representatives from the employers' union and the largest trade union failed to come up with interesting suggestions, and the ones we got from other experts exclusively dealt with women and gender equality. The Norwegian organisations, therefore, were quite average. In the case of Israel, we even got a neo-traditional sample of technically oriented organisations with men working very long hours. In Bulgaria, where the issues of men and gender equality were even more unheard of than elsewhere, the researchers changed the sample procedure to include individual men only, regardless of company affiliation. Interviews with interesting individuals were also made in addition to the company sample interviews in some countries (e g in Norway). These measures pushed the sample in the "advanced" direction. It is noteworthy in itself that relevant individuals were much easier to find than relevant companies.

3.2.3 The Project Sample

As a whole, the resulting sample can be characterised as average-to-advanced rather than purely advanced. In some ways, this weakens our ability to reach conclusions from the project. On the other hand, it also has some advantages.

76

Considering the early stage in the development of the project's topic, a really advanced sample might have become too abstruse or out of touch with ordinary conditions. As it was, the sample came to include much of the important variation on the European map, e.g., men who overworked as well as men who had reduced their hours.

Not knowing exactly what the sample represents is a fairly normal situation in an exploratory project. Another common problem is a lack of strictly comparable studies. In our case, some comparisons and postulated change patterns can be questioned in this light. Although we did have a lot of indirect evidence, usually a scattering of small qualitative studies plus some limited surveys, strictly comparable data were limited. At this point, the gender geography of Europe is again relevant; there were usually more existing studies in the north and the west than in the south and east.

The total sample consisted of interviews with ca. 200 individuals, including 60 expert and trial interviews. 140 men took part in the main interviews. Of these, 104 men are in the core organisational matrix sample where we have solid organisational as well as individual data for each person. 10 organisations are well described in the sample, with more individual and limited information on around 40 other companies and organisations.

3.2.4   The Interviews

The men in each organisation were selected for best practice reasons. This part of the selection process was less problematic than choosing organisations, although a tendency towards 'pragmatic normalisation' existed at this stage also. Obviously, if the organisation has only a vague idea of the topics involved, the suggested sample will not be very precise. Most of the men in the companies were selected for work hour reduction reasons – men in part-time work, and men who had used parental leave are the two core groups in the sample. As mentioned, in some countries we also used individual sampling to improve the strategic focus. In Norway for example, individual interviews with innovators and leaders were used in addition to the rather non-strategic organisational samples. However, we did not have the time and funding needed to develop this in a consistent way in all the six participating countries.

The interviews with the men were conducted mostly by the researchers, partly by other well-qualified interviewers, using a semi-structured interview approach. Although there was some variation regarding the degree to which the interviews were structured, the main outline was followed in all countries. The interview questions concerned the workplace, focussing on new work forms and reduced hours among men, as well as gender and family issues. These interviews started with the men's background and experiences of work, including reduction of work, reasons for reduction, use of parental leave, and conditions and culture of the organisation. Many topics were included - who does what at home, attitudes to gender roles and personal orientation. Several brief questionnaires were also used to elicit more information about company culture, gender role orientation, and sense of coherence. Interviews usually lasted one to two hours.

3.3 Results: An Overview

3.3.1 Organisation Types and Work Cultures

Based on the main task orientation, we included four main types of organisations in the study. These were production organisations (mainly companies), production service organisations (same), reproduction service organisations (partly state, municipal, etc.), and reproduction organisations (mostly state, etc.). The following table 8 shows these in comparison with the rest of the gender-relevant variables in the study, focused on overall support for men and gender equality, with clear company cases filled in.

Table 8: Four Organisational Types

Task orientation \ Gender equality for men	Very low support	Low to some support	Medium to high support
Production		Norenergy (Norway)	Hafner (Austria)
Production services	IT-firms (Israel)	Interbank (Germany)	
Reproduction services		Mobcom (Spain)	Coomundi (Spain)
Reproduction	Helfen (Germany)	Lia school (Norway)	Revoc (Austria)

Many organisations were mixed, e.g., a bank serving private/reproduction customers as well as corporate/professional customers, yet a main tendency could still be discerned. The technical-to-social dimension of the organisation's main tasks played a considerable role in the men's work adaptation and work learning. Men in social/reproduction work were the ones who most clearly fit into the "work changes gender" hypothesis. Here, we saw men's caring-related work role learning extend to private life, for example in an organisation favouring men's parental leave and allowing flexibility and shorter hours (Austria, Spain).

78

Traditionally, the production/reproduction dimension has been linked to gender (production = masculine, reproduction = feminine). Further, it has been associated with wage and non-wage labour, and with high and low levels of capital per work unit. Therefore, several overlapping dimensions are obviously involved when we look at organisational task orientation.

The importance of task orientation was also supported by Sigtona Halrynjo's correspondence analysis showing differences between the four main adaptations (see Chapter 4). One group, the alternative patch workers, were often young people. A high proportion was engaged in reproduction work. Time pioneers were also often found in reproduction or reproduction services work. On the other hand, overworkers and breadwinners were most typically employed in production and production services work.

Care and career combiners were more widespread and did not fit this 'task decides' picture. Their rate of incidence, instead, depended more on national/regional and institutional variation. Norway, the country with the most extensive welfare arrangements in the sample, also had the greatest proportion of care and career combiners, as seen in the Norwegian production company as well as the reproduction organisation. If the European future leads to a better combination of care and career, it will turn out as no surprise that national results at this point varied according to the gender geography map outlined above. In general, the tendency was stronger toward the north and west than the south and east.

In all countries, perhaps excepting Bulgaria (but including Israel), active fathering was a central "signal relation" for the care dimension.[20] Parental leave was an important symbolic issue for many men, apart from being a more concrete issue for some. Part of this issue concerns a man's opportunity to take parental leave (e.g., in Norway) and not to have to "beg" for time that the law states belongs to the mother (e.g., in Spain).

A main trend in the interviews was "common European," in line with a trend found in other recent studies. This research finds many shared traits of women and men in similar organisations and work-family situations across countries and regions (Gershuny 2003). Our overall impression is that region- and country-specific gender tradition and culture play a less prominent role today than they did a decade or two ago.

Besides task orientation and country variation, many other organisational and institutional variables played a role in creating different paths and adaptations among the men. Company-related variables were often important, especially when they interacted with work-family arrangements. We were sur-

---

20 The difference concerning Bulgaria was not that active fathering did not exist on a personal level – we have good evidence that it did, and played an important role there as elsewhere – but that it was so little thematised and formulated as a cultural agenda, notably less than in the west. This may be due to the active fathering role being too close to the traditional household head role, as well as other gender system differences.

prised that organisations in presumably rather 'backwards' regions in the European gender geography could be more active and positioned more on the forefront than organisations in better-developed regions. These active organisations highlighted the possibility of a more dynamic role assumed by the labour market and social partners in creating gender-equal work and welfare arrangements.

According to our evidence, a man will take parental leave more often in reproductive-oriented organisations than in production-oriented organisations, other things being equal. But task orientation can be overruled by other factors like active management and gender equality policies that include men. A main rule appeared at this point: A lower level of organisational discrimination toward men who choose the option of taking more parental leave and reducing hours correlates to a greater incidence of men choosing this decision. Active management, highlighted in some of our cases (social development organisation, Spain; metal firm, Austria), can clearly change the workplace climate and increase the acceptance of caring men.

Education levels, often higher in the services parts of the above table (type 2 and 3), will push a bit in the caring direction too, although education is not very strongly related. The mixed effects of education appear in our study as they do in others. Although education by itself usually points towards gender equality, the job situation of highly educated employees often resemble a "honey trap," in which partly self-imposed work demands reduce time for caring and domestic tasks (Sørensen 2003).

Organisational culture and work-family flexibility were quite strongly attached in the study. This was partly due to the lack of formal organisation regarding men's gender equality and the need for the pro-equality institutionalisation discussed above. In Spain for example, with a demographic downturn and lack of statewide parental leave, kindergartens and other support, organisations adapted as best they could in the competition for the best employees. One important factor behind changes in companies – notably in Spain/Catalonia in our study – was the emergence of new attitudes and ideas among potential employees. Young employees increasingly looked for good work-family balance and long-term welfare as well as material benefits. In other countries as well – like Norway – recent surveys and debate show that work-family balance has become a more important employee issue and perhaps also a new viewpoint on more traditional problems such as work stress.

In some of our company cases, work-family reconciliation went together with diversity management, but this link was not very clear, marking perhaps a rather unstable correlation. The reproduction-oriented organisations were sometimes "gender-equal" in the sense of "women are best", according to the men in these organisations (e.g., Revoc, Austria).

From the men's point of view, many organisations and companies were characterised by a rather superficial "in principle" treatment of gender equality. Gender equality as part of image building was pronounced in some cases, with a rather insecure or fluctuating real support for equality. This was highlighted in some of the company expert interviews as well as in employees' stories of how the company had reacted to their care-related needs.

Although difficult to pinpoint exactly, there were differences in how the men situated the three main themes of the project: work, gender and quality of life /welfare. Men with an alternative/patchwork form of adaptation seemed less inclined to associate welfare and gender than the rest of the men. Gender seemed more peripheral. This tendency was present, e.g., in the German study, but it is hard to say exactly what trends it represents on the larger European level. As mentioned, this was a heterogeneous group. Sometimes the adaptation was clearly periodic or age-based (young men, urban lifestyle), sometimes more permanent. The other three groups of men were more 'gendered' in their approach to welfare and quality of life issues, although they posed this relationship in different ways. In the Nordic model, there is a widespread norm that gender equality is a key to welfare and quality of life. In the Southern European model, gender is again very important, but it is connected to a more traditional concept of gender-segregated balance, with women and families as the main framework of reproduction.

3.3.2 Facing the Company

As a result of new conditions and change factors, the men in our sample have faced the organisation or company in new ways. Official statements of gender equality came to the test. At this point, we found a rich flora of gender equality statements that were rhetorical in the sense of legitimising the organisation's passivity. "Discrimination issues are non-existent. There have never been problems or issues on the basis of gender discrimination by either side" (manager of a male-dominated security company, Bulgaria). Often, numerical considerations were used to reach the same conclusion. "The organisation is gender-equal. In my division there are ca. 50/50 men and women." (Conrad, Norenergy, Norway) On the other hand, if there are 100/0 men/women, this can be seen as gender equality too – commonly justified by the explanation that women do not apply:

Maybe there are some job positions that are not very attractive for women. I think so, because no woman has ever applied for the position of technician, for example. Maybe this is the only position that requires a stronger physique. But we have women in the administrative department, so I can say the recruitment process is totally qualification based. (Hristo, private TV channel, Bulgaria)

There is nothing wrong with the company here; it is only that the qualifications are sex-divided. Another justification employed is to say the numbers do not matter, because the wage rates are the same: "Despite the inequality in the number of male and female employees, there is no discrimination against women. They earn the same salary as men." (Mike, Israel)

The eagerness to 'prove' gender equality among many organisation experts and managers by focusing on one isolated fact or the other stands in stark contrast to many employees' experiences. Among the employees, many were critical of these types of pronouncements and image-making gestures.

This conflict was often triggered by events that might seem small and insignificant at first. A common theme was that a man felt degraded as a caring person. This experience was most typical in companies that had invested little in family reconciliation. "I do not believe that the organisation pays attention to the personal and family life of its employees...The only care issue for this organisation is the work to be done" (Joel, Israel). "The organisation does not care about the personal and family life of its employees" (Yossi, Israel). It is important to note that this theme appeared in quite different contexts— stretching from overworked employees in technical firms in Israel to 'normal' employees in peaceful countries like Norway. "Even if they work with children, the school and jobs are not very family-oriented. They do not arrange for the needs of the families" (Jonas, Lia school, Norway). Our study shows that the issue of men and caregiving is not a luxury issue found only in some countries or conditions.

At this point, many interviews gave detailed experiences of how the company had reacted to the man's new situation. Often, there was an "I happened to arrive...and then found out" kind of process. In Spain for example, one employee described what happened after he became a father.

When his child was born, he and his partner decided that she should take all the parental leave. He used one month of his vacation to stay at home and help. After the leave period was over, he wanted to reduce his working hours. He turned to the Human Relations department and asked to be able to use the offer of reduced work hours (period of 6 – 12 month). The HR, however, responded negatively. (Juan, Mobcom, Spain, from the report)

Another example from Israel: When the daughter of an interviewee was born, they collected money to buy her a present, but afterwards there was no concern about his difficulties, i.e. having to work the whole day without sleeping at night. The common theme was that the men found out that the employers do not see men as caretakers.

He indicated that lately he has been feeling stress at work since he has many duties, and he cannot spend enough time with his family. However, after periods of work when there is a lot of pressure, he cannot compensate his family by taking vacation as he is forced to take his annual vacation in August. In general, he feels that the HR department is not interested in his family welfare, as this issue is never raised in periodical meetings. (Yossi, Israel, from the report)

Again, it is noteworthy that all the items indicated by this Israeli employee – overwork, time with family, health problems – were also indicated by men in Austria, Germany, Norway and Spain. Often they even used the same words, despite the numerous cultural and national differences. This was clearly a common European trend. We shall describe exceptions and better practices among organisations later. For now, a main point is that even in our fairly advanced sample, an organisational response of non-recognition was quite typical. As we shall see, this non-recognition was not really neutral.

3.3.3 Relational and Organisational Gender

A model of relational and organisational gender can clarify the men's stories concerning how they were treated by companies.

The men in new circumstances were characterised by a new sense of relational gender. The relation to the child, partner or spouse was a central matter and motivator for change. Even the men who were mainly motivated by the third main change factor (diversity, quality of life) often stressed the relational aspect – relations with friends, social competence, etc.

On the other hand, what the men encountered at the company level can be characterised as a more traditional organisational gender. This included gender concepts and stereotypes that were deeply lodged in the organisational practice and culture, partly because of the kinds of inertia reasons described earlier. A main component of this picture was the absence of new organisational measures in most of the companies we studied.

Obviously, a division between relational and organisational gender is a bit artificial. In practice things are mixed. Yet it has theoretical relevance as well as empirical support.

Relational issues have been central to gender equality and gender research as a whole. The relation between man and woman has dominated the picture. A main reason why gender equality remains partial is due to the persistence of non-recognised organisational structures that reinforce traditional gender divisions, even when the ideology surrounding them has changed. Indeed, the notion that man and woman should be equals, considered as a dyadic relational pair (in a quite abstract way), has become quite 'hegemonic' today. Therefore, a huge gap appears between the relational gender-equal ideal on the one hand, and the not-so-equal organisational practice on the other.

The new men and the more traditional men in new circumstances are pioneers trying to close this gap. They embody the tensions between new relational orientations and older organisational structures. It is not surprising, therefore, that the interviews contained a lot of information about the costs of gender equality for men. These men faced a combination of 'standard' devaluation of caring- and women-associated tasks and 'extra' devaluation because they are men.

Why were relational and organisational gender so out of tune? The reason is not only that domestic and care-related changes tend to run a bit ahead of wage-work changes, as described earlier, but also because of a "women-only" compensatory factor. The subproject found an organisational pattern to the effect that "as soon as it is gendered or family-related, it turns to women." This can be seen as a new adaptation of traditional organisations over the last decade. Gender has become allowed as an organisational issue, but only as far as women are concerned.

The Mobcom company (Spain) was such an example. This company was one of the best in Spain, offering different kinds of measures for work-family balance, yet even here the gender policies were concentrated mostly on women.

I believe that in general we have policies that benefit the worker. The policies we have implemented here are more radical with respect to what is normally found in the market. There are more ties to the women, or perhaps they have greater weight among the women.... The impact is much greater among the woman than the men. (Mobcom expert)

As a consequence, it often remained hard for men to be recognised as care-givers, even if the organisation had gender-equality policies and had implemented gender mainstreaming. That was the case in the Redsocial organisation in Spain. There, the first man to actually use the formal right to parental leave and to ask for reduced hours later said a few years later that he had met many difficulties along the way. "It has cost a great deal." He emphasised that he had had to fight for his right to care for his child and work reduced hours. Yet he also noted that there had been improvements and positive changes as of late. He said that the organisation was becoming more used to and familiar with employees spending more time caring for their children (Jose Manuel Ortiz, Redsocial, Spain).

The dividing line between relational and organisational gender was clearly evident, especially in numerically male-dominated companies and among companies nearer to the production end of the task scale. It was more complex in the female-dominated and reproduction-oriented organisations. This was shown especially in the women-led organisations, like Revoc (Austria). There, women made up 80 % of the two top tiers of leaders. In the organisation, a "women first" relational pattern was superimposed on an otherwise quite traditional and hierarchic structure. This led to a split treatment of men. The men reported that the organisation had an active policy regarding fathering and men's caregiving, but on the other hand, their career chances remained low.

A former employee at Revoc argued that men were discriminated against as men in the organisation. "The mixture between being critical and being a man is enough for not making a career in the company. That was the main reason why I quit the job." That women were preferred before men to top jobs was confirmed by current employees as well. "Not gender equality, but women's support" was the characterisation of the main policy of the organisation. Another man, Edgar, put the equality orientation in the organisation in quotation marks, since for him it provided "excellent conditions for women but not for men...The company is very active in equality issues. But the company is led by women and it's rumoured that men are not really able to get into key-positions. It's funny, but it's just the opposite of the traditional way." (Edgar, Revoc, Austria)

Although this reversal is interesting, it should be noted that the "traditional way" appeared much more frequently in the study. The typical company profile was, for example, that "in an official way there is gender equality, but the company prefers men rather than women in some top positions." (Alberto Garcia, Asisa, Spain). Alike: "women have no real chance in the firm, since there are two standards for male and female. When one of my friends, who is a physicist, asked me about a vacant position in the firm, I recommended to her not to apply for the job, because she would not have a real chance." (Joel, Israel)

3.3.4   Traditional Role Models as Obstacles

Gender models and relations in companies seem to be rather inflexible, traditional and do not meet the changes in the societal relations and gender roles described above. Women as well men, political actors, institutional structures and commercial regulations are still by and large based on the traditional model of masculinity. This impression requires a more detailed explanation.

Applying the work of Pfau-Effinger (1998), we have already made reference to the various levels at which models exert influence. These levels include the dominant societal models for the family and for the gender-specific division of labour, the institutional level, the changing relation between individuals' goals and culturally defined models, as well as the level of social actors (cf. ibid.).

In his concept of 'hegemonic masculinity,' Connell (1995) addresses the changing relations among these various levels. In addition to the distribution of political power and emotional bonding patterns, the relations of production, according to Connell, is the essential factor in the ordering of the sexes. The particular configuration of this order is in a changing relation to the particular predominant models of gender, which are used by the subject for self-orientation and thus serve as guides for identity and action. Because the social structuring capacity of these models is power forming, Connell refers to hegemonic masculinity as "that form of masculinity that assumes the position of power in a given structure of gender relations." (Connell 1999: 97)[21]

---

21   The basis of hegemony is not restricted to direct power structures but is also grounded in the consensus among the men and women upon whom it exercises power. This acceptance is reached on both sides through positively loaded concepts containing real or supposed power. Even though the hegemonic model is in fact lived out by only a few men, it is, nevertheless lived out vicariously by a large proportion or of men through imagination or transferred aggression (cp. Carrigan, Connell & Lee 1996: 62f).

Hegemonic masculinity contains the following attributes (among others).

Table 9: Hegemonic Masculinity

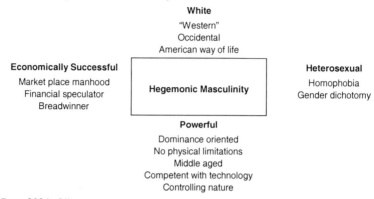

(*Döge 2004: 64*)

Although these standards do not correspond to the living situations of many men in Europe in relation to their work and private life, men are still nevertheless rigidly depicted in terms of their profession and careers by actors in the commercial sphere, e.g., stakeholders, equal opportunity commissioners and colleagues. Other forms of masculinity receive hardly any recognition, are regarded as exceptions, or are simply not given any notice. According to Lange, "this leads to discrimination against women especially, but also against men who either cannot or will not adopt the competition-oriented masculinity." (Lange 1998: 52)

Thus, almost all the men we interviewed had the experience of being perceived as eccentrics, exceptions, etc. Many emphasised that their professional deviation has hindered their careers.

Georg H. (Interbank, Germany) has worked part-time for over ten years. Upon being asked about his career opportunities, he answered as follows:

Good question. The chance is zero. I knew that the moment I decided to do it. The moment you decide to go part-time, you are – career-wise – dead. You're dead.

Current governmental unemployment policies still regard men as occupying the roll of breadwinners. Frank S., an unemployed father (Germany) who cares for his daughter half the week at his house, was required by his caseworker to apply for positions around the whole country. When he said he took care of his daughter several days per week and thus had to remain in the city, he was told: "Other fathers would change their residence for their children, to be able to work and support their families."

This loss in potential standing, power and income is not however always interpreted negatively: a career is exchanged for having time for oneself (*Zeit-*

wohlstand) and the "demand for a complete life." Men who cease fixating on professional employment reap a lack of understanding from other men but at the same time establish a new relation to their environment. Being content with life and not money becomes the important point of reference. At the same time, a limit is set to the pressure to function and the amount of time put in at work. Despite recurrent doubts and the ever-present "inner voice of hegemonic masculinity," the men we interviewed showed a great deal satisfaction with life. For all of the interviewees, the reduction in work time led to a higher degree of satisfaction with their arrangement of work and life.

In our investigation, it was apparent that advisory councils, personnel managers and equal opportunity commissioners do not assume that men can have work-life compatibility problems. It was also discovered that measures supporting gender equality (such as company agreements) often have regulations that not only clearly favour women, which is important in many cases, but also, focus *only* on women – although gender mainstreaming is supposed to apply equally to men and women. It is often assumed to be self evident that only women can have compatibility problems; men are perceived as completely identifying with their professions. By and large, men are only included as promoters of accepting gender equality. Their participation in child raising and housework is called upon in order to relieve the burden shouldered by women and is not formulated as being in a man's own interests. Thus, equality policies have to a large degree overlooked the interests and problems of men. Men are almost exclusively viewed as agents hindering equality policies. Thus, we have often looked in vain for seminars devoted to a topic such as: "How do I, as a man, reconcile both career and family."

As soon as we entered the workplace, this view became immediately apparent. Often when we asked about men who work part-time, we were told: "We don't have anything like that here." Only after inquiring deeper – for instance about employment data – did it come about that there were in fact men working part-time, and this came as a surprise to the contact partner.

3.4 Organisational Change

3.4.1 Proactive Practices in Organisations – The Phases

Besides obstacles, many men described positive changes. New relational trends became gradually more accepted and adopted by the organisations. Three main phases could be distinguished in this process, based on the thematic analysis.

Table 10: Organisational Change and Gender Equality for Men

Change phases	Change forms — Organisational process and conflict	Typical expressions
1 Early phase	Individual, relational, isolated Negative social sanctions	Neutralised discrimination of caring in general and caring among men in particular Frequent subdued discrimination (e.g., polite non-recognition); sometimes open discrimination (e.g., new men seen as effeminate or deviant)
2 Middle phase	More extensive Relational Mixed social sanctions	Gender troubles in the organisation More manifest gender conflict Acknowledgement of needs for work/family reconciliation
3 Advanced phase	Relational and organisational Positive social sanctions	More effective support for increased gender equality Lower gender equality costs Employee motivation and loyalty

Again, the division is simplified. Often, issues had some of each phase trait. This became especially evident after considering the region and country variation in the study. On closer analysis, it appeared that the European regions were 'advanced' and 'backwards' according to different criteria; they had different strengths and obstacles regarding men's gender equality and quality of life. Here however, we focus on the company level and common traits in each phase.

In the first phase, the men are mainly alone and feel subdued by their changes. In the second, more men become part of the change process. There are more mixed tendencies in this larger group, and also, more men who are confused, and bring up their ambivalence.

In the third, they are more actively creating new standards. This can be seen as a process from psychological to sociological change and analysed according to the "conditional matrix" described by Strauss and Corbin (1988). The process of change starts in the centre of the concentric circles described in this matrix, in the individual's primary relations, then shifts outwards toward secondary relations and more collective forms of change.

3.4.2   First Phase

We speak about proactive trends in the beginning phase when gender equality recognition has begun to take its course. We start with the pioneers before we move to the more integrated, common cases.

What do we see in the early phase? Regarding the gendered substructure in organisations, we meet the first men in women-associated fields. Their situation can be described as quite unbalanced and insecure. It is not stabilised at all, because the organisations are not prepared, while the men are.

In some cases, on the contrary, we found men who did not follow up on the organisational advances. They worked in organisations providing good conditions for gender equality and work-family balance, but the men were not willing to assume an active caregiving role. Some of them think about it, but more in the sense of a wish that will come true when a benevolent fairy comes along. Lacking concrete plans or practical ideas, this is the "you never know" and "maybe once in life time" attitude.

Concerning gender equality, positive actions for women gain attention, but the organisations are still a long ways off from taking appropriate social action. These first considerations, as already mentioned, do not include men and are mainly restricted to women's support.

The first, early phase was characterised by low or non-existent organisational support and isolated relational changes, often working mainly on an informal and personal level, subdued and not officially recognised. The men reducing work for caregiving reasons were isolated, perhaps excepting "a few soul mates in the company who think alike." They encountered social sanctions and showed many signs of having to adapt to a polite but devaluing organisational culture. For example, part-time men often talked about work compression or having to do more in their shorter schedule in order to be perceived as equals.

As described in the above table, traditional companies in the early change phase were characterised by discrimination against caregiving in general, plus there was an extra burden incurred by male caregivers.

A woman who says she will work 80 % (of a full-time schedule) in order to take care of the kids often receives admiration from her colleagues. The man who says it doesn't. But their actions are not much in the open. They are not very visible. I think many men sacrifice a lot for their children, but it is not valued much by society. (Company-internal expert, Telon company, Norway)

In 2002, my baby was born and I asked for a two-hour reduction for breast-feeding leave (with 100 % of wages).[22] This is one of the benefits that the company has. But this was the first time in the company that a man demanded this kind of benefit. The managers were very surprised and they decided that the benefit was for women only. (Ramon, Mobcom, Spain)

In the end, the man got the two-hour reduction, but with a proportional wage reduction since Spanish law allowed for this; later, however, he was fired

---

22   This is an example of the problem that many terms connected with babies and care are restricted to women. In fact, this case does not only touch on pure "breast-feeding," but caring in general.

during company restructuring. This was another typical risk factor in reducing work.

Support from colleagues was important in this situation. It can be rather minimal in many companies, especially if the man's absence means extra work, but we also found exceptions. In Bulgaria, a 34 year old widower who took sole caring responsibility for his two children said: "I work mostly with men and I don't know someone in the same situation. But my colleagues support me very much. They always help me when something happens and I need to stay home with kids. I do not have any problems taking paid vacations or 'sick child' leave." (Ilian, Bank security officer and taxi driver, Bulgaria)

Leaders are important in organisational change, especially in new fields or with novel types of change. This was confirmed in our study. We found a frequent "it-depends-on-the-manager" theme:

Do you think it will be harder in the future to combine work and family?
Yes, I believe so, I believe it will go the wrong way.

Because the company is in trouble?
Well I don't know. Bad leadership. I have a (woman) manager who has four kids, you know, and then it is no problem.

So the boss is important?
Yes very. (Conrad, Norenergy, Norway)

In another case (Spain), one of the male employees in the company had wanted to take fathers' leave. He went first to the manager (role model) with the appropriate request, and second to his direct superior, who seemed to follow a rather traditional gender role attitude. "By the time he got a positive reply from the manager, he did not bother about the more critical reply from his superior." (Jordi, Mobcom, Spain)

Often, leaders were more positive towards employees who were seen as important for the company:

My working schedule depends on me and my own task organisation. This gives me a possibility to plan my time and to attain work-family balance. This flexibility is not formally regulated and allowed by the company's policy and procedures, but the managers are liberal towards such flexibility as long as it doesn't hinder the achievement of goals. (Account expert, Bulgaria)

Lack of information was part of the organisational climate, especially in phase 1, contributing to a type of change on the level of informal relations:

The organisation doesn't want to communicate more than necessary the rights and opportunities that employees have as regards parental leave / reduction of working hours. In my opinion, the reason is the problem of replacements. When I negotiated with the company about work hour reduction, this was not an 'official communication.' I know a couple of other men in the organisation who experienced the same thing. (Victor, Coomundi, Spain)

The lacking of information and men's problems with availing themselves of their caregiving rights were sometimes attributed by management to the men themselves:

I believe that it is not necessary to promote this subject (fathers' parental leave). They know that they have it and if they do not request it, it is because they do not need it (our emphasis). I believe that it is a cultural subject, not a company matter. Here (in Spain), like it or not, we live in a sexist culture. It is more 'logical' that the woman sacrifices her professional career than the man. (Mobcom expert, Spain)

Although most men preferred a companionate or dual career model of marriage, there was much ambivalence under the surface, contributing to the inertia and small-scale change in phase one. A few articulated this:

Some of the men I have worked with have wives who don't work. They live in quite another world...These men don't quite know what life is. Perhaps they live the life we all should have... that just one person works. I am thinking, my wife works 100 %, I work 100 %; we have two children. If I had worked 100 % and she had stayed at home, the world would have been quite different. We would have had a much more quiet life. Now, we're supposed to go and fetch and (ask ourselves) do we have time for this and that. (Conrad, Norenergy, Norway)

But most men put some distance between the breadwinner ideal and their own choices: "Personally I don't want to use all my time for work. I have two small children. I want to use the flexible hours and home office possibility in my company in a positive way." (N1 Telon, Norway)

Negative organisational culture was another main obstacle, especially in the first phase. Negative sanctions were connected to the culture of overwork and an informal ranking system with the overworked employee at the top and the reduced-hours employee at the bottom:

He would have liked to work 45 hours a week, however he feels that the organisational culture rejects employees that leave the workplace too early. For instance, when he leaves his workplace an 17:30, he is asked in a funny manner whether he is working part-time. (Haim, IT company, Israel, from the report)

Due to negative informal sanctions, this man ended up not using his actual possibilities for taking time off from work. We found this tendency in new as well as traditional companies.

New media are signified by a pseudo-familiar working culture, informal structures, and lack of cooperative decision. Very noticeable is the tendency toward an unlimited work schedule – 60 or more hours per week. (Trade union expert, Germany)

Many men described an increased flexibility of hours; the men's working time was increasingly left to individual regulation. This was good, yet in some jobs it also meant an increase in overwork:

The problem with flexible schedules is that in the end people work more...It gives an enormous freedom to the individual. We started this policy with very young people. It has made people very responsible for their work. The machine, the clock, does not control you;

the control is from your colleagues.... In the end, the control tool is your own colleague. (Mobcom expert, Spain)

Flexibility was also seen as an alternative to long but rather empty work hours. The fact that long work hours can mean less work per hour was mentioned by many men:

You're away from home a lot but you don't work all the time. You are travelling or living in a hotel...The way the family sees it, you are away, but perhaps you are not so productive for the company. (Conrad, Noronegy, Norway)

Sometimes the negative social sanctions were more direct. In one case, an expert described the reactions to men asking for parental leave:

Generally the employees are ignorant. They think that this is a measure for women only. Also, it is a cultural subject. There are comments like, 'Are you going home now to breast feed the boy?' Most people don't understand that a man can take breast-feeding leave and give a milk bottle to the children. (Mobcom expert, Spain)

3.4.3   Second Phase

The transition into the second phase is initiated by a critical development or change: a new company culture might have developed, a management change, a process of restructuring that leads to excellent conditions for men willing to reduce their work time, or certain new institutional rules may have reshaped certain equality conditions in the company. We encountered a lot of different reasons that account for proactive trends. By the time gender equality measures or family-work balance measures had become visibly evident, the companies were facing gender competition. This is an important difference in relation to the first phase. In the early phase, we were able to still find gender segmentation, which leads to disadvantages for women in the companies. In the more advanced cases, we were able to discern gender competition. Ohlendieck (2003) refers to the important role of gender trouble in the process of gender equality. The occupational competition between men and women is a new phenomenon and it is not quite implemented yet—as we can see by looking at the statistics. Facing gender trouble in organisations means that women and men compete, that they are not segmented anymore, and that women are no longer relegated to disadvantageous positions. These are the more advanced cases in our model, where gender differences and gender gaps become evident and turn into gender trouble. In that sense, gender trouble is a sign of discrimination against women as well as a sign of successful equality processes (ibid.: 184). When we cannot find any form of gender trouble, we are facing organisations in the very early phase of gender equality.

Proactive practices in the middle phase are characterised by gender equality measures that focus on support for women. Men are recognised but not involved in these measures in an active way. Men's involvement seems to be a secondary effect that accompanies certain companies' reconciliation achievements as well as support for women. In that sense, men are supported in their endeavour to take an active role in the family, which is brought about by their female partners' needs.

In the second phase, the new men were no longer so isolated or viewed as deviants. Reactions were mixed in the organisation. Many men looked towards these men and at how the organisation reacted, and thus new observer roles were created.

In some cases, we found top leaders trying to change the organisation in gender-equal ways, often facing the organisational inertia described above. "The manager's commitment to men who take an active caregiving role does not correspond to organisational structures," a production company expert told us (Austria). Even if the leadership was committed, the organisation might continue to run in quite gender-traditional ways. Mid-level leadership sometimes appeared as an obstacle – a common finding in work research – although we do not have systematic data on this.

If we consider the sanctions, obstacles, relational coincidence and organisational inertia described by the men (especially in the early change phases), it is not so surprising that most of them held a positive attitude toward clear and strong institutional measures regarding parental leave for fathers. The "fathers' leave is good" theme was frequent among the men across very different contexts. Some examples: "When he was asked about the possibility of father's parental leave, he replied that it seemed like an excellent idea to him." (Shabtai, Israel, from interview report) "When he was asked about the possibility of parent leave for a father, he replied that this seemed like a good idea to him. He added humorously that he would have liked to have parental leave instead of his wife...." (Efraim, Israel, from interview report) In Norway, young teacher T did not take the paternal leave; he was a student and working at the time when he had children. But later he regretted it: "I really wish I had used that period. I would have thrived." (His children were 11 and 7 at the time of the interview.)

Furthermore, if parents share parental leave equally, employers would have no reason to discriminate against women: "The HR Manager said that it is a huge problem for the bank branches that too often the young women there get pregnant and take maternity leave for a year or two." (Dimitar, Bank, Bulgaria). A related line of thought is "it is better if the law does it." A regulation to ensure male parental leave would probably be respected by employers. "In his opinion, the organisation would probably confirm a request for a father's leave." (Efraim, Israel, from interview report) "If there existed a law for father's parental leave, then there should be no problem with that." (Israel Moshe)

But if the man's personal or "face value" is the deciding factor, chances are he will lose: "He thinks that if he had asked for parental leave (on a personal basis), the management would not have agreed." "It is enough for them that I have to leave for my military reserve duty…" (Efraim, Israel) If the law is there, negotiations are easier, as in a Norwegian example where a man used the paternal leave – 1 month for the first child, 2 for the second: "I managed that deal…. I wanted 3 months but settled for 2. It was my wife I was negotiating with, not the company. For them, you can take as much as you want, as long as it is within the law…It is not looked highly upon, but it is accepted." (Company manager, Norway)

Conversely, firms often face problems when the law or regulations are not in place. In Austria, for example, we heard this: According to the manager, there are still tough obstacles standing in the way of fathers' leave. These affect income and career paths. The company does not give work-place guarantee (same work position) to employees who take parental leave, says the quality manager. Referring to personnel recruitment, the possibility that an applicant is going to take parental leave is still seen as a negative factor, he says.

We found in our study the desire for better and clearer laws across countries, education and management levels, etc. A Coomundi expert (Spain) said:

I would like a law that gives fathers a fathers' leave of their own. As long as there are just some organisations that try this, they must assume all the costs, but if it is legally implemented, it will be more shared. There are a lot of costs for an organisation as it is and few resources. To assume all (responsibility).... is difficult.

This is a highly significant statement since it comes from one of the most advanced organisations in the sample, one that has invested considerable effort to bring about a form of gender equality that includes a new perspective on men and a company culture where fathers are somewhat encouraged to take parental leave. One important practical indicator of whether the company is moving ahead towards phase two is whether employees on leave are temporarily replaced or not. In many companies, they have no replacement, and therefore easily create an extra burden for the others. "When you have a lot of people taking leave to breast-feed, it forces the others to work more." (Mobcom expert)

The changes concerning men cannot be viewed in isolation from the changes concerning women. This was evident in the second phase in particular, where the company faces "gender trouble," a sign that gender has become part of the agenda, often through conflicts and complaints. Competition between men and women increases; women are no longer only in segregated positions in the work hierarchy (Ohlendieck 2003). In this phase, the main gender issues remain focused on women rather than men, but men were somewhat more acknowledged. ("Women and gender" could be one term for this halfway entrance of men into gender issues.) For management, a main point was seeing women as a new resource; for women and employees, new rights and organisational conditions were important. A typical management statement was that "the company should no longer discriminate but take advantage of talent on both sides."

As a broad tendency, women's advancement in the organisations was associated with men's advancement. This link was highly complex, however, and sometimes contradictory. Some companies defined gender equality as support for women in ways that was experienced as detrimental by many men, as a kind of reverse discrimination.[23] In the main pattern however, improved status of women in the organisation was associated with gender equality for men. In some cases, women were gatekeepers for men's change.

The mixed situation of phase two was also a reflection of broader forms of ambivalence in society and culture at large. Sometimes, non-standard arrangements in the organisation met traditional expectations, e.g., among customers. During a meeting with mainly male customers for example, a male secretary served coffee to the customers and his female superior. "This did not go very well," said the female top manager. The customers were annoyed; the relation seemed to be strange to them (Revoc, Austria). In other cases, innovative tendencies in the organisation were hampered by institutional inertia. This was the case in a women-only focus in gender mainstreaming that did not help the company to address the issues of women and men together (Interbank, Germany). Obviously, many factors came into this picture. These can only be mentioned here but include gender conservative aspects of the law and regulations, protective attitude towards women, traditional masculinity patterns, informal ranking in culture and private life, and the ambivalence of many women towards new men, etc.

3.4.4 Third Phase

While proactive trends in the middle phase mainly focus on women and gender equality, both genders are addressed in the advanced phase.

The gendered substructure in advanced companies can be described in the following way: Work is not regarded as independent from private life/family life; it is more considered as a completion in terms of "work-family balance." Therefore, we find proactive trends away from the overtime culture – a characteristic indicator for organisational structures influenced by male dominance (Acker 1991, 1992) – as well as supportive work conditions that should guarantee the balance between these priorities.

Wage work more often seems to be taken as the source of men's privilege as well as the subject of restriction on men's opportunities life. A gender policy that focuses men has two ideals: establishing gender justice while re-

---

23   We found the 'matriarchal' interpretation of gender equality especially in one company (Revoc, Austria), but also as a quite common complaint among men in numerically women-dominated jobs, e g men in kindergartens.

ducing male dominance and improving men's opportunities in life. The improvement of men's life therefore has to be oriented toward a turn away from a form of male life that is disproportionately grounded in wage work, a significant involvement of men in family and care, as well as an equal work-life balance (Lehner 2003).

On the individual level, an interesting difference is to be noticed. While the pioneers and outsiders in the companies refer to certain values, such as a fairness discourse when taking parental leave or work-time reductions, men in more advanced companies do not really mention any values. They seem to be much more integrated and typical in these companies. Men in the more advanced companies do not have to justify their requests on the level of fairness; a common reason seems to be "good enough." When their requests are atypical however, men have to provide justifications in a way that can hardly be questioned and discussed critically by others, i.e., in terms of a common sense approach to fairness). But in the more advanced cases, the men do not have to find such "unquestionable arguments" to justify their decisions anymore when their requests turn out to be common benefits entitled to male employees in the company.

When companies actively address men, then they can be described as providing gender equality conditions. They are not only affected by positive actions on behalf of women (as can be found in the middle phase), but they are addressed separately (reduction of overtime work, support of active fatherhood, etc.). The advanced organisational processes and the practice of social interaction tend to be perceived through "gendered eyes." To some extent, the companies are aware of gender-specific social structures in the organisation, the production of inequality in everyday life, as well as gender role expectations. Diversity sometimes overtook gender equality concepts and "new men's" culture received more attention in the process. The individual cases – the outsiders in the beginning of the change process – have gone; the "new men's" community slowly but increasingly takes shape.

In the third phase, the earlier innovations and new practices received more institutional and organisational support. New policies and measures were implemented. Gender and family issues were addressed more equally towards women and men. Earlier, more isolated and temporary changes turned into more lasting proactive changes.

Proactive changes have been studied in restructuring research (Holter 1998). Restructuring is a shake-up period for the company. It is often costly and hard for the employees, but it also has a positive side – if anything new is to come along, now is the time to do it.

Although restructuring was often associated with gender inequality in our study (as in other studies), there were some important positive exceptions that demonstrated better practices. Asisa (Spain) in the early 1990s, for example, had a negative culture towards women, but restructuring and globalisation in the ensuing years as well as a court conflict over gender discrimination made the company change its course. In 1996, it became part of a national gender-auditing program. This contributed to a growth period for the company. "(Today) we think positively of women. For example, when there is a free vacant position in the Systems Department (where there are more men), we put a woman's picture in the supply publicity to encourage women to apply for the vacancy." (Asisa expert)

In Austria, a large information technology company (Inno) was forced to cut back due to economic problems a few years ago. Rather than downsizing though, the company carried out strategies that focussed on reductions in work-time and the creation of new forms of work. Freelance and limited contracts were reduced, and the company made generous offers for part-time work. As a result, different models of part-time work were created and part-time employment strongly increased in the company. The new offers were taken mainly by men. The part-time rate of men more than doubled, and the women's part-time rate also increased slightly. The company was also pleased when employees took parental leave, because this was seen as a cost-saving measure (when employees were on parental leave, the company did not have to pay their wages). The high demand for qualified IT employees was an important part of the background behind these policies. As the economy improved, the company could change part-time jobs to full-time jobs, retaining their employees.

Very few companies in our sample could be regarded as phase 3 companies. The best of them tended to display some phase 3 traits while remaining less advanced in other areas. Since the advanced phase was less visible in the study than the previous ones, the material is more like fragments than a coherent picture. It can be seen as early examples of broader tendencies that are not well known yet. Phase 3 points to a wider connection of gender equality, diversity and innovation; although the conditions of this development are uncertain today, we know that this phase will be characterised by greater interconnection of formerly (seemingly) isolated issues. This has been pointed out, for example, by research on work. Isolated attempts towards innovation can create broader change when they work together. Role changes on several levels are needed to create breakthroughs; democratic innovation together with gender change constitutes one of the key factors (Thorsrud 1973).

A broad proactive trend pointing towards change can be connected to the increasing proportion of services in the labour market and thereby – by implication at least – the increased value of reproduction. More complex work means more emphasis on cooperation and social skills, and as a background tendency, increasing gender equality (Holter 1997a). This has recently been described as a more "relational" working life (Fossestøl 2004). We know that work has many socialisation effects (see, e.g., Kohn and Schooler 1983); today, some of them have developed in a social direction and have become more widespread. Social relations are more important in the workplace across different branches and sectors.

> What the individual does, how she or he cooperates, has become more critical. We can see this even in quite traditional firms as well as in production-oriented firms. Also, it has to do with increased service orientation. (Norway, employer expert)

The socialisation affects in work appear on the organisational as well as the individual level. An example is Coomundi (Spain). This company implemented gender equality issues internally in its own organisation, a move based on the social work and development work its members did for the organisation in other parts of the world. Gender equality appeared as a necessity considering practical tasks in the field, and on this basis (with an element of 'learning from the developing/poor world'), the organisation developed an internal policy that came to include men as well as women. This example shows the importance of work and task-related challenges for change. The orientation and character of the work means a lot, especially if other conditions are also fairly favourable.

A third long-term change dimension had to do with work itself – new work forms and innovation. A common theme in our study concerned the possibilities for working shorter and smarter.

> If you set your schedule so that you work till, say, four o'clock, then you don't think about the possibility that you could have done things quite differently, that you might not need to be there till four. Do we have schedules just to have schedules, for example? Are they useful? Are we doing anything useful? A lot of people think we schedule common working hours just to get information we've already received through e-mails, etc. Is it necessary or is the meeting just for the meeting's own sake, because somewhere it says we should have it? Or could we become more effective? These are the kind of things that have to do with our private lives. (Jonas, Lia School, Norway)

Employees with strict schedules were influenced by increasing flexibility and more 'loosely' structured schedules elsewhere in working life. Increased quality of life and family-work balance could be achieved by working smarter and more innovatively. Other long-term tendencies were more negative or possibly dangerous:

> The place of work and the place of living are becoming more integrated. How do we protect the living places in relation to the workplaces? People become more 'nomadic,' and shift between different tasks. Organisations become more amoeba-like. Firms are building up and down and moving. Restructuring has become normal. The car industry is an example, quite transparent and per se quite traditional, but also innovative. The whole society is become more transparent or borderless. There are no borders between living and working. (Norway, employer expert)

Although we found differences between a family orientation and a gender equality orientation, most men associated the two. For example:

> I think the company is good in terms of gender equality, because there are the same opportunities for men and women, and they do positive discrimination in favour of women to try

to balance gender in top positions. The company is also good because it helps employees with families. (Marc Busquets, Coomundi, Spain)

More transparency on gender-equal terms could mean better work-family policy, helping employees to set limits to "invasive jobs" and "honey traps." The benefits of proactive policies were especially evident in this company.

Training and material for fostering gender equality among employees are good. It is good for two reasons: there is an effort to be aware of gender equality in the company and in order to be more aware at home and in society (ibd.).

An expert in the company said:

For our organisation, it would be positive to have more men taking fathers' leave or other work-family balance measures. This is positive for gender-role equality in general. Our organisation can help demonstrate that there is an added value, that people use it, and people can seek shelter. This also can change society. It demonstrates that if we can do it, others can also do it – like a model or an example of different forms of operation.

A manager in another Spanish company said, "the advantages are that we are a tremendously attractive company, where people are very engaged with their projects. People are motivated." (Mobcom)

Attracting the best employees through social benefits was a key in this context. The benefits were "an added value compared to other companies." [24] "We cannot compete in terms of wages; the only thing we can offer to the employee is motivation and a positive atmosphere in which to work. And also you have compensation policies, work-family balance, and more flexibility than in other companies. And this also generates added value."

Benefits could, to some extent, replace wages. "Our salary is not very high. Based on the qualifications of the people and kinds of jobs we do, we should be receiving higher wages. So it is necessary to compensate for this, and they do it with time."

Social competence was clearly valued in the advanced companies, for example in recruitment. "If we have two profiles, the one without any social path or collaboration or dedication in social matters but with a technical profile, we prefer the second, someone who is motivated about social issues."

Many men emphasised gender equality and family reconciliation as motivation and loyalty factors. Companies who provide these benefits will increasingly profit from it in labour market competition, according to our study. "I like a more dynamic kind of job. I think I am a hard worker and my bosses appreciate my achievements. So I feel secure here with this company." Private and family reasons are becoming more important, and Boris (multinational company expert employee, Bulgaria) continues:

My partner and I have lived together for 4 years. I feel very happy and complete in this relationship, and I am strongly attached to my partner's son, whom I've accepted as my own child.

---

24   Here are following quotations from different Coomundi experts and employees.

So I am responsible for the care of the child, taking him to and from the kindergarten, staying at home with him until his mother returns from work. Also, I am responsible for the shopping and very much engaged in cleaning the house and washing dishes. I am inclined and willing to take on all these responsibilities, because my partner comes home later and she's too tired to have time and enthusiasm to cope with all her tasks. Helping – well, my partner helps me, because she supports me in my work and the stressful moments there. I have a budget to deal with and it's not easy to achieve all the objectives and yes, this is very hindering.

But all in all, he is happy – more men are seeing gender equality as a benefit rather than a cost.

3.5 The Status of Domestic Work

Compared to other countries, Austria may serve as a less advanced example concerning the status of domestic work. Men in Austria make a clear distinction between domestic work and caregiving work. Taking care of the child is much more emphasised than domestic work. According to the respondents who took parental leave for a limited period of time, men seemed to be busy taking care of children, while these men describe women in the same position as "busy keeping the house clean, rather than looking after the child." That assignment-pattern was to be seen especially when men spend a limited period of time in parental leave.

Men who spend an unlimited period of time with family work ("domestic men") did not make such a strong gender assignment. On the contrary, they compared their situation with the situation of other women as the result of their self-concept adaptation over time. The "short-period-parental-leave-man" did not compare himself to women, but rather distanced himself from women. This early stage of "misplacement" and "Gender Status Insecurity," described in the "Austrian pre-study-report" (Scambor, Scambor and Voitle 2003), sometimes even took derogatory forms.

Men's strong constructions of the gender distribution of domestic work and caregiving work have to be connected to the different value and social acknowledgement of the respective areas. Men performing family work get into a socially devalued position that is associated with women and mainly connected to domestic work. The men's strategy of differentiation towards "domestic women" ("housewives") can be interpreted as an effort to heighten gender status security by "distance regulation to women." Masculinity cannot be understood as a quality or essence; it is more of a (practical) project, and it is reproduced and established in the process of social interaction (Connell 1995). When a man assigns devalued domestic work to women and valuable caregiving work to himself, he is able to leave an uncomfortable B-position, getting back to a traditional paramount position in the hegemonic relationship between men and women.

This strategy only makes sense as long as the perspective of men consists of a phase of domestic/caring work that has a definite beginning and end. Under these circumstances, men may make use of "supporting discourses" to maintain their self-esteem while performing less acknowledged tasks. In Austria, such supporting discourses that are accepted and used by men tend to exist more for "active fathers and father-child-relationships" than for homemaking. When respondents mentioned that they attached a high value to family (sometimes with religious connotations), they were linking the construction of the family as a relational area in the first place and emphasising to a much lesser degree the family as a domestic-work-area. "Fairness" and "justice" concerning the distribution of unpaid labour between the partners play some role, but this is definitely of less importance compared to the "father-child-relationship" pattern of argumentation (cf. Scambor, Scambor and Voitle 2003).

3.6 The Costs of Equality

3.6.1 Work Compression

Part-time employment for men does not always mean part-time performance. Particularly men in part-time employment in traditional companies – characterised by traditional "gendered processes" in terms of work time, workplace and expected attitudes toward work (Acker 1991) – are often informally forced into a doing a full-time output equivalent. That means that part-time employed men compress full-time performance into a part-time job. The results are high work pressure as well as less contact with colleagues. It seems to be an informal deal, in the sense of a 'tit for tat': "I will work as much as possible if I get the chance to reduce working hours." Or alternatively, "you will be able to work part-time if you perform well."

Paraphrasing Peinelt-Jordan (1996), the process of "work compression" can be described in the following way: There are several important conditions for a successful reduction of work time. First of all, part-time employment already exists in the company. Another important aspect for schedule reductions is a good relationship with the superior, one based on trust as well as continuous employment in the company. On the individual level, the reason for "work compression" can be understood as an individual strategy to maintain the occupational function of serving identity development. The intensification of work performance in part-time employment has certain negative aspects for the employee, such as fewer possibilities to influence work processes, less of a chance to participate in informal communication (social isolation), as well as the loss of status.

When the good conditions (as described above) do not exist – for instance, assuming the manager expects the traditional male full-time model, the company offers other possibilities for flexible work, or the company is not used to flexibility in work – men employed part-time are somewhat forced into "work compression" for company-related reasons: 'tit for tat'-reasons, pressure from colleagues, or pressure from the manager (refuses new appointment). In general, managers as well as male colleagues seem to lack any sympathy for caregiving men in part-time positions. Female colleagues more often appreciate the fact that men reconcile work and family.

3.6.2   Career Break and Downhill Mobility

As soon as men get into women associated work conditions, they seem to become affected by traditional women-associated barriers, such as low career prospects, low job positions, and low income:

"Part-time employed men cannot become leaders!" As the Austrian examples show, part-time work for people in leadership positions is a very rare exception. The only part-time working manager in the sample is continuously confronted with the head of the department's request to increase his working hours. Referring to the question of career, most of the experts in our sample cannot imagine that management activities can be done in part-time employment. Up to now, the demands on people in management positions have seemed to be orientated toward a traditional male breadwinner model. Even organisations with a strong focus on gender equality do not provide good career conditions. One of the Austrian reproductive-oriented companies offers advantages for certain men, namely, men with less career orientation and the motivation to reconcile "whatever" with work. The company does not provide good career opportunities for men, but it is a supporting environment for men who reconcile work and family/life.

"Fathers' leave can be followed by an occupational 'downhill mobility.'" The Austrian companies give an example of what happens if formal rights do not exist. At Revoc (reproductive-oriented) and Hafner (productive-oriented), a guaranteed position after parental leave is not provided. That means that when employees come back to work, they cannot expect to do the same job they did before. Although a position guarantee is regarded as an important matter in terms of women's support, even Revoc does not provide appropriate conditions:

The company supports men taking parental leave. They really try to make it possible. But they cannot guarantee the father will get his position when he comes back to work again. This affects the hierarchical position as well as the work activities. There is no guarantee. And there have been people waiting a whole year to get back to their old positions....And it can happen that people come back and get a job in the administration department. Imagine, well-educated people have to work in the administration department (note: he refers to 'downhill mobility') (Magnus, Revoc)

Referring to personnel recruitment, the possibility that an applicant is going to take parental leave is still seen as a negative factor for some companies. Sometimes men taking care of their children are confronted with 'invisible' discrimination in the company. They become a member of a B-team in their working life. They are discriminated against, because their superiors and/or colleagues equate family-orientation with reduction in efficiency. That leads to disadvantages in a male dominated working system (Peinelt-Jordan 1996). A part-timer, considered his career opportunities as "zero" and added,

The moment you decide to go part-time, you are – career-wise – dead. You are dead. And you mustn't have any illusions about that. It would be naïve to think about it in any other way, to think you still had a chance.

In his experience it is not accepted

if you still have personal interests. And someone who dares to bring their personal interests out into the open, he is, in the eyes of the company...in the company, you only get anywhere if you say: 'I'll sleep in the office' or 'I'll come in the morning with my tooth brush and pyjamas.' (Georg H., Interbank, Germany)

The "costs of masculinity" (Lehner 1998) – strong competition and stress with psychological and physical consequences – might have been a strong motivation for some men to begin focussing on gender equality and making appropriate changes in their lives. The "costs of equality" should not change their approach. What can we do to minimise these costs for 'models of good practice'?

Men have to be involved in organisational measures to guarantee gender equality. In that way, the jurisdictional field of equality representatives should be extended to include men, and management consultants should be able to understand organisational processes from a gendered perspective.

Furthermore, institutional regulations and formal rights are necessary conditions to prevent discrimination (job position guarantee after parental leave).

3.7 Concluding Remarks

Two theoretical issues have been highlighted in this chapter. These are the need to develop change perspectives concerning men and masculinities, and the need for more organisational awareness of gender and masculinities concepts.

Caregiving men represent a new relational gender vis-à-vis the company's traditional organisational gender. Tension accompanies this development, leading to increasing conflict and a pressure towards new organisational developments. In our 'best practice' cases, men's needs for gender equality was more recognised, but as a whole, this process was in an early phase.

We have emphasised the 'neutralisation' of gender discrimination against men. What is in fact related to men's caregiving and new roles is expressed and practiced as if it had no special gender meaning or consequence. When a man in one of our interviews stresses that "career-wise you are dead if you take a part-time job" – an experience shared by many – it does not mean that the organisation is out to get you if you are a caregiving man or represent some special masculinity. That may be the case too, since in some companies, traditional organisational gender leads to cultural sanctions in the form of degrading remarks for example – but this is not the main pattern. Instead, the 'user interface' of unequal organisational gender is neutral and legitimised in non-gender terms. It is not as if management is anti-care. It simply does not care, according to many of the men. Gender models, practices and regulations seem to be determined by "hegemonic masculinity" and traditional masculinity standards. Even in gender-advanced companies men as gendered beings remain in the blind spot.

New leadership in particular brought about the change possibilities highlighted in our study. A paradox arises when the traditional organisation gets a new man as a leader, as in Hafner company in Austria. In this case, there had been a strategic shift from paternalistic to strategic management, and the new manager created several measures to flatten old hierarchical structures, involving class divisions as well as gender issues. Transforming unskilled to skilled employment was company policy. The company had developed a system to change unskilled employees to "workers with skilled employee status," a voluntary measure in the company that enhanced security for these workers to some degree.[25] The manager argued that the employees were all qualified for their jobs and that the term "unskilled" devalued their work and position in the company. The distinction between skilled and unskilled work also caused a gap between employees and management, allowing class division to form in the company. The manager's target was that the term "unskilled worker" should disappear in the company. For many reasons, the importance of the leadership role was highlighted in our results, and leaders' possibilities for change and gender equality improvement emerged as an important research issue for the future.

---

25 In Austria, there are "workers" and "employees," and the employees are better off in some respects.

4. Male Job and Life Patterns: A Correspondence Analysis

Sigtona Halrynjo and Øystein Gullvåg Holter

With Vera Riesenfeld, Klaus Schwerma, Elli Scambor and Christian Scambor

4.1 Profile

This section first describes the main profile of the men in the study and the context of reduced wage work.. Next, four main adaptations (or empirically constructed ideal type) concerning work-life are outlined based on the two independent major distinctions among the men in the sample: position in working life and degree of care responsibility.

Despite internal variation and some rather average subsamples, it is clear that the project sample as a whole differs from the European average in some important respects. The education level among these men is high; almost half of the men have a university degree. The number of men here who earn less than their partners or wives is higher than the societal average (although the majority in the subsample still earns more than their partners). Lastly they work more often with women at their workplace.[26]

4.1.1 Attitudes

The cultural demise of the breadwinner ideal was quite clear in the sample. Only 10 % of the men supported the notion that "a husband's job is to earn money; a wife's job is to look after the home and family;" 81 % disagreed. And as much as 96 % supported the notion that "children need a father to be as closely involved in their upbringing as the mother;" only 3 % disagreed. These attitudes are probably somewhat ahead of the European average. They point to a conflict in many men's lives between ideals and practices, with the issue of active fathering assuming an especially strong ideological change factor. But despite the dual career ideals, 70 %of the non-single men earned more than their wife or partner, 10 % earned the same, and 20 % earn less.

Gender role attitudes were mixed with a sceptical attitude toward assigning a primary place to wage work in life, especially among the men with re-

---

26 The results reported here are the results from multivariat analyses of the core matrix (N=104) that were also confirmed in more qualitative ways through analysis of the interviews.

duced work hours. This is important since it meant that some of the gender role attitudes could not be taken at face value. For example, many men were critical of a statement that said that having a job is the best way to happiness for a woman. However, they were just as critical to similar ideas regarding men. The men were sceptical towards extensive work in general, especially among parents of young children. There is probably some ambivalence to women's wage labour lurking behind this finding. The interviews showed that most of the men wanted income balance, yet many also expected women to take responsibility at home. These somewhat incongruent trends seem to offer a fairly good illustration of the ongoing European changes in the gender system and dilemmas. Against this background, it is not surprising that most of the men agreed with the statement that "employers should make special arrangements to help fathers combine jobs and childcare."

Stronger gender-equal attitudes were associated with social rather than technical jobs, shorter wage work hours per week, reduction of work hours in periods, income balance in the marriage and relationship, higher levels of male caregiving in the home, and having younger children. (Gender role attitudes also varied country by country, most likely because of the sampling variation reasons discussed above.) Based upon our sample alone, Israel appears to be the most gender-traditional society, followed by Germany, Austria, Norway, Spain. The men in the Bulgarian sample shows least gender traditional results).

The men who were active in child care were younger than the rest, more often had young children at home, had more pro-equality gender role attitudes, and were more critical to how companies valued their private-life caring.

4.1.2   Work-family Practices

Somewhat surprisingly, we did not find a strong connection between reduced wage work and more domestic work. This is discussed below. Some associations did appear, however. The men with reduced wage work said that they assumed a larger proportion of caring at home and had somewhat more pro-equality attitudes. They also argued more often that employers should make arrangements for both fathers and mother's family involvement.

In terms of work hours, quite different groups were present in the sample, for reasons discussed above. The men worked 35 hours per week on average, but the conditions varied significantly. Around 40 % of the men belonged to the reduced work group (working 30 hours or less per week). On the other hand, 25 % worked 45 hours or more. The Israel sample deviated from the others in this respect. The men in this sample worked much longer work hours, most of the men working 45-55 hours. Furthermore, the Israel men made up three quarters of the men with very long work hours in the sample as a whole. Long work hours were associated with production-oriented jobs, and

– less strongly – with education and a higher position in the company. There was also some association with marital status, and perhaps a more sceptical attitude toward women's employment, but we did not find any clear connection to other gender attitude items or to the personal orientation items.

The men who worked reduced hours were not a homogenous group. This finding is in line with the results of the socio-economic subproject, showing that this group is a mix of different subgroups (it can also be related to the third male employee type in the labour market overview, above). Our sample has three main groups of men working reduced hours: men with domestic caregiving tasks, students and multi-job workers.

The men who worked long hours were often dissatisfied with it. Many would prefer to work less – the association to the statement "I would prefer to work less" was very strong. Many found it hard to reduce hours. They were less satisfied with social life and leisure than the other men in the study. However, some of them also seemed to work more at home; at least, caring work was not reduced proportionally. About three quarters of the men worked in unlimited work contracts. Of the rest, some worked free-lance, some with fixed-term contracts, and a few with other or unknown contract forms.

Half the men worked in social and education jobs, the other half in technical or financial jobs. The orientation of the work between technical/production oriented work and social/reproduction oriented work had a quite strong connection with other variables in the study, confirming other research in this area.[27] At this point, a direct interpretation of the project's "work changes gender" title seems appropriate. Production-oriented work was strongly linked to long work hours as well as a high proportion of the household income. Not surprisingly, social competence was less valued here than in social and educational jobs.

Two thirds of the men were married or living in registered partnerships. 21 % were unmarried, 4 %divorced or widowed. The married, cohabitating and partnership group differed from the rest in several ways. They were older, more highly educated, had more years of employment and a higher average position in the company. They did not differ much, however, regarding gender role attitudes or personal items. 80 % of the men in the sample were in relationships. Of these, 6 % reported living with a male partner, 90 % with a female partner, and 4 % was not clear.

Regarding domestic work, the division of housework was more traditional than the division of care work. Again, this is in line with other studies. 60 % of the non-single men had partners who assumed the main responsibility for the cooking in the home. Only 12 % mostly did the cooking themselves. This high-

---

27 For example, a representative survey of men and gender equality in Norway 1988 not only showed the impact of social/reproduction work among the men, but also indicated that their wives or partner's job orientation played a role regarding the men's gender equality attitudes (see Holter 1989).

lights "average-to-advanced" rather than a "very advanced" character in the sample.[28] Almost a third of the non-single men had paid help to do the house cleaning. Very few men (8 %) said they mainly did the cleaning themselves.

Almost all the men with children in the household contributed to caring for the children, ranging from 5 to 50 hours per week, most frequently around 20 hours per week. The men's part of childcare was strongly associated with whether the men have taken parental leave or not. This is an interesting finding, highlighting the importance of parental leave for the domestic work division in general. Not surprisingly, the caring men were more often dissatisfied with how the job recognised their private caregiving tasks. In other areas, however, the effects of caring for children were less clear (not much difference in gender role attitudes, orientation, etc).

Except for the association between long work hours and less life satisfaction, we did not find much direct connection between life satisfaction and personality items, on the one hand, and the other items of the study, on the other hand. For example, the gender equality items did not have any clear connection to the personal items. This can be interpreted in terms of 'relative costs' of gender equality (more on this later). However, we did find that the men's satisfaction with their marriages or relationships was much greater than their satisfaction with their social life. This has been found in other studies also.[29] As we shall see, it helps explain an important part of the men's change picture, discussed later—why changes in marriage or relationship are so often important for the men's decisions in other areas, such as their job.

4.2 The Contexts of Work Reduction

As we saw, reduced work was less clearly related to increased domestic caregiving than one might suppose. One might expect a similar but opposed pattern among men and women. Among women, increased wage work has been associated with decreased domestic work, especially in the last decade. Among men, according to this logic, we should find the inverse pattern – less wage work, more domestic work.

---

28   The figures can be compared to a representative survey of men and women in Norway 1994, where 7 % said the man did most of the cooking, 17 % shared or fairly equal. Surveys from 1989 and 1994 showed that the woman took most of the cooking in ca. 70 % of the homes in Norway (Holter 1994). In this perspective, we see that the current European sample is a bit more balanced.

29   E.g., the representative survey *The Norwegian Man* (1998) where men were asked who they could talk to about personal troubles. The great majority answered "my wife/partner," while other alternatives – friends, therapists, etc. were much less frequent. It seems that for men, marriage is still a "haven in a heartless world".

108

There are several reasons why this pattern was not found. First, the theoretical basis for the assumption is problematic. Arguing that men are also gendered does not imply that gender means the same for men and for women, or that gender means the mirror opposite for men compared to women. These are fairly typical mistakes. One main reason why there is no symmetry or mirror opposition is that social class enters the picture differently for men and for women. Women's adoption of new gender roles has mostly meant increased upward mobility in terms of class. For men, it may not mean downward mobility, but there are much larger risks that it will lead in that direction, and also a much larger chance that the men's changes will be interpreted in this way and opposed on that basis.

Empirically, two main factors weakened the association between lower labour hours and higher domestic and caring participation among men. One has been mentioned already: the men who worked reduced hours were a very heterogeneous category. Only some of the men in this position in the labour market at any given moment are in it for caregiving reasons. Others are part-time students, have hobbies they try to develop into jobs, combine several jobs in a fluctuating "patch worker" style, or are simply pushed into part-time against their will, due to company reductions. The three first subcategories were common in our material. Once more, this result may be seen as a lack of strategic focus in the project (we were not able to select only the men who combined reduced work and caregiving), while also giving a broader and perhaps more realistic scope. At this point it should also be noted that in none of the countries we studied had part-time for men been promoted or much discussed as part of a gender equality strategy.[30]

The other factor was a "work more in both spheres" tendency, which could be found especially when we excluded the most overworked subgroup of men. In other words, many men with a normal to fairly long workday also contributed a lot to domestic work. Variation in gender attitudes and roles was important in this context. The men who worked much in both spheres were often gender-equally oriented and approached the "care and career" adaptation described below. Personal background and preferences are undoubtedly also part of this picture, although their meaning was not clear in this study. A common trait was that the men were married to career women and faced demands at home as well as on the job. This, however, does not necessarily mean that the men's domestic work was only a "passive effect" of their wives career choice; this relation is more complex, since, in our study (as in others), we have many indications that these men actively chose this type of relationship in the first place.

But does reduced wage work, by itself, have an effect on domestic work? This is possible, and there are some traits in this direction in the study, but not

---

30 Germany may be a partial exception, with more discussion of part-time than elsewhere, yet often in an alternative or health related framework, not gender equality as such.

very strong ones. It probably varies with the socio-cultural context and gender climate. Traditionally, research has not found increased domestic participation among men who are forced to work reduced hours or who are laid off. In fact, the contrary is more typical. Households with men who are unemployed in the long term tend to show increased social problems, including gender-related troubles and violence at home. It is true that voluntary reduction may be another matter, especially if it is clearly connected to a gender equality strategy, but as mentioned above, this was not a main issue even in our advanced sample. In our sample, many men had thought about parental leave and the need for fathers to become more active, but this discussion had not (yet) been extended into a more general awareness of the need to reduce work time. At this point, quite different models and ideals also appeared on the horizon, including the 'care/career' and the 'time pioneer/alternative' model, as will be shown later.

4.3 Four Adaptations[31]

Correspondence analysis was used in a further attempt to clarify the main dimensions among the men. In this type of analysis, the variables that explain most of the variation in the material construct axes in a diagram that might reveal distinctive positions. The purpose of this analysis is to reveal patterns[32] and underlying structures within the material. The analysis showed that four main adaptations could be distinguished based on different positions in relation to the axis, as shown in fig. 26.

This shows the two independent dimensions that construct the largest variations in the material? The horizontal axis (work dimension) is constructed of variables connected to work; *work reduction / work time, work position* and *career prospects*. Not surprisingly, education and social status also contribute to this dimension.

---

31 Further analysis and developed discussion will soon be published by Sigtona Halrynjo.
32 With patterns we mean the structure of available position that are empirically constructed by the significant dimensions in the social space.

Fig. 26: Men and Work-Life-Reconciliation

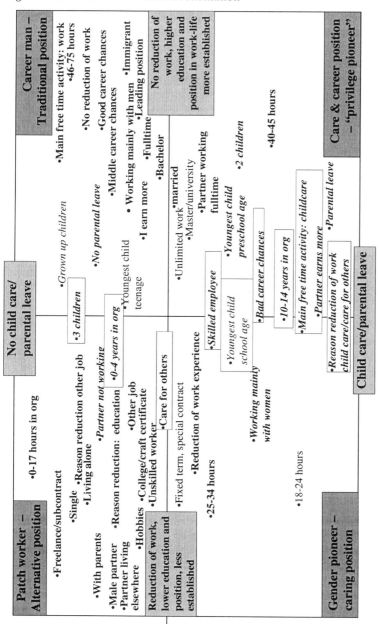

111

On the east side of the figure, we find the gravity points (average place-ment) of the high positions in working life, higher education, work security, unlimited work and good or average career prospects. Here we find "man-ager" and "no reduction of work." The typical civil status on this side is to be married with a full-time working partner, but to still be the "main breadwin-ner." On the west side of the figure, we find lower educated, unskilled work-ers and a reduction of work experience. On this side, it is more typical to be single and live with parents and to not be the main breadwinner.

The vertical axis (care-dimension) is constructed of factors based on child care, and care for others as the main free-time activity, parental leave and reduction of work for caring reasons. South from this we find the gravity point of childcare as the main free-time activity and the main reason for re-duction of work. Other reasons include taking parental leave and working mainly with woman.

In the northern section, we find no childcare. On the northwest side of the figure, we find *grown up children. –*The *main free-time activity is work (46-75 hours of work).* and there is *no parental leave.* On the northeast side of the figure, we find short working hours in the respective organization, but the reason for work reduction has to do with freelance or "other job." The actual working hours might easily be high, but the job security is still low. Here we also find other reasons for reduction in work, such as *educational reasons* and *work* or *health reasons that were beyond the control of the individual.* A little further south, we find *quality of life reasons* for reduction in work and *fixed term/special contract* (in other words, lower work security).

The average man and his characteristics in this sample (described in the previous paragraph) will disappear in the middle of figure, while the more radical positions are visible in the corners. We see four "ideal" or "pure" types (to use Weber's term). These can be called the *career position* or over-time worker (high wage work, low care work), the *caring position* or gender pioneer (low wage work, high care work), the *care and career position* (high wage work, high care work) and patch worker or *alternative position* (low wage work, low care work). As mentioned earlier, many traits were quite common among the men, including a rejection of the traditional breadwinner ideal, but as we will see, when it comes to practice the situation vary. These positions can only be understood in relation to the other positions and must be interpreted as extreme points.

When we combine the top end of the work/career dimension with the low end of the caring dimension, we find *The Career Position* or what we may call the traditional masculine position

Typical characteristics of this position are very long working hours (45 to75 hour work week), no reduction in work, leading position, higher educa-tion, working mainly with men, technical work, earning more than the wife or partner and high job security in terms of unlimited work contracts. In this position, we also find the highest anticipated career chances among the men (good to medium career chances in their own view.) Further typical characteristics include not taking parental leave and "work" as the main free time activity.

Then we turn to the opposite position in the figure: This was not originally meant to be in the selection, but due to pragmatic reasons, it turned out that many men in "modern organisations" were situated here. In a relational perspective this position is important to clarify the other positions. In order to see and understand the "new men" or the "possible new positions," it is useful to see and make clear the traditional position, which makes the new ones "new" or "different.

In the southwest corner of the figure, we find what we may call the *Caring Position:* One main characteristic in this position is experience with reduction in work. And the reason for reduction is *childcare, care for others* and *quality of life.* In this position, it is typical to *work mainly with women in an educational/social/health organization.* The main free-time activity will typically be *childcare* and *family and friends.* Here we find more use of fixed-term or special contract (lower job security). The typical man here will be a skilled employee with bad career chances (from their own point of view).

This position is, in some contexts, considered to be a position for *time pioneers*, as they are said to challenge the traditional male working pattern. But this position does not necessarily challenge the hegemonic position or the time and privileges structure as a whole – it might actually presuppose it. It can be argued that the career position and the caring position imply each other. These two positions illustrate the traditional way of handling the productive and reproductive responsibility in a society and in a family. The challenging part here might be that in this case we find men in the *traditional "female" position.* They might be *gender pioneers*, challenging our natural way of conceptualising male and female adaptations to work and family life. And that might be of great importance, but these men do not necessarily challenge the privilege structure, which is accompanied by a proclivity for the hegemonic position in working life (based on overwork and "outsourcing of life") to the care position. The traditional career position needs the care position to be able to be self-sustaining. While the gendered structure in society might be challenged by men moving into "female positions", the overall time and privilege structure will not.

In the southeast direction on the figure, we can identify *the Care and Career Position* with a medium to long working week (40-45 hours), a wife or partner working full time and the youngest child in pre-school age. The typical background is higher education. Here we find the most common experience with parental leave. The availability of this position is probably very closely connected to national law in terms of regulations on parental leave and father's quota, combined with corporate cultures that allow prolonged

113

father's leave. In contrast to the care-position, job security in this position is not reduced. The contracts here are dominated by unlimited work. Corporate cultures seem to allow parental leave without the same degree of punishment in terms of job insecurity as they do when reduced working hours are considered.

On top of working full time and raising small children together with a full-time working partner, the most common free-time activity mentioned in this position is reconstructing or building a house (in addition to childcare).

In the care and career position, we find men who present themselves as encumbered with caring duties, but they do not accept that caring duties should mean to give up on the traditional worker privilege of work security (unlimited contract, degree of establishment and positions in work life). They see themselves to losing something in terms of career options, but they do not accept the old paradigm with its strict dichotomy of care or career privilege.

When we look in the quadrant that combines *little care experience* and *lower position in working life* we find *the Patch Worker or the Alternative Position*. Typical characteristics here are *freelance* or *subcontract, unskilled worker* and *minimally employed in organisation (0-17 hours a week)*. Reasons for reduced hours in this position are not caring tasks, but other forms of work or studies or further education. Characteristics of being un-established are also found here, e.g., living with parents or alone, single or partner living elsewhere. This position resembled the third heterogeneous cluster of younger, temporary and part-time employed men found in the EC study mentioned in the overview (EC 2003: 139) with frequent transitions to unemployment. In this sample, the male partner is also most common here in this alternative position.

This is the only position where we actually find what we normally would call *free-time activities* like *hobbies, sport, music* and *volunteer work* (in addition to *studies/education*). This position could be seen as transitional (a typical student position) and we do find most of the young men here, but the position also includes grown-up men with lasting alternative adaptation. In the analysis based on objective positions like this one, *age* or *generations* often constitute one important dimension in social structure. But in this case *age* is not contributing to any of the axis. This means that in addition to the transitional student's position that might lead to other positions as time goes by, the "patch worker" can also be understood as a more permanent position for rejecting *the traditional structure*, including the hegemonic privilege of career and standard families and creating ones own.

Close: The Gendered Structure of "Work" and "Care"

When we consider the dimensions and the scattering of characteristics on the figure, it might be easy to explain all the disparity by "gender differences."

But this is a "men only" sample. The point, in accordance with Michael Kimmel's argument that inequality of power creates gender differences, not the other way round (Kimmel 2004), is that when we go behind the "gendered curtain" we might find other active structures like the structure of care-responsibility in society, which is historically gendered. These gendered processes are not situated inherently in the task or in the gendered body, but based on historical distributions of responsibilities, tasks and symbolic capital or privilege. Some researchers and politicians see the solution in situating men in female positions and vice versa. But maybe some of these power structures will not cease to exist if we just put some men into the old female positions. Maybe some of these symbolic capital structures have to be identified and dealt with on a structural level.

5. Towards a New Positioning of Men

Christian Scambor, Klaus Schwerma and Paco Abril

With Yair Amichai-Hamburger, Margarita Atanassova, Marc Gärtner, Sigtona Halrynjo, Øystein Gullvåg Holter, Stephan Höyng, Margareta Kreimer, Selma Therese Lyng, Ralf Puchert, Vera Riesenfeld, Elli Scambor and Violeta Velkova

5.1 Introduction

In the psychological subproject of the *Work Changes Gender*-project, the focus was shifted from economic, institutional and organisational perspectives to individual men, to the possible variations concerning how individuals deal with new work forms and discontinuities, and to what chances for individual contentedness and gender equality lay herein. We asked if men could find ways to exploit the new situations in the labour market and use the new work forms in constructive ways, and under what conditions such constructive variants of dealing with the changes could be developed. 'Constructive' means here that a man can partly replace a work orientation by some other element in his self-definition and self-concept, and do so in a way that he himself has evaluated positively and that helps to foster gender equality. Such elements might include caregiving, community or political engagement, quality-of-life aspects in social contacts and partnerships, personal interests and 'identity projects' (Keupp et al. 1999), health and so on. Although, as described in the chapters before, the whole sample turned out to range between 'average' to 'advanced'in terms of difference to what one can call a "mainstream of masculinities", it but left enough for a more advanced focus: to select exceptional male individuals who 'deviated'[33] from prescribed patterns of work-life-arrangements and found alternatives to traditional masculinity standards. We were ultimately interested in learning how the transformation processes concerning their self-concepts worked. Looking for the 'deviations' or 'positive examples' meant that the psychological subproject resembled an outlier analysis, a compilation of case studies on rare cases. The intention was to record and describe variations in male self-concepts, the focus being on

---

33   We use the term 'deviation' throughout this text to emphasize the difference of the men's behaviour and the respective norms, but we want to reject any possible negative connotation of the term. In contrary: note that these 'deviations' constitute 'best practice.'

- successful variants of dealing with labour market-related changes, variants that led to contentedness in the change,
- alternatives to traditional masculinity images,
- gender equality.

These self-concept-variants were intensively investigated and described in terms of 'best practice' at the individual level.

5.2 Theories and Concepts

The approach described above does not imply that we concentrated on isolated individuals however. On the contrary, our requirements were to work in an interdisciplinary way and to link the focus of the psychological subproject to the other subprojects (economic and sociological level, shown in the previous chapters) in order to address the topic in a comprehensive way.

These requirements had consequences for the theories and concepts that were used to address the research questions. They had to provide broad interfaces to the described perspectives. Some of the relevant concepts that were used are outlined below. Throughout chapter 5, links and references to concepts and theories stemming from social psychology, self-psychology, sociology and household economy will be given where appropriate.

For a basic integrative approach, we used the framework of 'reflexive social psychology' as it is presented by the Munich research group Keupp et al. 1999. 'Reflexive social psychology' is an interdisciplinary approach that primarily combines psychology and sociology and works mainly with qualitative methods. Within reflexive social psychology, analyses of societal frameworks and individual processes are connected. Since the area of our analysis was the *'interface of the inner and outer worlds' of the individuals*, reflexive social psychology was the theoretical framework of choice.

Apart from the concepts 'masculinity standards' and 'sprinkle system', which are described in the next section (5.2.1.), the most relevant sociological concept for this subproject was the *gender habitus concept* (Meuser 1998, 2000, Behnke 2000). It integrates the *habitus concept* of Bourdieu (1984, 1990), which emphasised *class*, and the concept of *hegemonic masculinity* (Connell 1995) with its focus on *gender relations*. Habitus can briefly be defined as a system of continuous dispositions, a principle of producing strategies that enables people to act in unpredictable new situations. People are not consciously aware of habitus but may become aware of it through conscious reflection or finding themselves in an alien environment or situation. Life according to the (gender) habitus means living in habitual security. The *gender habitus concept* has enhanced our understanding of *Gender Status*

Insecurity in a situation of trespassing gender borders, as described below (section 5.6.2.).

For in depth analyses and interpretation, a variety of concepts stemming from social psychology and self-psychology were used (e.g., Filipp 2000, Greve 2000, Higgins 1987). Among these concepts, Linville's (1985, 1987) concept of 'self-complexity' played a central role in our research. High self-complexity, i.e., a high number of independent aspects or facets of the self, can be seen as a cognitive buffer against stress that may result from non-conformity with masculinity standards. A rich variety of self-aspects can help to compensate for self-related conflicts and foster re-arrangements of the self-concept.

The connection of these concepts and theories remained loose. For the sake of interdisciplinarity and of a common language among the research teams, we tended to use concepts for interpreting and connecting the different levels of the analysis in an eclectic way, rather than trying to avoid inconsistencies between the concepts. We consider this approach to be appropriate for an exploratory analysis that seeks to provide new heuristic inputs for future research. Our theoretical approach can be outlined as follows:

- The interface of the inner and outer world of an individual as an area of analysis and reflexive social psychology form the basic framework;
- Eclectic use of concepts from social psychology, self psychology, and other disciplines and the use their potential for developing models and for interpreting phenomena within an exploratory study;
- Tendency to look for the interfaces between theories and concepts rather than problematising concept inconsistencies;
- Worked within the framework of Grounded Theory methodology and the concept of theoretic sensibility (Strauss and Corbin 1998).

5.2.1. Masculinity Standards and the Central Role of the Topic 'Men and Caring'

Two starting points emerged out of the previous subprojects:

- The male standard work pattern (continuous, full-time employment, with the role or connotation of the main provider of the family) is affected by changes in the labour market;
- Work and labour still play a central role within the 'masculinity standards.'

'Masculinity standards' and gender standards in general can be derived from Holter's (2003a) 'sprinkle system':

The 'sprinkle system' consists of economic incentives that favour the provider or bread-winner role rather than the caring role. It keeps men out of care-related activities, professional caregiving work, as well as caregiving in private life...The sprinkle system is not just an economic system favouring the breadwinner. It is also social, cultural and psychological. It is connected to social sanctions against unmanliness, to contempt for weakness and to a struggle for 'model power.' The two basic ideological messages of the system rest on the premise of the man as the hard outgoing instrumental type – the 'go till you drop' syndrome. One message is that men are expendable. The other is that men do not care....When a gender ideal like the breadwinner one is partially realised through such a sprinkle system, including economic rewards in working life, it takes on a normative quality. It persists and has a larger impact than one would otherwise expect..." (Holter 2003a: 25).

The basic ideological messages of this system ('men are expendable, hard, instrumental' and 'men are non-carers') are implemented on an economic, social, cultural and psychological level. We want to call these ideological messages and their concrete implications 'masculinity standards.' These standards exist 'inside and outside' individuals. This view allows us to link this concept to the 'identity work' of reflexive social psychology, because 'identity work' is defined in this framework as people's efforts to co-ordinate their inner and outer worlds. Furthermore, masculinity standards contain the common features of the male gender habitus.

In the psychological subproject, we interviewed men whose work-life-arrangements do not correspond to these standards, either because new developments have occurred, or new situations have been sought out and created by the men themselves as an active (partial) rejection of masculinity standards. We wanted to reconstruct these men's identity work, to look at how they dealt with friction or conflicts between masculinity standards and their actual situation, inside themselves as well as outside.

Masculinity standards are built into institutions, into every day life, into gender relations within and between the genders, and function as gender-norms within subjects. For the individual, these standards appear as preferences and attractions, as ought and ideal selves, as 'what I prefer and would like.' The masculinity standards can be seen as 'ideal self' or 'ought self' in a self-system that contains the following perspectives:

– what I am (actual self),
– what I would like to be (ideal self),
– what I should be (ought self).

The above breakdown follows Higgins' self-discrepancy theory (Higgins 1987). Important masculinity standards are:

– work and career are the central facets in men's self concepts; other facets are subordinate and created around work and career,
– men are expendable, hard workers,
– men are non-carers concerning working life,

120

– men are the main providers of the family and non-carers, if they live in a family – which they should – implying the norm of heterosexual orientation.

These masculinity standards clearly reflect a specific gender relation, the one of industrialised societies, marked by the strong distinction of work and home, paid and unpaid labour, etc. Like Connell's concept of hegemonic masculinity (Connell 1995), they reflect the historical, economic and cultural organisation and development of society. It is argued that these standards are increasingly dissolving, according to economic changes, and are doing so in certain 'sociotopes' more than in others. The pattern of what can be considered as hegemonic masculinity may be changing, and cultural, societal and economic changes, as well as democratisation and modernisation may have fostered a diversification of masculinities. This diversification, in turn, casts doubt on masculinity standards. Nevertheless, we argue that for most men such standards are still valid, at least as background orientation patterns, and that all men in a society know what these standards are.

It can be expected that masculinity standards show significant inertia against change, because they play an important role for the way the genders are organised within a gender system. Thus, they are implemented strongly into people's self-concepts as elements with significant weight and importance. They are affirmed and reproduced in daily life by *doing gender* (West and Fenstermaker 1995), and the basic imperatives hold across milieus and countries as actual standards or as well-known pattern that one is leaving behind.

In our study, men and caregiving constituted one focus. Although our effort was to look for individuals who differ from masculinity standards in general and not only for men who have taken over some caregiving tasks, we want to outline briefly why we consider the topic *men and caregiving* as *paradigmatic*. We argue that the combination *men and caring* challenges the way in which the genders are organised *in general*. Despite differences, the labour markets in every country in our study show a gender-specific segregation. Men or women prevail in certain professions, forms of work are distributed unequally (e.g., part-time work), and women's share of domestic and caring work is higher than men's. These gender specific disparities are the result of a complex development process that assigns and distributes *areas to genders*. As Holter (2003a) has pointed out within the concept of the *sprinkle system*, various levels play a role in organising work and gender (economic, social, cultural, psychological). Elements on all these levels work together in complex ways to maintain certain features of how the genders are related to each other (and how relations among subgroups are organised, e.g., dominant and subordinate masculinities).

The way in which work is distributed to the genders relies on a preference system that has emerged historically and that is influenced economically and

121

culturally. The preference system predefines people's decisions in a gendered way, although people consider these preferences as their own and as individual (technical versus social inclinations of boys and girls, resulting in gender-specific occupational choices and the assignment of different responsibilities for paid and reproduction work to the genders in relationships via inclinations that have been pre-defined within male and female self-concepts). Paid and unpaid labour is distributed unequally among the genders, which results in competitive disadvantages for women in the labour market. The reproductive arena is mainly assigned to women, as is the outsourced segment of reproduction (in the form of services in the domain of caring work). This increases horizontal segregation, since more men are found in the higher paid technical occupations, and more women in the lower paid human/ social occupations. Moreover, the assignment of reproductive work to women fosters the vertical segregation as long as organisations can predict that *she* will have most caring duties at home, and *he* will not. This assumes, of course, that the learning effect of domestic and caring phases is valued less by organisations than the availability of employees; this demand for *total availability* in times of *digital capitalism* has recently been emphasised by Böhnisch (2003).

For the above arguments of a more economic perspective, we regard the topic *men and caring* as a *paradigmatic case* for our research project. Men who take on caring tasks challenge the distributional rules by which work and gender are connected in many societies.

5.3 The Study: Overview

The following section contains an overview of our methodological approach in the psychological subproject. We have decided to explain our approach in more detail here for several reasons:

– The psychological subproject started last, and the theoretical elements and results of the economic and sociological subprojects had to be integrated in an interdisciplinary sense. The way to handle this complex task should be outlined here in order to provide the rationale for our conclusions as well as to present a methodological model for similar projects to come.
– Because only an insubstantial amount of relevant literature is available, researchers may also be interested in the methodology we employed in comparing qualitative data from different countries.
– In order to give the reader the chance of assessing our results and generalisations, it is imperative that our methodological approach is presented.

Readers who are not interested in methodological issues may skip section 5.3. and go to section 5.4.

The study in the psychological subproject consisted of an analysis of *best-practice examples* of *male self-concepts*. In contrast to representative studies on men that aim at statements of the kind *'what is the case in general,'* the perspective this subproject were the *'progressive outskirts of the distributions,'* i.e., those male exceptions where orientations away from masculinity standards were present. *We took a closer exploratory look at some of these exceptions,* i.e., men who were developing away from culture- and milieu-specific attitudes and practices that determine people (the respondents themselves, other men, women) to predefined gender roles, and developing towards gender equality and health.

On a structural level, a *best-practice approach* meant that we were *not* primarily interested in new variants of hegemonic masculinity (i.e., the ways in which hegemonic masculinity adapts to structural changes), but in aspects of new masculinities that integrate elements which correspond to the explicit values of the research project, that is, those values that:

- Foster gender equality,
- Foster health in the broad sense of health promotion, including psychological and social well-being.

Our level of analysis were the *psychological processes on an individual level*, i.e., self-concept change processes, although we tried to make connections to the other levels of the Work Changes Gender-project. The main feature of the study in the psychological subproject was characterised by starting at level of *practice* and moving on to *self-concepts*. The selection criteria resulted in a sample of men who behaved in interesting ways and held progressive attitudes. The comparison pattern was the case of the 'standard' employment and masculinity standards (with some variation across the countries). After having recruited a best-practice sample in this way, *self-concept change processes* were investigated. The study in the psychological subproject was exploratory and served the purpose of generating hypotheses. Our methodology followed Grounded Theory, as outlined by Strauss and Corbin (1998).

The psychological subproject was constructed in the following way:

First, a *pre-study* in Austria was performed. The focus here was 'men in caring situations' or men who have taken on caring roles for their children or relatives – at least for a certain period of time (Scambor, Scambor and Voitle 2003). This initial focus was selected because it could be seen as a 'paradigmatic case' for the definition of 'best practice' (see section 5.2.1.): Men with caring roles contradict the standard distributions of paid and unpaid labour among the genders; they also show a relevant development into the direction of more gender equal arrangements in terms of behaviour. As far as their working situation is concerned, they show atypical behaviour, such as reducing work or taking leave, thus making some use of new forms of work or showing breaks in their working biographies. The sample in the pre-study consisted of 15 men, 12 fathers with a high share of caring and domestic work, and 3 contrasting examples (men who reduced work with interesting identity projects, but without caring obligations). The men were mainly between 30 and 40 years old and had heterogeneous socio-economic backgrounds. The main findings of the pre-study were expressed in a model of self-concept change of men in caring situations (*'Misplacement Model'*).

In the main study – which was performed by all partners – this model was used for men in caring roles in all countries so that we could compare and develop it further. As the project progressed, we covered a more diverse range of men's lives, and new focuses in addition to domestic and caring roles were integrated. In the end, a reformulated Misplacement Model concerning men in caring situations resulted, as well as two more general models of self-concept change that are able to integrate *'caring'* as well as other best-practice cases. The research teams in every country performed qualitative interviews with a small but carefully selected sample of men (about 10 interviews per country).

5.3.1 Sampling Strategy and Samples in the Main Study

Models of Good Practice

In our search for new work and life arrangements of men, we started looking for men who deviated from standard full-time work, i.e., men in part-time or with other new forms of work such as freelancing. Men who reduced working hours or took leaves for caring reasons were of special interest for the focus *men and caring*. We started with the assumption that these men might have developed strategies to deal with the new conditions in the labour market or experiences of discontinuity and insecurity. Moreover, they contributed to gender equality by breaking gender-specific distributional patterns (distribution of paid and unpaid labour). Note that what is *atypical* concerning working patterns is not the same in every country. In countries with a more difficult economic situation, the pattern *'he only works full-time, while she takes the overworker position'* might form the exceptional pattern for example. This aspect refers to good practice on the level of *working hours*.

On the level of *self-concepts*, we were looking for individuals who replaced *'work'* with other elements like caregiving, social commitments, self-fulfilment and the like, assuming that these men had developed into the direction of a *multi-facetted self* (Linville 1985, 1987), in contrast to a self-concept that is only or mainly based on *work*.

All in all, we wanted to obtain a sample of men in every country who showed a self-concept-development into a certain direction, which was based on atypical practices or situations in working and private life. This direction or pattern was evaluated as 'good practice on the individual level,' and it was basically defined by the following features:

- subjective well-being (indicator: scoring relatively high in the Orientation to Life Questionnaire, Antonovsky 1987; the main basis for selection was the data of the men in the sociological subproject),
- gender equality orientation (indicator: BHPS-inspired items, see below),
- increasing distance from masculinity standards (various indicators from the questionnaire and the interview within the sociological subproject, see below),
  - appeared together with some kind of new work form or non-standard situation concerning working life (information from the question-naire and the interview within the sociological subproject).

Selecting the Case Examples

In two thirds of the cases (41 cases out of a total of 69 interviews in the psychological subproject), the company samples of the sociological subproject served as a pool for selecting respondents. The *qualitative interviews of the sociological subproject* were used to acquire the information referring to *best practice on the individual level*, along with the *questionnaires* that were used there:

- Items on gender role attitudes, inspired by the questionnaire of the British Household Panel Survey (BHPS),
- Items on satisfaction with various aspects of life, again comparable to the BHPS-items,
- Orientation to Life Questionnaire by Antonovsky (1987).

In the other cases, the individuals were selected using other methods, e.g., by snowballing procedures and similar strategies, so only scant background information about best practice-aspects was available prior to contacting these individuals, thus resulting in higher 'miss rates' (i.e., an individual was deemed not suitable in terms of the *best-practice criteria* after the interview in the psychological subproject; on the other hand, we were able to include them as contrasting examples, as the Bulgarian team did.) Because the distributions of company-access/ alternative-access were not the same in all six countries, *'way of selection' and 'country'* are confounded, which means that country-specific biases become likely. The 6 subsamples represent different cultures as well as different sampling strategies. The *company access* worked better in Austria, Germany, Norway and Spain than in Bulgaria and Israel.

The initial idea of the approach to the individuals for the psychological subproject via the organisations and companies that were investigated in the sociological subproject included the concept of a *'dual shift-biased sample,'* two subsequent shifts in a progressive direction (in the sense of the above mentioned *best-practice* definition). In other words, the sample of men in the sociological subproject was already biased in this direction: First, the research teams were looking for interesting organisations and companies, and there, men with interesting work-life arrangements were selected for the interviews in the sociological subproject. Thus, the analysis in the sociological subproject contained a sample of men that was *intentionally biased* in the direction of new work forms: we tended to include (though not exclusively) men with reduced hours, non-standard forms of labour, and the lot. Still, the men in this sample were a heterogeneous group, as can be seen from the sub-sample of men who worked reduced hours. Some of them were in this position for caregiving reasons, others were part-time students, had hobbies that they tried to develop into jobs, combined several jobs, or worked part-time against their will.

Taking the sample of men in the sociological subproject as the pool, those men who fit the criteria of best practice in terms of the psychological subproject (see above) were to be selected in a second step. Additionally, 1 or 2 additional case examples from outside the organisations were to be included to illustrate the variability of self-concepts in each country. As was outlined, this strategy worked better in some countries than in others (see table 11).

Table 11: Country samples in the main study[34]

	number of interviews	access via company	other access	youngest respondent	oldest respondent	university degree	'caring' was important
Austria	12	11	1	26	56	2	11
Bulgaria	10	1	9	27	59	9	8
Israel	6	2	4	31	60	6	4
Germany	10	6	4	29	53	4	7
Norway	21	14	7	30	55	11	17
Spain	10	7	3	32	52	10	8
Total	**69**	**41**	**28**	**26**	**60**	**42**	**55**

The resulting sample must be viewed as 6 country sub-samples that are not strictly comparable. Nevertheless, the overall sample in the psychological subproject consists of a unique group of men. Because we intentionally biased the sampling strategy of the samples in the best-practice-direction, we are not thus speaking about 'the average man,' but, on the contrary, about 'the excep-

---

34 Note: A) The higher number of interviews in Norway was obtained by including interview questions of the psychological subproject in the interviews of the sociological subproject. In these cases, some of the instruments described below were not used. B) The number of interviews is from the main study only, so the number of interviews in Austria in the table does not include the interviews in the pre-study (see above).

tions,' about those men who show behaviour and attitudes that the research teams deemed exceptional and interesting according to the above defined 'best practice'-aspects and with reference to their background knowledge about the respective countries.

Proceeding with caution, some differences between the sub-samples may be linked to the overall differences between the countries. For instance in Bulgaria, Israel and Spain, the samples consisted of men with higher levels of education than in the other 3 countries. As the Israeli research team concluded from their interviews, one could derive the *hypothesis* that a high level of (cultural) resources is needed to challenge masculinity standards in societies with difficult economic situations or high level of conformity pressure on individuals. Such a connection of *resources* and *best-practice* could result in the experience that it is easier to find case examples who have higher cultural resources, like in the three mentioned sub-samples. Irrespective of sampling inside or outside the organisations, the men with higher educational levels (or other indicators of higher cultural resources) tended to fit the best-practice criteria – if this hypothesis holds.

Moreover, high economic pressure could be related to difficulties in finding suitable organisations in general, which leads to the necessity of recruiting the sample outside of organisations. In this case, a possible connection of *resources* and *best-practice* as well as effects of sampling strategies like *snowballing* could bias the sample in the direction of higher education. (Note: In comparison with the other country samples, the case of Spain supports the idea of a connection between *resources* and *best-practice*. All of the 10 selected respondents had university degrees, although the company access had worked well in Spain and a pool of men with various educational levels was present. But the ones that were seen as fitting the best-practice criteria had higher levels of education. So *it may not only be the company access* that results in a more 'normal' sample in terms of educational levels in Austria, Germany and Norway. Correlations like *'the higher conformity pressure, the more resources are needed to resist'* could play a role here.)

On the other hand, Norway played a special role within the study, as a pattern of orientation. Norway is recognised as one of the more gender-equal countries in Europe. There has been some progress, even if equality has only been partially realised. In contradistinction to the other countries in the *Work Changes Gender* study, Norway has some institutional areas where recognition of 'new men' is being built into laws and regulations, and, e.g., there is a high acceptance of measures like *daddy's month* in connection with the topic *men and caring*. In terms of sampling, this meant that the individuals in the study could not be considered as exceptional, which they would in the other countries, just because they took parental leave for instance. A sub-sample of leaders (CEOs) in the research material tended to receive emphasis, since this group's integration of such topics could be seen as innovative.

5.3.2   Instruments

In the main, qualitative interviews were performed. They were recorded, transcribed and analysed by the research teams in each country. Additionally a set of different instruments was developed and used. These are described below.

The *half-standardised interview guideline* was developed for the pre-study and modified for the main study. It contained various questions concerning the man's biography (*initial biographical-narrative part*), work situation, life situation, and future plans.

A *timetable* was used to summarise the man's biography in terms of education, employments, private life, and life events. The objective was to get a graphic overview of the respondents' biographies as well as information about their time-use across their biographies.

The respondents were asked to give brief self-descriptions by saying 20 sentences that start with *"I am"* (Kuhn and McPartland 1954), thereby presenting a list of relevant self-definitions/ self-concept-elements.

A *social network card* (EGONET-QF; Straus 2001a, 2001b) was used to get information about the respondent's social contacts as well as their definitions of *'fields.'* They were asked to write persons' names on a card containing concentric circles, the centre of these circles representing the respondent himself. The distance between the name of the friend, spouse, etc. and the centre represented the importance of the relationship. Segments were drawn by the respondent that represented the *fields* in his life (frequent fields were *work, family, friends*).

5.3.3   Analysis

In the psychological subproject, we focussed on individual examples that showed exceptions and developments towards alternatives to the career and breadwinner concept of masculinity. To explain why and under which conditions such alternatives occur, many levels are relevant in the analysis, e.g., country-specific measures in social and family policies, organisational culture in companies, and social networks of individuals (like families and similar arrangements, groups, organisations). In the interview material, we discovered very complex connections between all levels, e.g., a man (actively) in parental leave – when asked about his motives – might refer to the benefit system, partnership arrangement, company measures, personal family background, milieu-specific influences like university peers, positive reactions from friends, etc. On the other hand, he might also refer to obstacles and have a personal variant of the masculinity standards well in mind, which leads to interpersonal tensions or conflicts. If the expected balance sheet shows a positive result, he might integrate the caring activities into his self-concept. To handle such complex information, we followed the logic of comparison from Grounded Theory (Strauss and Corbin 1998). Proceeding from a local research area and case (i.e., the *men in caring situations in Austria*) we moved to more general areas, i.e., *men in caring situations in all 6 countries* and *diversity of self-concepts in the 6 countries*, and we derived our statements by comparisons on various levels. To connect the various levels as well as to address the variation in our material, we used the concept of the Conditional Matrix of Grounded Theory.

The Conditional Matrix can be described as a group of concentric circles, each of them representing a certain aspect of the world that surrounds us. The circle in the centre is interpreted as an *action or interaction*; the outer circles represent more abstract, general levels. Each phenomenon studied is connected to all levels. For instance, the negotiation between a man and a woman about the division of paid work and domestic tasks in their household is embedded into a set of conditions that influences this conversation. Biographies, knowledge and experiences of persons and families are assigned to the level *'collectives, groups, individuals,'* a level with direct influence on the conversation. This level is surrounded by *organisational and institutional levels*, e.g., the companies where the two persons work. These companies define to a high extent the range and conditions for new arrangements concerning the work organisation of the two partners. Organisations and companies are encircled by *communities* with their demographic specificities. The even more general and abstract levels comprise the *national and international* ones, which contain aspects of politics, economy, legal regulations, values, history, cultural specificities, etc. These levels can also influence the conversation in question, e.g., legal regulations concerning wage compensation in case of a parental leave or other transfer payments can influence the household decision and occur in interaction with a gender pay gap, norms and values (Kreimer 2002).

In fig 27, the process of the analysis is shown in an overview. The pre-study together with the Austrian country report served as input for the research teams in all countries (in Austria, the pre-study served as an input for replicating findings and developing the model further). All teams tried to identify differences and accordances to the proposed Misplacement Model that were reported to the interpretation team (i.e. the Austrian and German teams) by *case study reports* (according to an *interview report format)*, together with *comprehensive summaries of each country* (that could contain a country-specific focus and proposals for interpretation). Relevant background information about the respective countries was provided within the research reports and working papers of the economic and sociological subprojects. The results of all research teams were integrated, and 3 models of self-concept development were formulated (SEMO, Misplacement variant of SEMO, PROMO; see below).

The whole research process can be summarised as follows:

- Development and proposal of a model referring to *men in caring situations,*
- Test of the model in all partner countries; test of the model in different contexts ('no caring tasks'),
- Feedback,
- Modification of Misplacement model; formulation of general models of self-concept change processes,
- Discussion and final version.

Fig. 27: Overview of the Process of Analysis within the Psychological Subproject

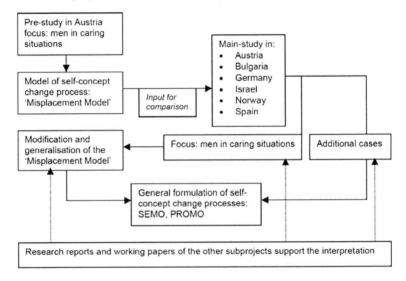

Admittedly, the concept of the research project and the research questions had a 'Central European bias.' For example, the Norwegian team would probably not have conceptualised *fathers who perform caring tasks* as *'exceptions,'* or the Bulgarian team would not have focussed on *'reduced hours'* as a starting point. Furthermore, a certain Central European bias emerged as we concentrated on relevant literature from the German speaking countries, especially in the beginning of the project (e.g. Fthenakis and Minsel 2001, Gräfinger 2001, Gärtner 2000, Werneck 1998, Zulehner and Slama 1994, Zulehner and Volz 1998, Zulehner 2003) which becomes evident by an over-representation of literature from the German-speaking countries even in our cursory reference list. But we do not see this bias as a disadvantage. The basic concept of the chosen strategy to apply the Grounded Theory-techniques of *comparing* and *asking questions* at this level as well means to *ask researchers from other countries to answer and react to 'statements' from our societies.*

5.3.4   Further Analytical Aspects

We have been using the concept of *masculinities* throughout our discourse, and want to add a few points in this connection. Masculinities are nothing that individual men 'have.' They are abstract categories for analysis that contain structural aspects, and so they can rather be assigned to milieus or fields of analysis, not to individuals. But individuals can be connected to masculinities: Elements that can be assigned to various abstract masculinities-categories can be found within persons (masculinities resemble structural ideal types, types of organisational/ structural units.) In this sense, an individual can be seen as a *'crossroads of various masculinities,'* and aspects of different masculinities can be assigned to him, e.g., expressed in terms of self-concept elements. Thus, each man in our sample *'carried his control group inside himself'* in the form of representations of the masculinity standards. Contradictory tendencies and elements should not be surprising here. This way of looking at the material stems from Grounded Theory, where comparisons rely on contextual variation; it is *not samples of individuals* that are compared but *groups of contexts and conditions.*

In quantitative forms of research, sampling is based on selecting a portion of a population to represent the entire population for which one wants to generalise. Thus, the overriding consideration is representativeness of that sample or how much it resembles that population in terms of specified characteristics. In reality, one never can be certain that a sample is completely representative. In quantitative research, however, certain procedures, such as randomisation and statistical measures, help to minimise or control for that problem. When building theory inductively, the concern is with representativeness of concepts and how concepts vary dimensionally. We look for instances in which a concept might be present or absent and ask why. Why is it there? Why is it not there? What form does it take? Because we are looking for events and incidents that are indicative for phenomena and are not counting individuals or sites per se, each observation, interview, or document may refer to multiple examples of these events. For instance, while following a head nurse around over the course of a day, the researcher might note 10 different examples of the use of power. Naturally, the more interviews, observations, and documents obtained, the more incidents that will accumulate (evidence of their validity as representative concepts) and the greater the likelihood of discovering significant variation (Strauss and Corbin 1998: 214).

Our journey started with individuals who showed some kind of exceptional behaviour. Within the analysis of the interviews, we found elements of various masculinities and contradictory tendencies *in each single self-concept* (e.g., behaviour seemed more progressive than attitudes or the other way round). These different elements that are found within *one* person can be assigned to *different analysis categories*, e.g., ideal types of men, discourses or processes.

As we have focussed on *self-concept change processes* in our study, we want to emphasise one more aspect that is relevant whenever *change* is concerned in studies with cross-sectional design. Repeated measures and designs are considered as the ideal pattern for studying *change*, regardless of whether qualitative or quantitative data is obtained. For the research questions in our study and in studies that work with biographies in general, such a design is not realistic. Following the quotation above, we want to make clear that our approach to the biographical material as well as to the cross-sectional data that we have obtained in the interviews.

When a single case is analysed, then we address *the man himself* as a *pool of biographical situations*: the man is seen like a *factor* to which a *sample of his biographical situations* is assigned (the sample consists of dependent situations). The statistical analogue for this way of approaching the material is a *multiple time series* (see the description of our 'time table' in the section 5.3.2 for illustration). The biography of a man can be seen as a 'qualitative time series,' and what is derived from one such time series can be replicated by other time series, e.g., effects of sudden impacts. Nevertheless, the problem resides in the retrospective data collection, where the *construction-reconstruction debate* is encountered. (We have tried to get reliable biographical data and differentiate constructions and reconstructions by using the time-table-instrument)

On the other hand, process models have emerged because we have clustered biographical sequences irrespective of the persons. The process models consist of the sequential order of these groups of biographical sequences. For instance, in a stage model, a 'stage' is a label that is assigned to biographical sequences, not to people.

5.4 Models of Change

Based on a correspondence analysis with a sample of men in organisations, Halrynjo (chapter 4) has proposed a classification of the interviews that we want to adopt as a heuristic framework here. The correspondence analysis discovered 4 positions - (a) overwork position; (b) care and full time work/career-reconciliation; (c) alternative/ patch work-position; (d) care and time pioneer position - that are (roughly) defined by amount of paid labour (from reduction to overwork) and caring task performance (from high engagement to no engagement). These positions don't mean types of men, rather a cross-sectional snapshot of work and life-situations of the men in the study. A developmental perspective was added assuming that men can change positions over time, e.g. an overworked employee can try to reconcile work and caring later on, e.g., after the birth of a child.

Fig. 28: Heuristic Framework Based on Halrynjo's Correspondence Analysis (Chapter 4)

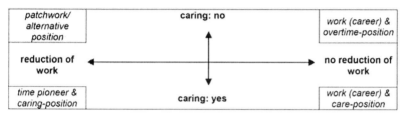

Note: Correlates are not mentioned here: higher or lower position, education, more or less established; domestic work; etc.

In the psychological subproject, the topic *men and caring* was of high importance. It could be seen as a paradigmatic case, as has been outlined above. *Caring* together with *working time reduction* have been regarded as one variant of 'best practice' within this subproject. But as was said above, additional cases could be selected by each team – cases that should show the existing variety of life concepts of men.

These cases did not have to do with caring situations necessarily, so these additional aspects are more covered by the concept of 'increasing distance to the career/ overtime-position' (in general), towards the patchwork/alternative position in the model above.

This 'alternative position' can be characterised as follows: low or minimal employment; the men hold lower positions and are rather unestablished; the reasons for work reduction or the corresponding areas of activities included other jobs, further education, hobbies (sport, music), art, voluntary work, commitment in various areas. As was mentioned in chapter 3, this position resembled one of three clusters of men in a recent study (EC 2003), i.e., the third heterogeneous cluster of younger, temporary and part-time employed men, often in the public and service sector, making frequent transitions to unemployment. Nevertheless, the cluster is characterised by higher than average education and access to job training. The other two clusters consisted of (a) highly skilled man in good positions with full-time work ('high quality employment cluster') and (b) younger low skilled men in full-time jobs, often temporary and low-paid ('low quality employment cluster').

The third cluster in the EC-study resembles the alternative position of the correspondence analysis (although the groups are not identical). The 'progressive shift' due to the sampling strategy in the sociological subproject may cause a bias towards the higher contentedness/higher life-quality examples, where *third cluster-cases* were selected. This is even more so in the psychological subproject. The 'second progressive shift' within the psychological subproject sampling procedure (*at least in tendency:* selecting those with higher satisfaction, more optimism, rather progressive attitudes, unusual behaviour concerning work-life-arrangements compared to the population of available subjects in the sociological subproject plus additionally sampled subjects in each country respectively) led to an intended over-representation of these features, i.e., a sample of men that is also suitable to show the diversity of rather unexpected and *well-functioning* male life arrangements that are already existing today – maybe not in the centres of societies but in certainly in various 'niches' and 'sociotopes'[35] that increasingly diversify today's societies (in contrast, the *work and care-position* can be considered as a mainstream theme). It is important to show this diversity under a good-practice-view, to counteract existing stereotypes and implicit concepts concerning male work and life-arrangements that conceptualise 'the men' as a monolithic gender block.

We turn to this diversity first (section 5.5.) when we present our results in the following chapters, then move on to the topic 'men and caring' (5.6.) and summarise these perspectives by presenting general models of self-concept change (5.7.), followed by concluding remarks and considerations (5.8.).

5.5 Diversity

Josep Balanyá (38 years) is a freelancer with a university degree (art history), who works as multimedia artist for a company. Josep comes from a middle class milieu and his family of origin lives in a small village. Josep is a gay man and lives alone. He shares the loft where he lives with other workers and artists who work there. He defines himself as a 'gay and queer.'

---

35 With this term, we refer to a structure in between a person's social network and a milieu. All persons in a social network are known personally, but dissimilar persons may be included. On the other hand, 'milieu' is a large-scale concept of similarity of persons who may have no personal contact. By the term 'sociotope,' a geographical/local aspect, perceived or ascribed similarity and the fact that people interact should be summarised. Like in a milieu, people in a sociotope share some features, e.g., certain attitudes. Like in a social network, people in a sociotope know each other personally or could be linked by a few connections. Examples are people living in a flat-share or in a rather homogenous suburban neighbourhood area as well as closer colleagues in a company or men's groups including similar other people from their social networks.

Until 1990, Josep had a standard biography for a student. He combined temporary jobs with his studies at university (art history and architecture). After this period, he started to work in architecture companies and as a barman in discotheques at the weekends. He lived with a boyfriend from 1987 to 1992. In 1992, an HIV-infection was detected, causing a severe personal crisis. The relationship broke, he lost and left jobs. At the same time, his father became ill and died. From 1992 to 1997, Josep did not work at all. He lived at his parents' place, broke off contact with friends, and was economically dependent on his family. After this period, he started to work with computers, combining art, technology and communication (visual art, web design, architecture), which he still does. He prefers to work in a self-employed capacity because he can control his time. This is important to Josep, who considers himself an artist and thinks that an important aspect of his work is to express creativity through work. Josep understands work as a way of self-realisation, not only in terms of the content of the work, but also in terms of the way of doing it. Except for his precarious income situation, Josep is satisfied with his working situation because he can control the rhythm and quality of the work and choose the direction where he wants to go with his projects.

For Josep Balanya, work and life are linked. He understands work as a form of life where he can control time, quality, creativity, etc. The areas *friends* and *work* overlap, because he does creative work with colleagues that are also his friend and live at the same place. *He lives in the same place where he works with friends.* Josep does not separate but connects fields (domestic tasks, work, personal interests, leisure time, friends).

It (the way of working) is positive at the health and spiritual level. If you can control and create, that means that you can grow personally. It is positive in the sense that work with other persons is easier, and you create new relations of work. You can join with others, in terms of new projects, work and life all together. If more people do this and create new guidelines with less work control and routine, maybe we will win in terms of the level of peoples' humanity. (Josep, Spain)

As was outlined above, we wanted to include a greater variety of work- and life-arrangements of men than only private caring situations. The selection criteria for interviews in the psychological subproject focussed on a distance from masculinity standards, which accompanies gender-equal attitudes and contentedness with life, combined with some non-standard work situation or working biography. Thus, a greater variety of cases could be covered, not only 'carers.' We were looking for individuals who were in the midst of a process of reducing the weight of the self-concept-element 'work/paid labour' and replacing it with other elements, i.e., to develop a 'multi-facetted self' (Linville 1985, 1987). As we will see later, we conceptualised two models of male self-concept change, one associated with significant external events and situational changes, the other covering cases where self-concept changes proceeded less dramatically, consistently moving away from masculinity standards over time.

In the interviews, the respondents gave a variety of arguments to explain why they worked in a non-standard way (i.e., reducing working time; temporarily taking time off from work; taking any form of leave; non-standard contracts, including freelancing; multitasking; flexible hours, etc.). Within the arguments, a possible classification consists of:

- *Motives*: here we refer to an 'active, self-chosen' kind of argumentation of the respondents ('active'),
- *Reasons*: here we refer to a 'it turned out that way'-argumentation of the respondents ('passive').

Sometimes, it is clear in the interviews how to interpret a certain argument: as motive or reason. But there is also the case when passive developments are *presented* as motives (i.e., an 'agency bias' of the respondent), or motives are *presented* as reasons (if for example, social desirability stands against an open expression of certain motivations).

Arguments (motives and reasons) given by the respondents for working in a non-standard-way included:

- caring for children or other persons,
- continuing education,
- quality of life,
- time abundance/'time luxury,'
- social engagement,
- leisure time,
- quality of partnership,
- quality of family life,
- found no other job,
- further education,
- maximising the household income, 'she earns more than he,'
- being independent, e.g., from employers.

These motives and reasons can be clustered within the following *fields*:

- work, with its demands, restrictions and opportunities for the individuals (including the area of education),
- closer social relationships (partnerships, family), including caring tasks,
- leisure time and unpaid activities (social commitments, hobbies) within social networks, or related to the own person.

And they can be related to the *circumstances that function as change agents*, as formulated within the sociological subproject. There, the clusters were defined as follows:

- Caring, especially for children: becoming a father as a event indicating a need to change one's work-life-arrangement,

- Women and equality: a frequent pattern was that the man changed his work and family balance because his partner had the better or more demanding job,
- Life quality, diversity, welfare: men who tried to find a better balance of material values and social values/ life concerns,
- Job-related changes like restructuring, but also gender-aware companies.

There was a variety of ways in which the respondents tried to balance the fields, including work, i.e., a variety of strategies to integrate other elements than work into one's life by assigning time-shares to elements, within a given life-arrangement (e.g., a long-distance partnership without children versus a more conventional family arrangement).

'Time squeeze' as frequent pattern in our material refers to the problem that only a certain amount of time is there to be assigned to the fields. 'Time squeeze' was introduced by the Norwegian team to describe the situation of men with caring obligations within arrangements that demand their contributions in domestic work and care. Time squeeze can be seen in the frequent pattern of lower satisfaction with the 'amount of leisure time' and 'social contacts,' in contrast to high satisfaction with the partner. It is obvious that these men have to save time and put their priorities to their closer relationships.

But time squeeze is not only a function of a private arrangement that includes caring obligations. To assign and organise one's time is a general demand that is relevant for all men in the study. In this context, we want to mention a proposed classification of "education time, working time, social time, me-time, and leisure time" (Nef 2001: 3) that points to the problem of *how to assign time to fields* for the individuals, i.e., a *balancing-problem*. The basic task is well expressed by a respondent from the Israeli sample:

I compare life to a juggling game – each one decides which ball is up: work, family, taking care of the body, taking care of the soul, creativity, commitment to the environment, community... I keep throwing the balls. There are times when all the balls are up in the air, but this is too much... I wish that all the balls would be in the air but I know that what comes up must come down. (Aviram, 42, writer/ translator and editor of literature, freelance, Israel)

The variety to handle time squeeze and the individual assignment of time to fields across the biographies in our samples included:

- reducing working time,
- changing form of work,
- having a 'break from working life,'
- passively waiting,
- connecting private life and work, mixing the areas, living at the workplace,
- shape and change private life arrangements: move in together, marry, establish distance relationships,

– negotiate and change distribution of paid and unpaid work within partnerships.

Often, a simultaneous balance is not possible, and people establish priorities in a sequential way. The metaphor of *'multiple field crop rotation'* introduced by Keupp et al. (1999) refers to the idea that the focus of individuals can lie successively in different central fields in life (work, partnership/ family, leisure time, other subjectively important fields). The focus can change over time. A person might work and invest in one field (caring and partnership), harvest in the other (work arrangement currently stable) and not care at the moment about the third (no time for leisure time and friends). In a future perspective, this person might focus on 'work' again and 'harvest' in the familiar field (due to past investment).

The men in the sample tried to reconcile various fields by applying different strategies, and increased the distance from a self-concept variant that is only or mainly based on work. They tried to develop variants that enhance their individual satisfaction, and for many of them, gender equality was a matter of course within their personal arrangements and ways of acting.

Moving away from traditional masculinity standards is a demanding task, but there are ways – as the interviews show. At least in a more passive sense, probably every man could come enter the situation of our respondents, for instance, in a situation of rapidly changing labour markets. From this perspective, it is interesting how a person in such a situation can find a constructive variant of self-concept change, what resources are to be provided, how model-processes run, and where the risks and chances lie. Not only is the practice of the men in our study *good practice* in the above defined sense, there is also a 'model-dimension' for other men in these examples, which shows how one can reconcile various areas of life.

5.5.1 Restrictions

At this point, restrictions and constraints for successful identity work have to be emphasised. Identity work is not only a process of individuals within their closest network, but also a process that is embedded into larger social contexts. According to Keupp et al. (1999), obstacles to identity work can lie in:

– social, political, economic circumstances in a society,
– dominating discourses referring to these circumstances, including values and norms.

These aspects can be linked to Bourdieu's concept of capital transformation outlined by Keupp et al. (1999), together with the question of distributional justice in a society. Labour and unemployment, and educational chances play the central roles. The discourses that are linked to these circumstances are

138

partly covered by the masculinity standards that are implemented into many discourses in a cross-sectional way.

Depending on what range of change is pre-defined on various levels (national laws, milieu and social networks, organisations, individual circumstances), people can perform their identity work in order to balance the relevant fields. The consideration above refers to the *range* as far as it is pre-defined in a large-scale-way (societies as the perspective). In the *Work Changes Gender*-project, we have tried to model this level in the economic and sociological subprojects, e.g., within concepts like 'gender geography' (see chapter 3). The material that we are reporting here consists of 'processed qualitative raw data,' i.e., the interviews were enriched by interpretations of the country by teams who were able to connect the case examples to social, political, and economic circumstances in the respective societies.

Each team interpreted the case examples in the psychological subproject on the basis of country reports and results of the previous subprojects. Based on this information, we can state that although there was a *considerable range of change in all countries*, we found *big differences in the scope of change for the case examples across the country samples*.

For example, it was obvious that the economic conditions were restricting people's scope in Bulgaria and Israel. In both countries, extreme time squeeze due to their long working hours was observed for the respondents, and this fact was linked to economic data by the research teams. Despite differences between the two countries, the constraints for identity work in both countries seem similar: people often hold more than one job or work more than full-time. For a standard household with two adults and children, it is very hard to make a living with one income. Many resources are needed to widen one's personal space for behaving differently from a standard way. Just as in the conclusion to the Israeli report, it seems that belonging to the societal elite is a necessary condition for challenging the pre-defined patterns of life. In contrast, e.g., the German sample contained men who lived in family arrangements where his part-time income was sufficient to maintain the breadwinner-position.

The Norwegian sample contained examples of men in atypical occupations, working on their *multi-facetted selves* by reconciling work with other personal projects, based on a safe material and cultural basis, like Knut:

I tested this (position of men in kindergartens) in a party on the west (rich) side of Oslo. I told them I worked in a kindergarten. 'Oh yes,' they said, and then nothing. To some other, in another room, I said that I worked as a musician, and mentioned some well-known names. They wanted to hear more. I could have talked the rest of the night. I thought it was incredible to get such different reactions. These were people with education and good jobs! But what appeared was a very from-above-downwards attitude. It was a deep experience for me. After the party, I wrote down everything. I have fun doing such things. (Knut, 31, kindergarten employee and musician, single, Norway)

5.5.2   Socio-labs

These differences among the countries are not only due to differences in sampling. Although the sampling procedures both in the sociological and psychological subproject in the respective countries have led to samples that are not strictly comparable, the access to individuals via promising companies and organisations was a basic approach. We argue here that this access assured a bit broader scope of what examples were found than if we had concentrated on certain milieus from the start. Although the selection criteria led us back to certain societal niches/ sociotopes in some countries to a certain extent, it is important to emphasise that our access did *not* restrict us to certain milieus at the start. Where the company access turned out to be difficult, the sampling individuals was led by a strategy of seeking a heterogeneous sample. Together with the information from the economic and sociological subprojects, the case examples in the psychological subproject can be seen as indicators for the range of how diverse life-arrangements and self-concepts in each country can be (in any case, they define the *minimum* of this country specific range).

As an example of the use of the range of change that is offered by a society, we want to turn to Klaus Alberts of the German sample. Klaus has caring duties as well, so with this example we are moving from the 'alternative position' into the direction if the 'time pioneer and caring position' in fig. 28 Klaus, 43 years of age, separated from his partner. They have two kids together and the two parents are both involved in raising them. Klaus has a new partnership with a woman who has two children. Klaus lives alone in his household, a squatted flat. Klaus has a working class background. He attended an apprenticeship as an industrial clerk, later on worked in the area of social work and attended some further education in this field. Jobs in the alternative segment (autonomously run enterprises) and participation in labour-market policy measures and programs followed. His last job was as a DJ and light designer in a cultural centre, and this is where he is working today, albeit on a self-employed basis. He is working around 30 hours a week, which is sufficient to live a modest existence. All in all, he has a patchwork working biography and could well be assigned to the third cluster mentioned above. Klaus takes part in men's group meetings: in this group, he and other men reflect on their situations and lives. Klaus emphasises his family orientation and defines himself as a 'non-traditional man.' Concerning his partnership, he emphasises his autonomy but also his ability to relate.

We argue that people like Klaus *reflexively* develop new forms of work-and-life-balance in societal niches, in his case a combination of part-time work as a self-employed, childcare, relationships and activities with political relevance. Together with his former partner, Klaus is successful in establishing a common caring arrangement for their children, although they have broken up. Such arrangements are of utmost interest because they provide models of how to establish the emerging new family patterns (serial partnerships, divorces, custody matters, etc.). The developmental activities within the identity work of men in similar niches and sociotopes are fostered by economic and cultural resources. In Klaus' case, society provides a framework that allows him to make a modest living with only one part-time job, although he does not have extremely high cultural capital in terms of his education. It is very questionable if this was possible in other countries with a lower level of salaries or poorer measures in terms of labour market and social policies. The men's group does give him access to cultural resources, and he considers it as supportive in times of crises (partnership breaking ups) and as a 'coaching facility' in terms of life priorities and practice. Again, it is questionable if Klaus would be that successful in coping with crises and developing a new form of work-and-life-arrangement without this resource, even if he could easily make his living with a 30-hours-job. Being able to make his living with a part-time job gives him *time* to integrate other elements, and among these elements is a men's group that supports him in his *identity projects*.

How did you deal with it (crisis)? What helped you?
In times of crisis, my men's' group and my children helped. I always had someone I could talk to. I mean obviously not with my children, but they simply helped me because they were there. I didn't drop them. It's because they love me and that will always be the case when a parent is there for them. That's how it is. Children love their parents.

And the men's group?
Yeah, that's also love. My brother goes to the group too, but I didn't identify with him as my brother at the time, more as someone who was a good friend from the days when we were political and from playing football together.

It is true that Klaus' sociotope is specific and does not represent the mainstream or the centre of society. With reference to men's groups like the one that Klaus takes part in, Meuser (1998) has been sceptical about their changing impetus. 'Insecure masculinity in permanent reflection' was observed for 'reflexive' men's groups (masculinity discourses in group discussions were analysed, and various patterns were found; Meuser 1998, Behnke 2000). It was rather *young skilled workers* who were assigned the closest discourse pattern 'security in pragmatic partnership arrangements.'

But despite an eventual habitual insecurity that is connected to reflecting masculinities, we argue that the reflective developmental work concerning work-life-arrangements in certain sociotopes may have minority effects (Moscovici 1976), given the condition that a special position is consistently emphasised. In fact, the common features of the 'products of these social laboratories' seem to consist of a critical distance to work and power, although considerable variance can be observed. At least the *critical* discourse is compatible to discourses related to women and gays' movements, and synergies to transport it into the mainstream of public discussion are there. In terms of behaviour and realised identity projects, there are men who experiment with work-life-arrangements and explore the ranges of alternatives under the above-mentioned conditions. In sum, the reflective activities of men in such societal niches influence the public discussion to a certain degree, and experimental/ alternative male life-concepts are presented as models. It is important that a discoursive pattern is provided in public discussion that contains alternative male life concepts (*'discoursive mainstreaming'*). Men whose situation forces them to deviate from masculinity standards or who don't have access to useful cultural resources can use these discoursive fragments when they need them.

A more advanced stage of a society or a milieu could be interpreted if structures like men's groups become more informal, as in the following example of Knut in Norway. An informal group of male friends meets and shares and reworks experiences:

We are a very diverse group of friends. Most have jobs, but quite dissimilar jobs, some in kindergartens, some are architects, one is an artist, some teachers and so on. For us, the title is not what counts. We meet to talk; we don't go out much on the town. We hold speeches each New Year's eve. We are a very open gang.

Are you different from your parent's generation?
Yes, this is important for us. We talk a lot about that. It is important for me that we don't hide things. Say things openly, and show feelings. We take it out and are open. (Knut, Norway)

5.6 Men and Caring: The Misplacement Model

We now turn to the topic men and caring, covered by the positions *'work (career) and care'* and *'time pioneer and caring'* from fig. 28. Due to the high number of men in arrangements that require some reconciliation of work and caring and the paradigmatic character of this topic for all participating countries, men and caring was the common denominator of all country samples in the psychological subproject.

The Misplacement Model refers to the topic 'men and caring.' It was developed within the pre-study of the Austrian team by means of Grounded Theory methodology. Men in caring situations were selected, using various ways of searching and getting into contact with these men. The selection criterion was formulated as strictly behavioural, i.e., selecting exceptional individuals who performed a high share of domestic and caring work. The initial sample consisted of 15 interviewed men (mainly fathers in the age group 30-40 years old, with heterogeneous socioeconomic backgrounds; 3 contrast examples). The main questions of the pre-study were:

- How do men get into caring situations at all? (aspect: 'entering the caring situation')
- What happens to them in terms of their self-concept once that they are in a caring situation? (aspect: 'process of implementing the caring situation into one's self-concept')
- What are the results and consequences of being or having been in a caring situation, again in terms of self-concepts? (aspect: 'implementation of the caring situation into one's self-concept')
- Which apparent influences foster or hinder the processes within the above three aspects? ('intervening conditions')

The teams of the participating countries used the resulting model in the main study as a comparison pattern. Thus, the model that is presented here is an extended and modified version of the initial model, having integrated the case examples of 'men in caring situations' in Austria, Bulgaria, Germany, Israel, Norway and Spain. In a fruitful form of a group discussion of the participating research teams, the Misplacement Model (as well as the ones that will be presented further down) was developed further. The presentation is not only based on single interview reports by each country team, but as well on summaries, interpretations and the inputs of all researchers of the consortium devoted to the psychological subproject.

As we will see, a phase or a situation where the man takes over a relatively large share of caring tasks together with domestic work tasks (compared to the average conditions in each country) means a demanding, major situational change in the men's lives. In sum, we found that a state of habitual insecurity concerning one's gender status, caused by the new and unexpected experiences of the men in the caring situations, was coped with by a reflection process in terms of one's self-concept and the rearrangement of social networks. The process could run well and lead to a de- and re-gendering stage, as in some cases; on the other hand it could get stuck in traditional concepts and tend to lead to perpetual crisis and a low level of satisfaction. Throughout these stages, there are in most cases positively evaluated experiences concerning the direct contact with the child. These positive experiences foster the maintenance of the caring situation and start to overlay the more stressful aspects.

Many intervening conditions played an important role, and the different conditions that were provided by the respondents' environments (milieus, countries) as well as his resources played the central roles. With respect to the condition of sufficient resources (e.g., a supportive environment, high preparedness before entering the caring situation, etc.), the results of the reflection process can be integrated into one's self-concept in a positively evaluated way. Self-concept elements like 'men are expendable performers' or 'men are non-carers,' i.e., masculinity standards are rejected, and one's caring role is integrated. If everything runs well, then 'caring work changes gender.' On the other hand, too few resources can result in severe crises.

Fig. 29: Process Model of Self-Concept Modification for Men in Caring Situations

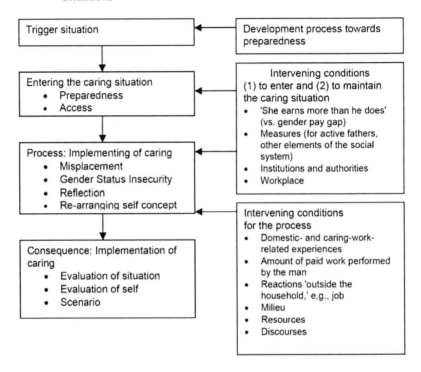

Our results concerning men and caring can be described within a process model of self-concept modification, summarised in fig. 29. The most important points in this model will be discussed below.

5.6.1 Entering the Caring Situation

From an interactionist point of view, we should expect personal and situational factors to lead to a decision like 'entering a caring situation.' Basically, if a man is willing to enter a caring situation and the situation is right, we should expect him to do so. The cases where this view was applicable was a subgroup of all cases: those with a personal inclination to take over caring tasks (and often, the related domestic tasks). It is of special interest to try to reconstruct the development of such an inclination throughout the man's biography. The development of this inclination can often be described well by 'small steps, progressively;' but also life events or crises can change a man's

144

"goals, values and beliefs" (Marcia et al. 1993), and foster the development of such an inclination. An appropriate situation would foster the man's decision to take over caring tasks.

But as we have observed in the interviews as well, there are men in caring situations who are hardly to be classified as initially 'inclined.' In contrast to men who had worked on the situational aptness themselves to have a suitable situational framework to enter the caring situation, for some of the men the situational context just turned in a way that left them little choice (for instance, they lost their job, but partner was still working, or the partner died). Somewhere in between were men who 'in principle' could imagine taking over caring tasks or had planned to be in a caring situation some day when a situation occurred that was not planned and led them to enter the caring situation (e.g., planned to go abroad and unplanned pregnancy; or hours at work were reduced). In sum, the situation sometimes was not considered as appropriate by the interviewed men, but rather seen as circumstances that they had to adapt to. In this case, 'situational aptness' should rather be interpreted as the 'presence of a trigger situation' that made a person adapt to it.

These differences led us to conceptualise the two dimensions of *entering the caring situation*:

- preparedness for caring situation,
- access to caring situation.

The two dimensions were formulated to represent the variety of cases in terms of how it came about that the men had entered into caring situations. The first dimension, *preparedness for caring situation,* represents the individual's personal inclination for caring. In this dimension, we collected all the aspects that were related to the person (personality, motivations, experiences...). We found men with very high preparedness, as well as with very low preparedness, and everything in between. The second dimension, *access to caring situation*, represents the situational aspects, expressed in a certain level of planning to enter the caring situation. Again, we found highly planned accesses of men as well as purely contingent circumstances, and everything in between.

That was the initial reason – my daughter being born. But even beforehand, I always had it in mind...it was too much for me with (the child), the amount I worked and...it didn't work really well....That's why I had already wanted it for a long time...beforehand I found it more difficult to go that way. (Heinz, 38, physician, reduced working hours, Germany)

A primary result on this conceptual level concerns the 'active/passive'-distinction. We found that this distinction often is not sufficient. What is called an 'active approach, active fatherhood' etc. might be the 'high preparedness/ planned access'-cases; the passive approach might be the 'low preparedness/ unplanned access'-group. But all the other combinations exist as well, and there is much in between the poles on each dimension. We argue that the

145

variety of personal factors and situational circumstances (and their combinations) that play a role in the decision of a person to take over some caring tasks must not be overlooked by reducing the area to a simple active-passive distinction, or by focussing on the cases with active approach to caring only. (A secondary result here is that this classification system creates a kind of typology of men in caring situations, if groups of 'preparedness/access combinations' are regarded as types.)

5.6.2 Process of Implementing the Caring Situation into the Self-concept

After the men have entered the caring situation (each one with his respective pattern of *preparedness* and *access*), a process to integrate this situation into one's self-concept has begun. For this process, we have reconstructed four subsequent stages:

- Misplacement,
- Gender Status Insecurity,
- Reflecting,
- Re-arranging self-concept.

People proceed in this process by performing 'identity work' in the sense of reflexive social psychology: they act and react in their 'inner world' as well as in their 'outer world' (e.g., social networks). As will become clear in the following sections, the movement in this process can be described by certain types of action and interaction of the men. These activities can be clustered in the following way:

(1) Identity work in the men's 'inner world' consists of psychological distance regulation to women and men (as genus groups, or to sub-groups), questioning gender models and standards, reflection based on (gender-) normative conflicts, and mixing the elements of masculinity and femininity standards.

(2) Identity work in the men's 'outer world' basically means 'networking,' i.e., re-arranging one's social network and increasing/reducing distance (contacts, form of relationship) to other people. A non-sanctioning, supportive network should result and does so under the condition of 'doing something different than most of the others,' which means a conflict with the norms/standards in many social environments.

It has to be mentioned that the *context* that surrounds this process has to be kept in mind in order to understand what the respondents expressed in the interviews:

There is a difference if a man is in a continuous caring situation, or if the caring situation is a phase with a pre-defined end point. This aspect was called *content of implementing*, referring to the question of what elements had to be implemented into the self-concept: *single phase, repeated phases, or continuous situation.*

Furthermore, the *time-dimension* was important for the interpretations. The caring situation could be a past situation, a present situation, or a future plan (*point of time*). The *duration* also had to be taken into account (short sequences within measures like the *daddy's month* in Norway, or continuous open-ended arrangements that appeared in all countries).

In general, a balance of paid work and caring for the man mitigated the stressful aspects of the implementation process, and *'caring only, no paid labour'* accentuated the stressful aspects, especially in the beginning of the process (the *'amount of paid work'* was assigned to the *intervening conditions*, see below). We now turn to the phases in detail and give a couple of examples.

Misplacement

Most of the men talked about stressful aspects and problems occurring at the beginning of the caring situation. At this early stage, the objective is to keep the self-concept constant and to fit into the caring situation. Being in a caring situation brings along new, unexpected situations for men. The narrative can be summed up here as, 'I am in the wrong context/situation.' An example that is frequently mentioned by the respondents is the one of being at the playground with the child, 'alone among the mothers.' At this stage, the respondents try to keep their self-concept stable *by increasing the psychological distance* to women/mothers. This *distancing from women* sometimes takes on devaluating forms, where the men stress their 'genuine interest' in the child, contrary to the women/mothers, who on the playground are only interested in their children in a peripheral way, chatting (and forming a group that the man does not want to belong to). It is interesting that the men's early reactions in the case of such an unusual situation is to increase the psychological distance to women, which in a way is like re-assurance of the male gender by emphasising a non-female outlook.

At the playground, we didn't have anything to talk about. I hadn't imagined it to be that way. I thought that I would have normal conversation with the mothers. But that doesn't work....So, I sat there alone amongst the mothers. (Ingo, 35, graphic artist, in parental leave, Austria)

Yes, indeed it's a little bit strange to be one of the few fathers coming every day to the kindergarten. In the beginning, it was a bit confusing... (Boris, 27, full-time accountant with flexible hours, Bulgaria)

Gender Status Insecurity

Experiencing misplacement can result in insecurity if few or no models for the desired behaviours seem to exist for the men. The normal, standard male self-concept facet 'working/paid labour,' is reduced or not present, the caring situation is new and unfamiliar. Crisis, based on Gender Status Insecurity, can follow if resources are missing or cannot be activated in the respective situation.

Well, it does make me make me feel insecure when I stay at home...I can also see my dark side in the area of child rearing. Like today for example, I am very nervous, very nervous. My nerves are frayed, I shout, yes, I can't stand it anymore, well – it is not that extreme, but well... (Andy, 37, social worker, in parental leave, Austria)

The men experience or assume social rejections that increase their insecurity. A Spanish Mobcom expert, describing the reactions to men asking for parental leave, said:

Generally, the employees are ignorant; they think that this is a measurement for women only. Also, it is a cultural subject. There are comments like: 'Are you going home now to give the teat to the boy?' Most people don't understand that a man can take breast-feeding leave and give a feeding bottle to the children. (Mobcom expert, Spain)

In some cases, counter-devaluation or problematising people who exert social rejection was a strategy to react, and to maintain a positive self-esteem.

They called me a 'family man'...but I feel sorry for them....My supervisor – he has two little daughters and he spends only one hour per month with them ...I feel sorry for him, that he misses out and I also feel sorry for his daughters who never spend time with their father. (Daniel, 32, full-time employee in high-tech company, refusing overtime, Israel)

Reflection

Given that the men cannot or do not want to exit the caring situation, they activate identity work-related resources to *work on their self-concepts* or to *alter their social networks*. The objective is to overcome insecurities that stem from self-discrepancies (inner conflicts) and social rejections of their social networks.

Well, other people are often surprised when I say I was on parental leave. They ask whether I feel confused and uncomfortable staying at home and my wife being the bread-winner in the family. I don't find it extraordinary – yes, it is uncommon, but that's the way things like that (having a child) should be settled. Everyone is free to decide whatever he wants. I feel comfortable and it's the decision of my wife and me. My wife and our close friends and relatives appreciate my help very much, and I am proud of being a caring father. (Alexander, 33, marketing manager, was on parental leave, Bulgaria)

In the reflection stage, the men start to reflect on existing masculinity models. They compare their own situation to the standard 'working-man' masculinity model. Being different from others becomes acceptable, and the men try to connotate this in a positive way. Normal patterns of masculinity are defined and rejected. The meaning of the term *work* in particular is often reflected on, redefined and related to one's own situation. As a derivative of their situation, the men's new 'processed' and reflected upon meaning of 'work' is similar to the meaning of the expression *paid and unpaid labour*: 'work' covers jobs, domestic and caring work.

Re-arranging Self-concept

In general, the men's reflections can lead to the last process stage where they try to integrate their domestic and caring activities into their self-concepts. They rearrange their 'inner and outer worlds' in a way that allows them to evaluate themselves positively and that supports their self-esteem. The men integrate the caring tasks into their lives in a stable way and re-arrange the 'emphases' of their self-concept-elements (work, child-care and family life, etc.; *time assignment* (actual or preferred) *to elements* could be seen as an indicator of these points of emphasis):

Personally I don't want to use all my time for work. I have two small children. I wish to use the flexible hours and home office possibility in my company in a positive way. (Conrad, 42, engineer, Norway)

Ascribed elements of masculinity and femininity model can be mixed, with an 'individualised masculinity version' as a result. We have called this stage: 'degendering and regendering.' A strict male-female-distinction is rejected and replaced by a diversity-view. One's reference group is redefined: similar others now become persons (men or women) in the same situation ("the other mothers and I..."). One could say that the reference-group-criterion *'same sex'* is replaced by *'similarity of situation:'*

Well, another woman from the middle management level and I reduced our working hours because of caring for little children... (Alexander, 33, marketing manager, was in parental leave, Bulgaria)

In most cases, we found positively evaluated experiences concerning the direct contact with the child (e.g., 'being close to the child,' etc.). These positive experiences foster the maintenance of the caring situation and start to overshadow the more stressful aspects along the whole process.

I think I'm in the same position as thousands of housewives. Housework isn't fun and you don't get any credit for it. ...But I'm not any different from a woman. It's the same for women who do that job; it's a lot of work. It's more than a regular full time job...I am definitely much closer to my child – closer than I would be if I had a job and a career....I know what I would miss out on if I didn't do it. My career, I can – well, I'm not going to take care of them forever. At some point they will leave home. It's just like with mothers. It's the same. And maybe I'll start my career then and go back to work....I'll keep caring for them until they don't need me anymore. And then, well, my dream – maybe I'll start working as a masseur. Become self-employed.(Frank, 38, masseur, part-time, Austria)

5.6.3 Consequences: Implementation of Caring Situation into Self-concept

A lot of conditions shape this process. Some conditions are established before the man enters the caring situations (e.g., conditions related to personality), others show an effect later on (e.g., social support or rejection in various fields). Every person leaves the process at some point. The results/ consequences of the process depend on when the man leaves the caring situation and how far the process has progressed.

In the stages 'Misplacement' and 'Gender Status Insecurity,' the self-concept is held constant. The task would seem to involve integrating one's caring situation into the former self-concept, which is hardly possible, mainly because of social reactions (perceived social sanctions). When the men experience that the strategy 'holding the self-concept constant while being in a caring situation' is not possible, and they cannot or don't want to leave the process, then they start to reflect on and re-arrange their self-concepts. Norms are questioned, the sanctioning elements are rejected. The subsequent stages 'reflection' and 're-arranging self-concept' thus deal with *change*. This change takes place in the inner world of the men (changing of attitudes) and in the outer world (changing one's social network); in our research, the scope for change often seemed broader in the inner world.

A driving force behind change is to maintain or establish a subjectively positively evaluated self-concept/ self-concept elements, i.e., a positive self-esteem. Furthermore, in most cases there are positively evaluated experiences concerning the direct contact with the child throughout these stages. These positive experiences foster the maintenance of the caring situation and start to overshadow the more stressful aspects over time.

This was an important moment for my wife's career, and we both decided I should take a half-year parental leave. Yes, I suppose this is not a common practice here, but it was not a compromise from my side. I am so happy to have a baby, and she is wonderful....It was not so easy to change napkins and to prepare the milk, and my wife needed to come home frequently till I got skilled enough. But now I am faster at these tasks. To be close to my family and to be able to support and to be of help is extremely important for me. I always wanted to have a child. (Alexander, 33, marketing manager, was in parental leave, Bulgaria)

With respect to the consequences of the process, the focus lies on 'what has resulted, what can be seen at the moment,' a sort of 'self-concept-snapshot,' like taking a closer look at what extent the man has integrated the caring situation into his self-concept and to what extent he has changed. We asked:

150

- How does the man evaluate the caring situation and its impact on himself? We concentrated on the men's subjective retrospective evaluation of the caring situation ('balance sheet'), with a special focus on reflections on the changing impact of the caring situation ('having changed/having been changed by caring').
- How does the man present and evaluate himself? Elements of self-concepts (facets) are presented by the respondents in the interviews, and evaluations are given by them. Often, *positive comparisons to the former situation or normality patterns* were made by the men to construct or maintain a positive self-esteem in the current situation.
- In addition, we used *'scenarios'* as a summarising category to typologise the whole process. Three scenarios were defined:
  - permanent scenario (stable implementation of the caring situation into one's life),
  - temporary scenario (the caring situation as a project with a defined beginning and end, yet with some persisting consequences),
  - iterative scenario (a temporary scenario with the intention to enter a caring situation again).

Here is an example for a permanent scenario with positive evaluations of the self and the caring situation:

I think of it this way: Once the children are grown up, I am going to work more again, because this is a job that I see as my vocation and I am involved in it, but of course I am involved in family life as well, as an active, practical father. (Klaus, 43, DJ and light-designer, reduced hours, Germany)

5.6.4   General Tendencies

The comparison of the presented model from the pre-study in Austria with 'men in caring situations' in the other countries was an important part of this subproject. Basically, this model holds, although the details bear out differences as well, as was expected. In the following section, general tendencies are reported, concentrating on patterns that appeared in the sample as a whole, across the country samples. Differences between countries and cases are emphasised in the next chapter ('Intervening Conditions').

The sense of similarity as *similarity of situation* can be considered a central result. Basically, it says that a man in parental leave, for instance, considers himself more similar to a woman in parental leave than to a man in full-time work without caring duties or with a strong career-orientation. (The same could be true for women: a women in parental leave could consider herself more similar to a man in parental leave than to a female manager without caring duties.) Similar situations, combined with diversity views on both genders, can be seen as a good basis for new alliances beyond the sex-based man-woman-dichotomy.

Another finding is that caring work changes gender. The majority of the respondents evaluate the caring situation as a positive phase in their lives. The last two stages of the above-described process were defined as 'change-areas.' Here, clear reflections about masculinities, the meaning of the term 'work,' social reactions, etc. take place and significantly alter the men's views. Most of them remain 'agents' who actively try to reflect on and rearrange their social environments.

Weak social relationships are of high importance. Networking-activities are more successful in the area of the respondent's closer relationships (like family, friends, closer colleagues at work, etc.). The weak relationships cannot be shaped that easily. They consist of relationships to people that one meets only from time to time, that are known from sight and the like. They can give stronger inputs, though, as the closer network is arranged in a way that is consistent with one's views, values or attitudes. The weak relationships, however, can reinforce or punish a behaviour or attitude in an unprompted way.

There are gender-specific rejections. A direct devaluation because of one's violation of masculinity-norms by performing domestic and caring behaviour is ascribed to other men (rejection type/perspective of others on me: 'gender-traitor'). In the respondent's eyes, women's uneasiness with these exceptional males is expressed in rather superficial acknowledgement accompanied by an underlying mistrust, regarding the man as an 'intruder' (rejection type/ perspective of others on me: 'gender-trespasser'). Both sorts of rejections play an important role in the implementation process.

All in all, the caring situation turns out to be demanding, especially in the beginning, due to reasons such as social rejection. The men report a feeling of 'sitting between the chairs.' What we have defined as Gender Status Insecurity and crisis deserves more attention.

5.6.5   Intervening Conditions

The above stated findings are generalised patterns that apply more or less to the different case examples. But one always finds a certain amount of variety that makes the cases differ from each other and differ from the general tendencies (expressed as main findings above).

In the terminology of Grounded Theory, the concept of the 'intervening conditions' refers to factors that influence phenomena like a man's entry into a caring situation, maintaining it, and the resulting effects in terms of the self-concept and the re-distribution of paid and unpaid work between the partners, which fosters more equal and balanced arrangements. Intervening conditions can have fostering or hindering effects and help to explain differences between cases as well as countries and cultures (or other levels of analysis).

Within Grounded Theory, one asks *what* makes the cases differ by collecting intervening conditions, and tries to show which effect these intervening conditions have in each case.

Looking for intervening conditions is a quite demanding task because this is the interface of the different disciplines' perspective, and analysing intervening conditions requires interdisciplinarity. To avoid stating that 'everything is influencing everything' (which may be true), it is recommended in the literature (Strauss and Corbin 1998) to concentrate on the factors that seem to be the most important ones.

The structure of the intervening conditions that were found and considered as relevant in the psychological subproject are summarised in fig. 30.

Fig. 30: Structure of Intervening Conditions

Intervening conditions for enter the caring situation:
- Gender pay gap
- Measures
- Institutions
- Workplace

Intervening conditions for maintaining the caring situation:
- Gender pay gap
- Measures
- Institutions
- Workplace

Intervening conditions for the process "implementing the caring situation," micro conditions:
- Domestic- and caring-work-related experiences
- Amount of paid work performed by the man
- Reactions *outside the household*: job, other living fields

macro conditions:
- Milieu
- Resources
- Discourses

It is difficult to tell if certain intervening conditions are responsible for differences between cases or for differences between large-scale-groups such as milieus or countries, especially if only small samples and little additional information from quantitative studies is available. Thus, we want to present our findings with a bit of caution and emphasise once more that we consider them as heuristic input for future research. Some of the intervening conditions were already discussed in the previous sections and thus will not be presented below.

Intervening Conditions to Enter and Maintain the Caring Situation

The high importance of the *workplace* for entering and maintaining a caring situation has to be emphasised, especially if you take the results of the organisational analysis in the sociological subproject into account, (organisations often possessing backward' organisational gender' (see chapter 3)).

Institutions and authorities of all kinds must be prepared for men entering into caring situations, which they rarely were. Most institutions and authorities had not integrated the idea of *men and caring* into their standards processes. The men in the study mainly reported the 'unprepared systems-type': „(E)ven when I went to the job centre I was seen as this alien." (Frank, 38, masseur in part-time, was in parental leave, Austria)

On a symbolic level, the lack of institutional preparedness appears in language that uses, e.g., policy terminology that connects 'caring' with 'woman/ mother' (as reflected by 'maternal leave'). As in many other aspects, Norway was advanced in these terms, although it's not all a matter of language. Some sections of the Norwegian population, women more than men, have responded by a *'the rest is the mother's'*-trend to men's increased caregiving as a consequence of the *'daddy's month'* reform. In the Norwegian case the man has to negotiate with his wife/partner about the 'parental leave' time which comes in addition to the 'father's quota' (also called the 'daddy's month,' which is one out of 12 months). Most women think that fathers should take their part, yet trouble often arises when the nominally gender-neutral period is to be shared. There is a marked cultural-symbolic undercurrent that says this is 'her time,' mainly maternal time, although not as strong or open as in Spain for instance. The same symbolic connection appears regarding compensation – until recently[36], the man got compensation based on his wife's income, not his own.

The *gender pay gap* was found to have an important influence. It was a hindering condition for a higher share of men's participation in domestic and caring work in the standard case if the man earned more than the woman (for measures to compensate the gender pay gap, see below). On the other hand, if the woman earned more or had the better job, the income difference fostered 'his' participation in reproductive work. Within a society, we can expect this effect have the highest significance in the lower income segments.

On a country level, this effect is most marked in countries with difficult economic conditions. In our sample this was mainly Bulgaria, but this effect was also present in Israel to some extent. The situation was described as follows: increased insecurity, risk of unemployment, the necessity to have at least two incomes to make ends meet. If *she* has the better job or a job at all, the pressure to make one's living gives little scope to decide in an 'irrational'

---

36 Note that the Norwegian 'daddy's month reform' was introduced over a decade ago.

way in household income maximising terms, i.e., she reduces work hours to take over domestic tasks. ('Irrational' in this respect means that the partner with the *lower* income has the *main provider role* for a time and the one with the *higher income reduces paid work* to take over more domestic and caring tasks.) On the level of interviews, these economic aspects sometimes enter into the argumentations of the men very strongly, as the following example of a Bulgarian man shows. His wife earns three times more, so she works overtime while he 'only' works full-time with flexible hours, taking over most of the domestic and child-caring tasks.

I accept my partner as an ambitious woman with good career opportunities. We are equal in terms of rights and responsibilities. I don't adopt the idea that men should earn money and women should take care of the children, household and cooking. I find the economic situation in the country too hard and insecure to be the breadwinner in the family. So when the two partners contribute to the family budget, they should both take care of all the additional tasks concerning household and children ... I really have to take into account the economic situation in Bulgaria. It is clear that the average man with an average job is not able to provide the necessary income for the family budget on his own. Very often the wife earns more than her husband. The same is the case in our family. I prefer to be able to earn more but I know my girlfriend respects me for my support at home. (Boris, 27, full-time accountant with flexible hours, Bulgaria)

This situation can *restrict* as well as *enable* unusual arrangements:

Enabling perspective: Normally, if *she* has the better job, it is more likely that *he* will take the reproductive part of the work. In contrast, in wealthier countries or in richer milieus (generally speaking, in a situation with better economic resources) the partners could *afford* to maintain a traditional arrangement under such a condition, if they wanted to. This was not so in most of the Bulgarian case examples. It seemed that 'the households' in the Bulgarian sample could not do with a loss in income, so the pressure on the man was higher to take over reproductive tasks in a situation where she earns more. This factor was clearly accentuated in the Bulgarian interview material, in the sense that men without personal preparedness tended to be in reproductive situations and these men had to adapt.

Restricting perspective: If he earns more than she does, the household can hardly afford to go without his income or with an overall income reduction when there are economic pressures. In some of the wealthier areas of society in the wealthier countries in the study, however, it is easily possible to do without the additional income in favour of a parental leave period for the man, for example. In this case, some money is exchanged for an experience that is considered important and '*worth the loss of income*' by the actors. In these cases, living according to one's values and beliefs was seen as 'affordable.' Generally speaking, economic pressure will tend to *force* men and women into caring situations or overwork situations. There is little scope for individual choices, priorities and negotiations. Thus, the pressure to *adapt* is higher, and so are the risks for people to get into situations that are too de-

155

manding. Here, *measures* for fathers/families become important (parental leave regulations, including wage compensation level, other measures in terms of social politics, campaigns, etc.).

In countries with a difficult economic situation, a 100% wage compensation for parental leave would be necessary to foster parental leave. Anything less would not work well. Today's best models are the Northern European ones, especially Iceland (Holter 2003a). In our study, the best practice example on this level was Norway. Well-working supportive measures combine the following features: rather short parental leave periods, sufficient and affordable child care facilities with high quality, wage compensation for parental leave periods that depend of the income, on a high level.

Such measures can have wide-ranging effects. The Norwegian experiences with daddy's month led to a high proportion of fathers who at least use this one month for caring. Thus in Norway, men and caring is not exceptional in terms of numbers, which contrasts with all of the other countries in the study. The same behaviour of a Norwegian father and a father in Germany, Austria, Spain, Bulgaria or Israel, is situated in a very different context: quite normal in the Norwegian case, rather or quite exceptional in the other cases. This statistical context has effects on how fathers assess and interpret their societal position. It seems that once a *'critical mass'* of men in caring situations is reached, phenomena like *Misplacement* and *Gender Status Insecurity* decrease drastically. As the Norwegian research team concludes from their comparison of the interview material, more normalised active fathering leads to reduction of Misplacement and Gender Status Insecurity. This is supported not only by the study but also by the climate in the debate since the Norwegian reform was made in 1993. It has definitely become more normal for men to do caregiving in Norway. In general, when the Misplacement Model is more applicable, the less men in caring situations can be found in the respondent's social environment (country, milieu).

In general, it should be noted that the Norwegian case is advanced in *relative terms*, i.e., in comparison with the other 5 countries. On the other hand, the Norwegian research team concludes that equality remains partial: "In summary, the material shows a Norwegian adaptation to partial equality that has neo-traditional and passive elements" (Holter 2004: 11).

Macro Conditions

Macro conditions are those that are broad in scope and possible impact with a less direct connection to the categories within the process. As possible macro-conditions within the process of implementing we have defined:

- resources,
- milieu and
- discourses,

that we want to briefly present in their interrelation.

156

As Keupp et al. (1999) have pointed out, it is essential for one's identity work to have a solid basis of *resources* to be successful. The resources of an individual heavily rely on the economic, social and cultural capital that can be transformed into resources in a given situation. Without resources, crises or demanding situations can hardly be handled and coped with. Antonovsky's (1987) considerations on the Sense of Coherence and the resistance resources to cope with stress and develop/ maintain health are also relevant here.

Although we focussed on the individual, we have also tried to take into consideration the men's affiliations concerning important social dimensions. We are inclined to follow Meuser (2000) in his proposal to reconcile socio-structural and social-constructivist positions by habitus combinations, emphasising social networks or sociotopes as areas where *milieus* can merge. We have not been able to include 'milieu' into our study in the sense the term was elaborated on by Vester et al. (2001) and Vester and Gardemin (2001) in the German case. Comparable literature on milieus in each country is missing. We have worked with *rough descriptions of social areas* for each respondent instead and tried to assess the influence of the men's pathway through such areas and institutions concerning their identity work.

As the men move along, they collect and convert capital and resources. This perspective gave us a broader understanding of their *argumentative and discoursive background*, i.e., the ways in which they used arguments. Sometimes the research teams had to interpret, sometimes the respondents themselves had clear reflections on what had influenced them throughout their biography. Furthermore, we have taken *social networks* into consideration, and the men's actual milieu could partly be defined by these networks.

Irrespective of their 'preparedness,' the men sometimes referred to arguments that they knew from some public (or other) discussion and that were useful to serve the implementation process and to explain their situation to themselves and to the interviewer. This *argumentative strategy* of the men was called '*discoursive resource activation.*' On a macro level, in each country various *discourses* can be identified. Discourses, seen as a *pattern/ structure of terms and arguments*, are *offered* by '*discourse providers,*' e.g., a fatherhood-discourse in some countries is offered by men's literature or groups and appears as a topic in mass media. In the interviews, the men referred to these discourses to explain their situation and views or to link their situation to positive, self-esteem-serving arguments; thus, they can be seen as '*discourse users.*'

We referred to the term *discourses* as public *argumentative patterns* shared by many people. Academic discourses with their specific ways to use terms and arguments (i.e., semantics) arrive in broader discussions, newspapers, consulting literature, and other mass media as background patterns, albeit in 'light versions' (and as such they appear with specific-reduced semantics). They are more or less accepted, combined and used in different

157

milieus, sociotopes or social networks. Individuals who mix and use these discourses often develop their own implicit semantics. In a society at a given point of time, a variety of different compatible and incompatible discourses on different topics is provided (work, societal changes, gender etc.), and thus – in principle – are available to the individuals. The task for the individuals is to select the ones that serve their purposes in their situations best in order to reconcile *inner and outer worlds*.

The chance to use available discourses in a way that supports one's identity work is *not equally distributed*. This is so because *resources are required* to get access to some discourses, e.g., high cultural capital is necessary for the more academic discursive variants. And of course, a good economic basis is needed to perform identity work well. Without a certain amount of social security, precarity rises for individuals in situations like the ones described. "Without participation in the societal living process in the form of meaningful activity and fair wages, the daily identity work becomes a precarious state of floating along, which can only be called a 'postmodern empire of freedom' from a very cynical point of view." (Keupp et al. 1999: 277; translation by Scambor et al.)

A basic starting equipment with economic, cultural and social capital is given to an individual by his family/milieu of origin; each can be higher or lower. On his way through life, the individual transforms the capital sorts into various kinds of resources in order to be successful in his projects. In connection with the use of available discourses, we consider cultural capital (education, information, variety of experiences) and social capital (networks and their reception of different discourses) as relevant on an economic basis that gives enough security to the individual to work on his identity projects.

5.6.6 Inertia and Partial Changes

Both discursive and structural support foster a man's identity work as he tries to integrate his caring situation into his self-concept. The two categories of support can work together. As we have seen, it is normal to take the daddy's month in Norway, so there is no 'normative offence,' in contrast to countries (milieus) where it is an absolute exception to take parental leave. Furthermore, the rather advanced countries in terms of 'gender equality and men' will not only show higher numbers of men in caring situations (e.g., parental leave as a rough indicator), but there is also some positive correlation to the public discussion about such topics: the more advanced, the more discussion, the more effects, etc. So the general atmosphere towards men in caring situations in one country can be more supportive than in others, providing more discourses and arguments, and thus more support for the individuals that they use in their self-explanations.

We want to conclude this section with a caveat concerning inertia against changes by taking an example from Norway, the most advanced country in our study in terms of *men and caring*. As the Norwegian research team concludes, two things can happen as active fathering becomes more normalised: Social sanctions and barriers are reduced, but they also can change form and become less open. The well-known question arises: *Is patriarchy dismantled or is it reorganised, and if some of both, what matters most?*

The Norwegian research team concludes that breadwinner ideals with father absence and other connected phenomena are becoming less popular among leaders, and active fathering now has such strong support that it can be seen as a new 'hegemonic' ideal. In Norway in the 1990s, the *daddy's month* became a signal for active fathering, and this arrangement has changed attitudes also among groups of men who, traditionally, have not been characterised by caregiving or gender equality practices. Within the Norwegian sample, a subsample of private business leaders (CEOs) with high awareness of the importance of the topic work-life-balance, men and caring, etc. were interviewed. One top leader in a private business company says:

I don't like housework. But changing diapers – that's good! All my friends (mainly, other male leaders) think so too....On this point there really have been large changes. (Marius, 48, CEO, Norway)

There are two ways of reading this quotation. The one is that caring has become an attractive element for this CEO. The other is the rejection of housework.

Many men in our study distinguished between a highly valued '*child caring segment*' and a devaluated '*domestic work segment*' within their home activities. This tends to be the case in countries and/or milieus where a 'supportive fathering-discourse' exists. Men can relate their situation concerning *caring* to this discourse, but *not* concerning *domestic work/ housework*. On this symbolic level, the borderline of the initial separation of spheres is redefined, and childcare is assigned to the highly valued area, while the domestic work segment remains *hers* (wife, female paid help).

In contrast, this differentiation within the reproductive tasks seemed not really necessary or not to make sense for men who did not refer to a supportive fathering discourse. The Bulgarian interview section already quoted above, can be assigned to later stages of the process, marking the transition between Gender Status Insecurity and Reflection:

I don't accept the definition 'softie' for my behaviour and role in our household. To take care of my girlfriend and a child is a kind of masculine, gentleman's behaviour. I accept my partner as an ambitious woman with good career opportunities. We are equal in terms of rights and responsibilities. I don't adopt the idea that the man should earn money and the woman should take care of the children, household and cooking. I find the economic situation in the country too hard and insecure to be the breadwinner in the family. So when the two partners contribute to the family budget they should both take care of all the additional tasks concerning household and children. Indeed, I don't have many friends who think it's strange to act the way I do. I am proud that my girlfriend's friends esteem and respect me and even envy her success to find a man who isn't prejudiced against household duties. (Boris, 27, full-time accountant with flexible hours, Bulgaria)

Household and caring activities are re-defined as masculine/ gentleman-like behaviour, focussing on the woman ("to take care of my *girlfriend* and a child [i.e., her child, his stepson]"), in order to deal with insecurity. But what is interesting in the context of *household versus caring-tasks* is the fact that this man *does not differentiate* between the two areas. He is not referring to a discourse supporting fathering (such a discourse is not very strong in Bulgarian public), but rather to an equality discourse (one might speculate if this relates to the possibility of 'recycling' the *ideological* positions of the former communist system concerning equality, since these *discourses* were there).

5.7 General Models of Self-concept Change: SEMO and PROMO

In the following chapter, two models of self-concept-change are presented. These two models were developed to describe the change processes that we have seen in the interview reports of the research teams in all countries. As described earlier, the topic *men and caring* was a special focus within the broader perspective of the project as to what constitutes a man's successful handling of new conditions concerning work. In general, we were interested in variants of identity work within the men's experiences in *working life in the centre*, and the men's efforts to combine and integrate other facets into a subjectively well-fitting individual male self-concept. The main tasks within this kind of identity work is to resist a preference system that would imply the integration of the elements 'I as expandable,' or behavioural dispositions like 'go until you drop.' This process of resisting relies on a sufficient amount of individual resources (i.e., transformed material, social, cultural capital), experiences and aspects of the personality.

The main question is: If we see an individual rejecting existing masculinity standards, why does he do that? This is not related to caring only, but to any significant deviations from masculinity standards.

The following models of self-concept change place the focus on the situational demands that are felt by the individual (i.e., how stressful and demanding the individual assesses a situation), and the available resources to deal with the situation. The first model, called 'SEMO' (Significant and Sudden Event Model), is appropriate for a narration (or a sequence) where a life event occurs (e.g., a life event like the death of a relative), or the respondent's situation changes considerably (e.g., entering a caring situation. Note that it is the *respondent* who defines if an event or situational change is 'significant').

The 'Misplacement Model' is a special variant of the SEMO for those men in caring situations who evaluate the respective situational change as 'significant.' Their evaluation implicitly includes their resources. To remember an event or situational change as 'significant,' 'demanding' means that a lot of resources had to be used to handle the situation, and the psychological situation was close to a crisis (i.e., a situation where the resources are not sufficient to handle a situation). On the other hand, handling such situations without any problems would mean that one's resources are sufficient.

The second model of self-concept change, called 'PROMO' (Progressive Model), was formulated to cover the narrative sequences in an interview where self-concept changes seemed to proceed less 'dramatic,' in small steps over time, consistently developing (instead of situational breaks). As in SEMO, the main point is that masculinity standards are partly rejected. In this respect, PROMO is connected with smaller steps than SEMO, and with the significant difference that PROMO is mainly associated with positive experiences reported by the respondents, and not with the SEMO-typical crisis-related experiences.

5.7.1   Significant and Sudden Event Model (SEMO)

As in the case of caring, increasing one's distance to masculinity standards or gender-norms can mean a major situational change involving high demands. How this demanding situation can be handled depends on the man's resources. In a way, this resembles models of coping, in connection with life events or crises, or health related models, e.g., Antonovsky's (1987) salutogenetic model. This is what we have developed for a very gender-specific situational case (men and caring). In general, any demanding event can have an impact on one's identity work and trigger a development in a direction away from masculinity standards. We have found crises, life events, and demanding situations of various kinds that play such a role, e.g., illness, death of children, cultural shock or losing one's job act as triggers for self-concept changes. Mostly, reflections on values and life goals play the intermediate role between 'occurrence of life events' and the 'self-concept change process.'

The main points of this model are:

–   A significant and sudden event has occurred, impacting the respondent. Any highly demanding situation can trigger self-concept changes.
–   The demands on the respondent to cope with the event are high. The situation after the event often resembles a crisis (higher demands than can be cope with by one's resources).
–   Normally, people do not seek such situations in an active way (e.g., life events), or they underestimate the situational demands that they will face

in actively chosen situations (e.g., entering a caring situation with high preparedness and planned access under conditions existing in most of the countries in the study).

- Within the coping process, various central self-concept-elements can be affected: values and life-goals are questioned, gender habitus crumbles. The significant event and eventual crisis trigger a reflection process. Self-concept-change has started.

- If enough resources are there or can be activated, then the individual manages to adapt to the new situation and emerges from the demanding situation with a modified self-concept. Survived crises strengthen the belief to manage future demanding situations (i.e., high sense of coherence). If resources are missing, we tend to expect frustration, giving-up, learned helplessness, etc. as results. It is a question of individual resources and social support if a situational demand can be handled or not.

The Misplacement Model is a special variant of the 'Significant and Sudden Event Model.'

Fig. 31: Significant and Sudden Event Model of Self-Concept Change

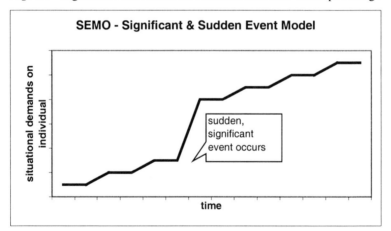

Within the events, we can differentiate between:

- Events with significant change impact, having a clear gender-related aspect (e.g., 'event' can imply a different situation after entering a caring situation, with Misplacement etc.)

- Events with significant change impact on general character and not clearly gender-related (e.g., Aviram from the Israeli sample: A 'cultural shock' in the beginning of a life period in Japan and the divorce of his parents seemed to trigger changes).

162

Often, the events are somewhere in between, as the following example from the Bulgarian sample shows. Iwan's son died, which caused an 'I was a bad father' reflection process. A change of priorities followed:

The critical moment in Iwan's life is the death of his 21 years old son in a car crash 7 years ago. This event was serious for every member of the family and unlocked the beginning of many changes. This period was marked by deep psychological withdrawal from any social contacts and closing into the family circle as well as a significant values re-consideration. As a result – a new focus on the family.

It is still very hard to talk about those times. I suddenly understood that it is so easy to lose my family, any member, my child.... Because maybe I wasn't the best father but I really love them very much. So many things changed. Just helping my daughter became the utmost priority. (Iwan, Bulgaria)

3 years later his daughter was divorced and returned with her baby-boy to live in the household of her parents. As a single mother she needed a lot of help. Her father supported her a lot with childcare. 3 years ago, he decided to reduce his working time in order to have more time to care for his grandson who is now 5 years of age. He encouraged the daughter to get a full-time job, as well as his wife (who earns more than him now).

5.7.2 Progressive Model (PROMO)

It is not only major events that can lead to self-concept changes. As we have seen in our material, 'small steps change gender' as well. There were developments or sequences in the biographies that are characterised by continuous distancing from masculinity standards. The respective self-concept change model is mainly associated with positive experiences reported by the respondents. Values, beliefs and life-goals play a central role, e.g., the motivation to live according to one's values can bring a person to change things in one's life or to enter new situations over time. The development itself of values, beliefs and life-goals as well as preparedness often can be described very well by PROMO.

The main points of this model are:

- The 'Progressive Model' (PROMO) is appropriate for 'small steps, subsequent self-concept-changes,' where *no significant and sudden event* happens, but *men move away from masculinity standards over time*. We found this model appropriate for many men who were in situations other than 'caring,' or where the new and unexpected situation in a caregiving context had *not* been the focus.
- Within the processes that can be described by PROMO, the situational demands never exceed the individual resources. The situational demands

that the individual faces over time remain moderate, i.e., the individual always has the feeling of being able to handle the situation.

– People actively seek situations with a moderate amount of situational demand, they create or move into situations that give them the possibility of developing further within their identity work (Keupp et al. 1999), e.g., discovering new abilities within voluntary social activities outside wage labour.

– Values, beliefs and life-goals play a central role, e.g., the motivation to live according to one's values can bring a person to change things in one's life or to enter new situations. The development of values, beliefs and life-goals itself often can be described by PROMO very well, in connection with familiar background, milieu and milieu changes, etc.

– Often, people give the impression of being curious, interested in their own development, equipped with a fair amount of ambiguity tolerance that allows them to move in new situations without too much anxiety.

– The change process in the PROMO often is connected with positive experiences. It is a slower and gradual self-concept-change process, and positively evaluated experiences with 'behaving in a different way' motivates people to go on.

Fig. 32: Progressive Model of Self-Concept Change

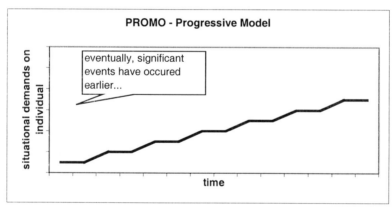

Example for PROMO:

Bernd Jürgens of the German sample has reduced working time to organise gay sporting events, to live his gay relationship, and his life in general (networking, meeting friends, maintaining his long-distance relationship etc.). Reducing working time did not appear as a significant event that would have led to any insecurity; nevertheless Bernd felt a little bit 'like an odd person' in

164

his company. The positive experiences are a much stronger factor than any negative, rejecting reactions that Bernd had experienced or expected. (A 'significant event' or more difficult situation could be assumed to have occurred earlier [Bernd's coming out-phase], which was not much of a topic in the interview.) For developing one's personality in this respect, increasing the distance from masculinity standards, a society must provide an open, supportive framework. Societies can be supportive or hindering for developments away from these standards when developing in any other direction. The amount of support or constraints to behave in a non-standard way in a country/milieu makes the difference.

5.7.3   Concluding Remarks on the Two Models

In many of the biographies of our samples, different phases of self-concept-changes can be found, some better described by SEMO, others by PROMO. Often, 'SEMO-PROMO-chains of identity work' seem most adequate. A good example for a *sequence of PROMO and SEMO* are the men in caring situations with high preparedness/planned access. Their *high preparedness* often has developed in a way that can be described best by the PROMO (e.g., step by step, in connection with their values that were developed within certain milieus etc.). Then they enter the caring situation and nevertheless find themselves in a situation with unexpected and demanding aspects or that is very different from what they have expected, (SEMO); *Misplacement/ Gender Status Insecurity* follows. Within the reflection process that follows, they can use their preparedness as a resource again; here, *more or less preparedness* makes the difference.

The events and situations that have an impact on self-concept-change-processes can be very different. The models remain open here. They are not restricted to a certain dimension, e.g., 'work' or 'private life.' The interview reports show that the various fields are strongly interrelated and that there is no easy general formula like 'work changes gender.'

Our samples consist of men who have been rather successful in coping with new forms of work, new situations concerning private life, etc., i.e., what we tried to define as 'good practice'-cases. The selection was based on rather high satisfaction and sense of coherence, gender-equality orientation, etc. The presented models, SEMO and PROMO, thus refer to these cases to describe and partly explain their development and self-concept changes. We want to emphasise that these situations/ processes emerge out of '*risky* chances,' and that at any point there could have been failure as well.

Both models, SEMO and PROMO, have to do with behaving under the condition of uncertainty, because people (actively) seek or (passively) get into situations that have to do with *rejection of masculinity standards*, either in terms of work- or private-life-related ideal norms (that in most cases remain as implicit norms in the background of people's self-concepts, as Higgins' (1987) *ought self*, or as knowledge of the masculinity standards). Under certain conditions, people manage to find ways to deal with these new, uncertain situations, or they even create them or move into such situations. These conditions mainly contain resources, either to cope with difficulties or to believe that one is capable of handling such self-chosen situations. Keupp et al. (1999) have given a compilation of 'prerequisites for successful identity work' that can be applied to the tasks of the men in the study:

- People need *material resources:* Under the label of individualisation, the task to make use of an increasing pool of chances and options is seen as an individual question. However, a material basis is needed to use these options. On the other hand, the principles of solidarity in societies is in question nowadays and arguments like 'modernisation, increasing flexibility, competition in a globalised world,' etc. are used to undermine social welfare systems. The distribution of material resources tends to show increasing gaps that work against the chances of the underprivileged performing successful identity work (keeping in mind Bourdieu's concept of capital transformation). Here, the question of distributional justice is touched upon.
- People need *social integration and acknowledgement:* People are increasingly liberated from traditional forms of social systems, which improves their chances of behaving in diverse ways. On the other hand, they have to invest time in 'networking,' with an increased risk of being left aside and left alone. People need social abilities for their networking-tasks in order to accumulate and transform social resources. Again, it is rather the underprivileged people who show deficits in networking. The development of the necessary skills and abilities depend heavily on a person's 'starting conditions' and social integration, and these conditions are far from being distributed in a fair way. Moreover, abilities like social competence, motivation, communicative abilities, etc. play an important role in today's labour markets.
- People need the *ability to negotiate and to overview options:* People move in multi-optional environments today (e.g., occupational development, friendships, partnerships, etc.) that have to be combined and reconciled. The pre-formed patterns increasingly dissolve, and new, individualised solutions have to be found (e.g., for one's partnership arrangement in connection with work. The partners have to move in a field of many possible variants of how to create what they call their partnership, and they have to deal with how they arrange it.)
- People need *ambiguity tolerance:* Ambiguity tolerance can be seen as the ability of a subject to explore other people and situations instead of being demoralised by diffuse and vague information. A high level of ambiguity tolerance is the key to remaining able to act in an insecure, only partially

166

predictable, and continuously changing (social) world. High ambiguity tolerance may be connected to a low level of anxiety, and vice versa.

This view is also supported from a more problematic angle, referring to the European research project SIREN (Hentges et al. 2003). In essence, the authors develop the following argumentation: Under the condition of a changing, increasingly neo-liberal labour market, people's often frustrating experiences within the field of work produce feelings of injustice and fear of 'declassement/loss of status.' These feelings can be addressed by right-wing populist politicians. But:

Right-wing extremist attraction is a minority phenomenon. In addition to the political conversions discussed above, it is necessary to consider other types of interviewees: retired workers involved in charitable works or in local politics, young workers involved in trade unionism, early retired managers organising cultural activities, or employees dedicating their spare time to family life. Some people are satisfied with their working situation, although often with a sense of resignation, and emphasise the positive aspects of work. ... Some people do not experience frustration, or if it exists they can cope with it. Those who are not attracted to right-wing populism and extremism (RWE) exhibited a kind of 'acceptance of real life challenges,' i.e., 'what can you do?' and hope that the democratic process will somehow be able to correct the economic and political conditions. (Hentges et al. 2003: 103f)

In general, less RWE-receptive people relied on different cultural and social resources to cope with socio-economic changes.

This is because they are members of social groups and networks with different cultural influences and they have available to them a wider range of experiences, discourses and arguments that can reconcile changes without reliance on RWE arguments. For example, they are more familiar with other cultures and ways of life....They can relate more to other identities than to that of the workplace and do not need to rely upon a sense of national identity for their self image and sense of place in society. Their ability to identify with multiple and differentiated groups within society eliminates the necessity for exclusive group identification. (ibid.: 104)

5.8 Men and Changes

As we have seen, male self-concept-change processes can be described well by the concept of identity work,

- as an ongoing, life-long process,
- as a continuous effort to deal with demanding situations that occur, or to move into demanding situations in order to develop further,
- as dependent on individual resources and social support.

As we found in our interview material, developments in all spheres of life – work and private – can lead to a remarkable variety of male life concepts.

There are men in the sample of the psychological subproject who can be seen as 'models' for how to deal with increasingly difficult conditions in the labour market in a constructive way, who use the 'risky chances' by reducing the weight of the self-concept element 'work' or 'career' and replacing it by subjectively relevant, meaning-making identity projects. Such developments are enabled by open, supportive frameworks on various levels. The amount of support and resources provided versus constraints makes the difference with respect to behaving in a non-standard way. But how are such developments permissible in the first place? What are the agents of change?

5.8.1   New Men, New Circumstances

We refer to two models of change based on main agents of change processes. One we may call 'new man model', the other 'new circumstances model'. In the new man model, a special group of men or a specific configuration of masculinity is seen as the agent of change. A mainly ideological process in close connection to gender role attitudes and gender-equal norms underlies this model. The new circumstances model emphasises new situations that most men experience. New socio-material conditions are experienced by many men and lead to large-scale tendencies. This model tends to stress the men's adaptations to ongoing changes on a more practical level. The new circumstances that change gender were summarised as follows:

- caring, especially for children,
- increased equality and more balanced arrangements in relationships to women,
- life quality, diversity and welfare,
- changes in the area of work, and job-related changes.

Evidence for both models was found in the interview material in the psychological subproject. Roughly, the new man model was addressed in the chapters on *diversity* and *socio-labs*. There, we summarised the results concerning our access to illustrate the changeability and range for change in each society (under admittedly exceptional conditions).

The *new circumstances model* was covered by the focus on men and caring. In the referring chapters, the case examples may not seem that exceptional, having sometimes rather unspectacular shifts in the distribution of labour within the couples. But this focus was chosen because the topic men and caring was seen as paradigmatic and challenges the core of fundamental transcultural masculinity standards.

We argue that *new men* and *new circumstances* can be linked. We have shown above that what can be called new masculinities or new men can influence the mainstream by having minor effects. Exceptional individuals and groups are visible, and their inputs seep into the mainstream discourses. The

168

more they differ from standards, the more they may be noticed. New masculinities can prepare the ground for men who get into new circumstances in an unintended way or who face unexpected situations. As we have seen in our material, these men profit from broadened discourses that have been developed by pioneers that can be best described by a *new men / new masculinity* perspective.

On the other hand, *new masculinities* emerge on top of *new circumstances*, and cultural and societal developments prepare the ground. It was the women's and gay rights movements that challenged hegemonic masculinity (Connell 1995), and democratisation and modernisation processes of the 20th century have set free a pluralisation of masculinities (Böhnisch 2003). In this perspective, the emergence of new men/new masculinities can be seen as *indicators* of social change and new circumstances.

In our study, we have concentrated on how *self-concept change processes* run, and the question as to what changes gender has been underlying our considerations. The compatibility of the *new man/new masculinities model* and the *new circumstances model* in our proposed *models of change processes* can be demonstrated, for instance, by the Misplacement Model. As we have argued, there is a development process towards *preparedness*. High *preparedness* and the connected pre-reflections have to do with aspects of the *new man/new masculinities model*. But no matter if a man enters with high or low preparedness, being in a caring situation belongs to the area of *new circumstances*. As we have shown, a variety of (new) circumstances can lead to this situation. More facets of what can be seen as *new circumstances* were formulated within the *intervening conditions*.

5.8.2 Generational Position

Another perspective that can be added to the new circumstances model is Meuser's (2000) argument concerning changes of masculinities by *division of labour* and the *generational position* of men. It basically covers the aspects 'changes in the area of work' and 'increased equality' from above, eventually in combination with 'caring tasks.'

As far as *division of labour* as a change agent is concerned, *dual career couples* and *shift-working couples* are of particular interest. In these, influences from the work situations of both partners demand a redistribution of domestic labour.

Concerning *generational position* as a change agent, Meuser argues that men in the age group from 20 to 30 years[37] have grown up in the period of the second women's movement. Women with equal status have become a matter of course for many of them, as have gender-related conflicts and friction that

---

37 Note that Meuser published this article in 2000, so the upper limit of the age range would today correspond to about 35 years old.

contain a certain potential for change. Younger men find their partners among younger women who already profit from the women's movement. These younger women are looking for the 'whole life' (Beck-Gernsheim 1994) and are less inclined than former generations to enter or remain in unbalanced arrangements. Thus, gender-related tension and frictions in case of discordant arrangement- model of the partners become relevant for the younger men. This tension and friction resembles the concept of 'gender trouble in organisations' (Ohlendieck 2003), which was introduced in the sociological subproject within a developmental model of the three phases of *organisational* change: *early, middle and advanced phase.* One can apply these phases to *private arrangements* as well, i.e., social networks, partnerships, families. *Gender trouble* is the central category in this model: it may be used for organisations, private arrangements, or individuals.

These aspects of *generational position* were developed chiefly in reference to the situation in western countries. The interesting case of Bulgaria points to the different meanings of *generational position* and additional aspects depending on *historical development.* The former situation of the older generations in Bulgaria was characterised by dual earner couples, in which the woman was additionally responsible for the reproductive work. An official equality ideology was counterbalanced by a de-facto-imbalance and inequality within the households, as well as a considerable vertical segregation. After 1989, the situation has changed totally, and the younger generation of men (in the sample, around age 30) who had spent their childhood and adolescence in the former system, entered the labour market under new conditions that are characterised by increased insecurity, risk of unemployment, the necessity to have at least two incomes to make ends meet, a high probability of having a patchwork working biography and so on. We have shown above that these difficult conditions can boost the redistribution of tasks among couples when the woman happens to have the better job and higher income. This is not the standard case but appears in our material because of the selection of exceptional examples. There is one cluster of Bulgarian respondents that was labelled *'behavioural change with little attitudinal change'* by the Bulgarian research team. It means that these men have to adapt and attribute this adaption externally. In their eyes, the circumstances force them to redistribute tasks within their relationships, and because of the external attribution, there is not much reason for 'gender trouble' that would emerge from men and women's different expectations and negotiations. Thus, cultural resources are even more needed to implement one's behaviour into the self-concept, or such adaptations will remain peripheral.

5.8.3 Total Availability and Split

The extremely time-consuming work situations of the men in the Bulgarian and Israeli sample are reminiscent of Böhnisch's (2003) concept of *availability*. Böhnisch has emphasised the role of *work* for gender-related changes in times of *'digital capitalism'*: Economy asks for *abstract workers* that are *completely available* all the time, irrespective of gender. Employees of either sex have to be available for work, free to move geographically, etc. Among highly qualified workers, the workload and pressure to be available increases, a mechanism that can boost changes in private gender arrangements if *she* holds the better, more career-promising job. On the other hand, it has to be noted that in the more advanced, equality and social welfare oriented cases, like Norway, the pressure for men to do more in both areas, work and private arrangements, i.e., experiencing time squeeze, becomes a topic in public discussion and starts to influence all segments of society. In our sample, there are Norwegian CEOs for whom the topic of work-life-balance is becoming increasingly important, where a certain amount of work-life balance, family life, and caring becomes a new norm, often resulting in *time-squeeze* (but note the caveat concerning a possible reconstruction of 'separate spheres' by introducing the *'household versus childcare-differentiation,'* see above).

On the other hand, apart from *dual career-couples*, experiences in the world of labour often mean disillusionment concerning lower qualified persons. Work is increasingly becoming a 'rare good,' in contrast to the previous 'everybody's duty.' In this respect, work is even more important than in industrialised times, but now with the connotation of a status symbol, not so easily accessible to everyone. Under these new circumstances, it becomes risky in terms of one's self-definition to rely only on work. Some of the interviewed men could be seen as first representatives of a process that 'disentangles' work and masculinity in order to reduce the risk of disillusionment, but only if the prerequisites for identity work are there, e.g., enough cultural/ discursive resources. (For the risk-perspective, see the SIREN report, Hentges at al. 2003.) Nevertheless, the distributional problem concerning labour is evident, not only between but also within the genders.

In this respect, and with reference to the *second* and *third cluster-men* (EC 2003) we should start to think about a *split* in the *male* labour market in addition to the *split female labour market* (in principal, not taking any numbers or gender gaps into account here). The concept of a split female labour market (Kreimer 2003) states that there are *highly qualified women without caring duties* who can compete with *men* in the labour market for the better jobs and positions, while women with a double burden cannot (caring obligations work against the person's offer of *total availability* concerning labour). In addition, high qualification that can be transformed into economic capital enables people to outsource a portion of their caring and domestic duties, which in turn enables them to compete in the above sense.

Böhnisch's thesis about the *new circumstances* of a digital capitalism that ignores gender but prefers the availability of abstract workers, men or women, can be introduced as a context. There are some who can compete, due to many resources, and others who cannot. Those who can and who stay in the labour market accumulate more and more experiences and other market-relevant values, while the others decline and give up. Some of the respondents had patchwork working biographies, including non-standard forms of work, work leave, changes in jobs or occupation *before* entering the caring situation. In combination with a low investment in their career, these biographies in some contexts led to a high *preparedness* for entering a caring situation when there was a certain amount of cultural resources, e.g., discursive resources. In other cases, when *preparedness* was not very high at the time that the men entered the caring situation, *caring* substituted for work as an area of experiencing competencies and success.

The proportion of men in such situations may still be small, and the well-known gender segregation of the labour market persists; yet, these men exist. Thus, our proposal is to conceptualise a '*split in the labour market.*'

– between the genders, to observe the basic gender gaps,
– and for both genders together respective for subgroups within the genders, in order to emphasise the increasing gaps as a whole that affect people in certain situations.

As in today's societies distributional inequality is increasing due to a vertical drift apart, disparities between the genders *and* within the genders increase *within this process of drift*. It is not a sufficient objective for political action that the distributions of resources and other variables of males and females should *overlap*, while the *overall variance* is increasing. We need to differentiate developments concerning gender subgroups, as well as problematise the increasing overall gaps. Gender is still a fundamental category for addressing social inequality – not *per se*, however, but in a framework of distributional justice. Approaches that aim at the same proportions of 'male and female heads' across vertical levels or horizontally defined areas only, while the levels themselves drift apart, would blur our view of the problem of an increasing structurally caused inequality.

5.8.4 Conclusion

In order to close with an optimistic perspective after the caveats in the previous paragraphs, we want to emphasise that we *have* detected changes in men's lives that indicate movement in promising directions. Today, men's concepts concerning work and life show a considerable diversity. The category 'men' is very different from the concept of a homogenous 'gender block.' (Such a monolithic view of men' has resulted from a past lack of approaching *men as gendered* and must be abandoned.) The actual diversity provides chances for constructive alliances aiming at more gender equality. In this context, we have placed a special focus on the issue of 'men and caring' (either for children or other persons, such as older, disabled or sick family members) where a variety of cultural undercurrents has prepared the ground for challenging the dominating gender systems. This gives us the hope that if we implement the correct social policies, major societal changes may eventually come to pass, and a more equal society may be created, one that favours all people.

Men are likely to benefit from broad social and cultural changes associated with gender equality. Less rigid stereotyping of masculinity can increase options for men and yield benefits in mental health and psychological well being for men and boys. A move towards gender equality is likely to improve overall social inclusion, with benefits for men and boys as well as women and girls. (United Nations 2003: 5)

6. Men are Gendered, not Standard: Scientific and Political Implications of the Results

Marc Gärtner

With Margarita Atanassova, Vera Riesenfeld,
Christian Scambor and Klaus Schwerma

Changes in labour and cultural patterns deeply affect gender relations, images and roles. Masculinity is now in a field of tension between change, dissolution and persistence. In this situation, men often remain, admittedly, stuck in old models that are sharply divorced from social reality or, at the very least, are unclear. Thus, masculinity is distinguished by differentiation and, in relation to the real lives of individuals, by prominent aspects of everyday discontinuity and differing requirements (Gärtner and Riesenfeld 2004: 99).

Our study documents men who are content with their lives in nonstandard employment conditions. There is a multitude of motivations affecting their decision-making process: partnership and family orientation, social engagement, caring work or simply the "demand for a whole life." At the same time, they face discrimination, are perceived and treated as exotics or exceptions.

The field of gender and the changes within it still seem to be mostly associated with women and femininity, not with men and masculinity. By and large, political actors and organisational regulations still operate on the assumption of traditional models of masculinity. For men, the latter imply that they are committed to their jobs and careers. A culture of work and policy based on gendered assumptions is the greatest hindrance to men making real changes in their life patterns or perceptions.

Adherence to these notions also causes men with alternative masculinities to be "marginalised" (Connell 1995), seen as exceptions, or are not perceived at all. Many of these men seem to face varieties of effemination:

In terms of career opportunities, a glass ceiling prevents women as well as marginalised men from entering higher positions. Many men in caring situations seem to go through a phase of gender role irritation that makes them feel they are not "real men." These traces of effemination demonstrate the profound relation between masculinity and labour.

In this chapter, we want to summarise briefly the most important results of our project and give comprehensive recommendations for political, organisational and social actors – and, last but not least, for individuals who are interested in productive changes in terms of the gender system.

6.1 Ways to Changes

6.1.1 Labour Market Changes

The occupational relations of men and women in Europe converge, in particular because male non-employment, unemployment and unstable work contracts increase. These unstable contracts, however, have not significantly increased. Even if part-time work is still dominated by women, the men's share has risen above average.

In the labour markets researched, gender segregation is still strong. Connections with forms of occupation have to be tested in more detail. Up to now, we can only presume where there are professions and business lines with exceptionally significant changes for males.

Domestic and professional work are still unequally distributed between men and women, but couples seem to share the whole amount of work in a relatively equal way. Some statistical factors increase the probability of men doing more chores, e.g., non-standard contracts and blue collar jobs.

The structural changes in male employment have a significant influence on the emerging new patterns of the working life course of men. The trend for men seems to be moving in this direction: more men are in discontinuous employment because of unemployment or higher professional mobility; men are working more in part-time and temporary work, and men remain longer in education and retire earlier. As a result, some men have what was previously considered an exclusively female 'patchwork' biography.

6.1.2 What Makes Men Change?

Structural Changes

The labour shift from the production to the service sector is embedded in various life and labour changes, including the deregulation of labour law, social policy and tariff arrangements, which lead to growing social insecurity, the individualisation of social risks (cf. Beck 1986) and a restructuring of life patterns in cases where traditional embedding structures like the family lose their cohesion.[38]

As global capitalism and markets lose their limitations, men increasingly face what Lothar Böhnisch (2003) calls "release"[39] From this point of view,

---

38 Sennett (1998) characterises the processes in post-modern societies with these key-words: high speed, deregulation of institutionalised patterns, social fragmentation, pluralised matrixes of interpretation. The longing for community is opposed by a hostile economic system (cf. Scambor & Scambor 2003).

39 German: "Entgrenzung" (Böhnisch 2003), i.e. breaking traditional boundaries of demands from outside, but also of individual choices and potentials. Both new risks and options are

best practice resources such as the higher level of ambiguity tolerance shown by some of the men in the sample may represent a scheme of coping with growing insecurity in general, but also with the demands of a restructured work life, one in which the demand for "the whole man" is present.

This "holism" reveals an ambivalent process of increasing options for men on the one hand and growing demands placed upon them on the other.

The traditional "job only" focus of men may become weaker over time. The men in this sample show functional, adaptive strategies leading to higher life satisfaction while focusing less on their jobs. Although there are undoubtedly exceptions, these cases very much correspond to the more theoretical thesis of modernisation theory, in which men are divorced from their traditional breadwinner role (cf. Beck 1986, Böhnisch 2003). Work-life balance is becoming increasingly important in cases where the economic situation does not undermine self-determination. At least the preferences of men and women demonstrate this inclination (cf.: European Foundation for the Improvement of Living and Working Conditions 2002: 92).

Diverse Motives for Changes

Initially, we developed three main aspects of analysis for the change processes in masculinity and men's self-concept: non-labour-based self-concept, gender equality, satisfaction with one's life.

Although other aspects remained important, we focused heavily on a "work less/work differently" issue. Among the men interviewed, there were a host of different motives for reducing their workload: partnership, realising caring duties or wishes, social commitment, or simply the "demand for a full life." The quality of life acquired in this way is consciously offset against a professional career.

A change in men's values is more clearly seen in the private sphere than in the professional world. In the European Union, a differentiation in the form of ways of life is taking place. The forms of life of the men interviewed were correspondingly diverse, ranging from single parents, singles, married couples, long-term relationships as well as communal living to homosexual and heterosexual "living-apart-together pairs." These forms of life lead to different distributions of work in these communities and also to new forms of emotional reproduction. In most cases we found that the interviewees had a positive attitude toward the equality paradigm that corresponded to their actual behaviour. On a practical level, it e.g. was a matter of course that both partners should be employed and that housework was shared, if the respondents lived with a partner in one household.

---

marked by this term, which fits to Sennett (1989) as well as to the "risk society" of Beck (1986).

Differing male labour histories often are not due to voluntary changes, but due to pragmatic reasons. This is shown in the milieu of skilled workers (cf. Meuser 1998) or, in general, among blue-collar workers (cf. Ramos 2003). Here we see good household contributions or comparatively egalitarian partnership arrangements. In Bulgaria, our sample showed arrangements and gender relations in terms of household/job-relations, which also turn out to be rather egalitarian. The framework here was determined by economic instability and pressure on the concerned couples where a female partner was employed in better conditions than the male one. Nevertheless, the cultural resources of men are a very important prerequisite for an equality-oriented modification of the male self-concept.

Best practice examples show male life courses deviating from a model based solely on availability, breadwinnership and devotion to labour (in a one or one-and-a-half career couple), which are rather "non-ideological" and not driven by "longing for change" in terms of the male self-concept. It is not completely certain whether gender identities in these fields are very polarised or not.

These "patterns of difference" however, are not to be conceived of as a new concept of masculinity. It's more the case that it remains, to a great extent, isolated. It is often not connected with a demand for equality either. Most of the men we interviewed do not define the position of men in society in a new way. Although they affirm and realise some elements of "new masculinity,"[40] many are also representative, to some extent, of traditional masculinity concepts. Distinct new patterns of interpretation are not being integrated into a comprehensive understanding of a different, new masculinity. For men, this is not possible given current social circumstances. In many European countries, non-conventional individual self-perceptions held by men have not yet been granted recognition. Thus, many men fall back on or persist in identifying with old role models that are, to a large extent, disconnected from the social reality around them. Nevertheless, contentment outside of the "normal work life" is possible if these forms of work and life are chosen by the individual. The sample, however, is not representative. It focussed on special types and individuals. It is clear now that they exist, even in regions and areas where there is scarcely a self-reflective discourse on masculinity (e.g. in Bulgaria).

Frameworks of Changes

It is not only men's modus of adaptation to structural changes that is the key to a work-life-change, but also the macro-cultural framework. Most of all, the organisational framework within a company – management, institutions sup-

---

40 Types of men and masculinity differing from the traditional, patriarchal models.

porting men in different work forms, and, not least of all, the informal culture – that is decisive here. It seems to work in such a way that "a willing man meets a willing company" to lead to the establishment of a more balanced form of employment. At the very least, an income attractive enough or sufficient for making a living is required – ideally within a framework of a societal redistribution of paid and unpaid work.

Many respondents but did not feel recognised in organisation-internal and external gender equality processes, so they developed individual strategies of realisation. But it may just be the traditional male model of "doing it on my own" which prevents the development of solidary structures and collective representations. So it seems that the social "legitimation" of the own interest has yet to be developed to help men to experience themselves as "concerned ones among other concerned ones."

At the level of potential integrative balanced working time structures, part-time work seems to shift from a phase (mostly in the early work biography) to a form of working life. It tends to cease being a transitory stage even for men. In Germany – and here, above all, in the west – part-time has traditionally been a female concept within the male breadwinner marriage. In Spain, we see best practice examples of men choosing part-time contracts in order to balance their lives in a better way.

Frequently in public debate, changes of men are connected to attitudinal change and consciousness. Such discussions are important to provide arguments for those who get into a situation where they can need discursive resources for their identity work. But structural changes, into the direction of adequate frameworks that foster care taking by males, are more important. Demanding changes of men without changing the structures means to ask households to behave irrationally (which they sometimes may do under certain conditions, e.g. if they can afford).

Nevertheless, the discursive resources must be provided, so the importance of arguments that continuously appear in public debate must not be underestimated. As e.g. the Bulgarian research team concluded, some of their respondents showed "behavioral change without much attitudinal change," and the respective men seem to be 'locked in tradition' despite their promising behavioral changes. Again, the ones that were more affected of this pattern were the ones with lower resources, including psychological and network-related aspects. We emphasise once more the necessity to provide resources for the individuals by improving their material and cultural capital.

Does Work Change Gender or Does Gender Change Work?

In the course of this project, discussions arose about the question concerning the key to the change that leads toward gender equality: Is it more an issue of couple arrangements and the private sphere, or are structural changes in the labour sphere more important? We found evidence for both, but, as expected, not enough to answer definitely. Changes in gender relations appeared on a cultural and an economy level, in the private and the public sphere. From one perspective, men's household and private life relations were seen as primary, while working life and organisational structures were regarded as secondary. Households appeared as more dynamic than jobs, at least from a biographical perspective.

The other perspective states that the labour market tends to be rather flexible and demands flexibility from "working men" and employees. Organisations, on the other hand, tend to be inflexible. It proved to be difficult to find best practice companies in terms of the project's basic question. This was due to organisational aims and structures:

The sphere of labour in general (and, more specifically, companies) demand employees' availability, which historically has affected men to a greater extent (cf. Böhnisch 2003). It is the system of cultural sanctions stemming from the social surroundings – the "sprinkle system" in Holter (2003a) as well as the male self-concept of expandability, availability and strength that still maintains the validity of the link between masculinity and labour.

6.1.3 What Leads to Changes in Organisations?

In a very general sense, one can identify organisations as obstacles to equality-oriented changes among men:

- Professional segregation is internationally still high. What is remarkable but also mysterious is that while "male jobs" seem to be the same in all the countries we analysed, there were no identifiable "female jobs,"
- Gender and organisational structure are closely related,
- Equality actors mostly focus on traditional models of masculinity,
- Expandability and availability are the premises of career options. This is not only valid for traditional masculinity and male life histories but still constitutes a very strong relation.

This leads to the question: What organisational logic promotes gender equality and the inclusion of a perspective regarding men?

Men have traditionally surrendered to labour and externalisation and often stand alone without institutional support when demanding "a whole life". Individually, they cannot adopt a new self-concept for themselves that is already in existence. Instead, they are forced to devise as best they can suitable individual strategies. Collective strategies seem hard to adopt.

Men showing a "lack of availability" and career-focus face not only a glass ceiling (usually described as a female career obstacle), but, because of their life choice, also effemination.

180

In general, the effemination of men is a cultural pattern of reproduction of masculine normality, shaped in the direction of hegemonic masculinity. But it also works through the economic sanctions or social devaluation. The appearance of diverse strategies of men in our sample seems to show that the cultural pattern loses relevance, at least in particular milieus and perhaps in general; there are even social groups where "un-male" strategies of men (caring, emotionality) are more accepted than traditional masculinity. "Misplacement" can be described as a sort of temporary effemination.

When social and economic devaluation becomes more and more of an individual risk outside of milieus and social groups, it should also become more and more de-gendered. This is indicated by the general decrease in standard work, a phenomenon that affects men at a proportionally higher level than women.

The quality of in-house gender equality policies seems to be only slightly dependent on the sector or the country, and more on the organisational culture. A pro-equality change among male employees on an organisational level appears to us to depend on three major points: the management, the informal organisational culture, and in-house institutions concerning men.

Best practice examples in the company sample, Coomundi and Hafner, are located in countries as different as Spain and Austria, which have different gender regimes and cultures. Coomundi is situated in the field of social services and Hafner in classical production trade.

Political regulations can centralise marginal groups or change the labelling of egalitarian-oriented men from "exotic" to "quite normal". In Scandinavia for instance, the interest in gender equality was great enough to establish parental leave regulations that represent an unrivalled form of egalitarianism. Here, active fathers are not a marginal group, but normal.

Best practice men in this survey can be seen as change agents if their example were to be used in counselling processes and gender training. This process will lead them to become "change agents."

It is very important here to change the label of gender from "female" to "concerning both/all genders." It is equally important to change the image of men from "standard" – the traditional male position in social and ideological terms (cf. Meuser 1998: 32-7, Kimmel 2004b: 339-43) – to "part of the gender system"[41].

---

41 Micheal Kimmel (1997) provides a striking biographical example of how the principles of standardisation work by the attribution of privileges, and thus cause the relational invisibility of the privileged: "During one meeting, a white woman and a black woman were discussing whether all women were, by definition, 'sisters,' because 'all women,' the white woman noted, had essentially the same experiences as women, and because 'all women' faced a common oppression by men. Thus, the white woman asserted that the fact that they were both women bonded them, in spite of racial differences. The black woman disagreed. 'When you wake up in the morning and look in the mirror, what do you see?' she asked. 'I see a woman,' replied the white woman. 'That's precisely the problem,'

In terms of career opportunities, a glass ceiling prevents women as well as marginalised men from entering higher positions. Many men in caring situations seem to go through a phase of gender role irritation that makes them feel they are not "real men". These traces of effemination demonstrate the profound relation between masculinity and labour.

For a long time now, men have not been perceived as part of the gender system; they have simply regarded themselves (and were regarded) as the "human standard". Women on the other hand were regarded as the "gendered sex" or simply as the exception from the male norm (cf. de Beauvoir 1972). This tradition helps to explain why men are not perceived as being addressed by gender policy in general and in organisations in particular. In our organisational research, we detected the following pattern: "Men in the company? They do not face problems" or "Men and equality? Never heard about it". At the same time, men are *the* labour standard gender, limited to wage work (cf. Böhnisch 2003, Gärtner and Riesenfeld 2004).

The "nothing wrong" attitude and the "expandable men" attitude complement one another. These attitudes also reflect the entrenched notion of men being standard/not gendered. That is to say, if men discursively leave the standard sector and "become more gendered", it should become more visible "what is wrong" in terms of work-life (im)balance, one-dimensional life paths, stress, health and mortality, quality of life, etc. Perceiving men as gendered and men as problematic sex category causes what Ohlendieck (2003) –referring to Judith Butler - calls "gender trouble" – at least on an organisational level. This might be a necessary transitional phase in the process leading to equality.

6.2 Equality in Gender Relations and Masculinity Models

It was one of the major aims of this research project to point out "best practices" in terms of a pro-equality change among men in a work-life context. A triangle of good change criteria was developed, comprising "satisfaction," "gender equality orientation," and "distance from traditional masculinity standards." Individuals acting with new strategies and effecting positive change accounted for the majority of our documentation. On the other hand,

responded the black woman. 'I see a black woman. To me, race is visible every day, because race is how I am not privileged in our culture. Race is invisible to you, because it's how you are privileged. It's a luxury, a privilege, not to see race all the time. It's why there will always be differences in our experience.' As I witnessed this exchange, I was startled, and groaned - more audibly, perhaps, than I had intended. Being the only man in the room, someone asked what my response had meant. 'Well,' I said, 'when I look in the mirror, I see a human being. I'm universally generalisable. As a middle class white man, I have no class, no race, no gender. I'm the generic person!' Sometimes, I like to think that it was on that day that I became a middle class white man." (ibid.: 187) there are lots of facts that describe a situation where men are left out of gender policy on a macro and organisational level. Starting with the thesis that "gender is female" and that men are traditionally seen as "standard, but not gendered," we argue for an different point of view in order to broaden the view of men and masculinities. In order to be effective, this perspective has to be implemented in several fields of policy and power structures.

"Good practices" were not a result of an ideological "break" with traditional identity nor an entire "new identity" or all-embracing "new masculinity" concept, but a sample of strategies pursued to cope with new situations in a good manner. Just because of these strategies depending on situations and contexts, conditional structures like state policy, labour regimes and organisation cultures, but also public discourses and cultural patterns build up a kind of opportunity structure[42] promoting a pro-equality change in gender relations. On individual levels and fields, we give recommendations, many of them derived from existing good practice examples. Thus, we can offer initiatives to be further developed as well as outlining ideas that describe what is currently happening.

6.2.1   Economy and State Policy Level

The Labour Market

Although, as we have argued, labour sphere changes promote beneficial modifications in gender relations and masculinity models, this not unequivocal. To some extent, changes can appear as obstacles or breaks. As we have shown, many pro-equality changes happen in the private sphere, while many companies remain neutral and passive to certain developments. Moreover, there are even real dangers for gender equality arising from labour market reforms, like in Germany. Here, social cutbacks and new job forms may lead to a re-traditionalisation of gender roles and arrangements (cf. Klopp 2003).

A process towards equality needs socio-economic security. This is valid in particular for egalitarian family arrangements, as a survey by Rüling, Kassner and Grottian (2004) suggests: "(C)ouples striving for a balanced arrangement are prepared to surrender a part of their wages. At the same time however, this type of arrangement is endangered by the risk incurred by a tight financial situation." (ibid.: 15, transl. M.G.)[43] As long as flexibility is not combined with

---

42   Opportunity structure as a term in the theory of action can be defined as a framework of rules people are encouraged to follow in order to achieve what is considered to be successful. In a structural sense, we might use it as a framework that provides opportunities for certain, intended processes.

43   Cultural developments in the west of the 1990s immediately suggest the conclusion that with the undermining of security, there is, in the course of the deregulation, a falling back on a purported basis of security that tends to rely on anti-modern concepts. Examples here

measures for social security, the way towards reconciliation of work and family life seems to be obstructed. New flexible work forms are mainly chosen by men with either good financial or psycho-social resources or in case of great pressure or as a result of a life crisis (e.g., death of a partner, disease).

Instead of promoting only flexibility among working people, the concept of "flexicurity" as a balance of labour market flexibility and social security of employees (Wilthagen 1998) should be promoted and implemented in labour policy. Adequate public compensation for the costs of bringing up children is necessary, so that financial losses do not have to be absorbed by over-work or taking on second and third jobs.

At this juncture, unions should step in and strongly demand a policy that reduces working hours across the board. Only this will allow for the work outside of professional employment to be done – namely, for the carrying out of the socially and individually necessary work of raising children, caring for the sick, and aiding the elderly. This would mean a shaping of the conditions of employment in accordance with their compatibility and coping with the vicissitudes of caring for those in need as well as dependents. The shaping of employment must not lead to a situation where discontinuous participation automatically relegates one to a career deemed to be inferior. Included here are measures that reduce the gender-related division of labour as well as the hierarchy of separate spheres of work.

Overtime hours should be cut back on or – contrary to current trends – made significantly more costly. Expenditure for children must be socially compensated so that financial losses are not made up for through more work (overtime, extra shifts, second jobs, etc.), which deny the employed 'individual(s)' an active presence in the family.

Although union representations of equal opportunity in relation to men are not sufficiently concrete or are marked by omissions,[44] their compatibility problems are increasingly being revealed in GM processes.[45]

As opposed to objective social policy, the general level of discussion of standard work tends to neglect the differentiation of work forms. The individualisation of people, especially men who work differently, could be solved

---

are the boom in esotericism or neo-nationalist 'sentimentalism' . In the 1990ies, popular gender representations have been based on a romantic critique of capitalism. For the discourse on masculinity, probably the most popular example is Robert Bly's Iron John (1993), but also Australian Biddulph (2003).

44 E.g., in the German trade unions' action programme Chancengleich (2003/2004), under 1. (field of action, occupational training/initial training) the culture of gender-specific career choice goes unmentioned and the perspective of an equality-oriented occupational preparation is totally unspecific. In advanced and additional training (2.) there is also no connection made to the area of men's problems. In any case, men are mentioned – albeit in a very general way – in connection with work schedules (3.) and (company) restructuring (5.).

45 The department in the German service industry union Ver.di that is responsible for questions concerning gender and equal opportunity conducted a study entitled: "Men Too Have a Reconciliation Problem."

by addressing those "non-standard" forms as limited, part time or, as Spitzley (2003) suggests, "shortened full-time" ("kurze Vollzeit") as different standard forms of employment.

Structural and Family Policy

Since gender models are a decisive factor for how men and women act and define themselves, it is not sufficient to limit initiatives to the socio-economic level. Normative questions concerning the family, parenthood and role behaviour (just to name a few areas) and corresponding measures aimed at degenderisation are necessary to render new and egalitarian models of gender-effective behaviour.

As in the past, German marital, familial and tax laws still support the image of the traditional housewife and female role model. This is clearly demonstrated in the case of divorce or the prohibition of marriage and adoption for homosexual couples. Tax laws, where they promote the traditional breadwinner arrangement should be changed. At least in Germany, the spouses' tax splitting[46] reproduces a main income situation and fosters men's traditional role in the labour market.

Beyond that, it is necessary to re-think custody laws in countries that emphatically favour the mother over the father, which was reaffirmed in Germany to a considerable extent over the past years. To the disadvantage of both sexes, handed-down attributes (establishing active motherhood and inactive fatherhood) are being reaffirmed.

Raising children is – as is the case with employment – not a personal pleasure but instead a socially necessary form of work. Based on these premises, it is important to make more funding and support available for child care facilities and all day schools and to construct the system of child raising along collective lines.

The Nordic regulations for father's leave should be considered seriously. Since 1993, 1 in 10 parental leave months has been "reserved" for fathers in Norway; since 1995, 30 of 450 days in Sweden; since 2000, 3 of 9 months are set aside for fathers in Iceland. This parity model was widely supported by the population at the time of its introduction.

Although one of this project's core recommendations, an equal parental law can only be a first step. We have also seen that fathers who reduce their working hours to spend time with small children almost always return to a full-time schedule after three years. Even with a better fathers leave system, policies fail in keeping active fatherhood without changing the work-life-

---

46 For spouses, both incomes are added, equally divided, and then the tax rate is determined. On account of this, one high earning person with one low earning marriage partner reduces their tax considerably (by thousands of Euros). A couple does not have to have children, but only be married to receive this benefit.

relation of men. In policy and in campaigns, it is important that men are addressed in all their diversity.

Men are taking different strategies to reduce working time or place work aside other components of life, and they differ a lot in their motives; we found caring-oriented (social) fathers as well as the socially obliged or the ones who want to have more time for partnership, others want to "stay alive", reflecting on the mental and physical risks of overwork. All these men may be door openers for change.

Although fatherhood can be, as shown above, a special and demanding change motivation in men's life, other reasons for non-standard work must be considered as well, like quality of life, work-life balance, closer relationships, social engagement etc. Frequently, discussions about change and support demands of men are restricted to fatherhood and caring. The results on hand tell us, that the other differing life concepts and strategies need support, too. These perspectives discursively should not be seen as competing to "caring". What is needed, is a differentiated view on different situations and demands of these groups in the process toward gender equality.

Gender Mainstreaming and Standards of Labour

The perception of men's diversity documented in this sample may help to break up the stereotype of a uniform masculinity.

In most cases, interviewees had a positive attitude toward the equality paradigm. Experiences outside of the breadwinner model are part of these men's lives and are not only ideas they hold. It is reasonable to employ these good practice examples as possible strategies in public discourse and in gender-equality processes.

On the other hand, men often do not feel recognised in gender-equality processes[47] – not least of all because of the "women only" or "gender is female" paradigm. The traditional definition of gender-equality processes was to promote women's options in the male work world. Men willing to change had and still have to develop individual strategies ("find my own way"). The traditional role model of "a man who has to do it on his own" prevents the construction of solid collective structures.

A discourse on gender policy that integrates men's perspective will help men to change from an isolated situation to being "concerned ones among other concerned ones." This increasing self-awareness probably fosters solidarity structures used by men to change their situation.

---

47   At the Berlin conference "Forum Männer in Theorie und Praxis der Geschlechterverhältnisse" (On Men's Role in Gender Mainstreaming Processes), July 9th to 10th 2004, company and gender experts confirmed that gender works as a "women only" issue; negative masculinity stereotypes were identified as obstacles blocking even willing men from taking part in these processes.

The instrument of gender mainstreaming "involves both women and men" and "makes gender-equality issues visible in mainstream of society" (Council of Europe 1998: 19). Taking men's issues more seriously would mean a particular promotion of change agents, integrating traditional female positions and activities such as child-care, part time work, or discontinuous work biographies.

Occupational choices are often limited in a gendered way and therefore should be broadened. The limitation for men is very obvious in caring and educational professions. Men in these sectors would not only provide new experiences for men in general, but also new male role models integrating caring activities.

Relevant indicators mentioned here should be included not only in gender-focussed management systems (like Gender Mainstreaming), but also in general labour and management standards like ISO 9001[48]. This is organised into sections like resource management, which includes the subsections human resources, infrastructure and work environment. All of these give space to include gender- and masculinity-focussed indicators, particularly human resources. In general, it deals with the quality and development of education, training, skills and experience. We recommend three steps to be followed in this operation:

1. Review of existing indicators in human resources with special attention to increasing flexible employment forms and gender-equal opportunities for men and women.
2. Enriching of indicators about work-family balanced policies in the organisation.
3. Enriching of indicators about flexible employment for men and women.

Although it is not entirely possible to standardise equality and balance promoting measures, several standard indicators can be developed and evaluated in practice. By this, processes in organisations dealing with the discussed topics can be made transparent and controlled. This may be one step toward ending the "individual strategies only" structure we detected in companies.

6.2.2 Level of Organisations

To a great extent, companies in this study's sample demonstrate a kind of gender equality rhetoric, legitimising the organisation's passivity in terms of including men in equality considerations and policies. The result is that men

---

48 ISO 9000 is a set of standards for quality management systems that is accepted around the world. Currently more than 90 countries have adopted ISO 9000 as national standards. Many companies require their suppliers to become registered to ISO 9001 and because of this, registered companies find that their market opportunities have increased. In addition, a company's compliance with ISO 9001 insures that it has a sound quality management system, and that is good business. The standards apply uniformly to organisations of any size or description.

who are actively caring or leaving the "breadwinning track" are forced to take a solitary path. This might restrict changes to groups of men with well-working private networks. But we also detected the importance of organisational cultures. For instance, when fathers leave, or specific structures relevant to men are set up or at least accepted (or not discriminated against), they are taken advantage of by employees. If it would become common to arrange internal information activities for (future) fathers, the company would signalise a different family and gender culture.

Active management – highlighted in some of our cases – can clearly change the climate and increase the acceptance of caring men. Because of this, "good practice management" can be found in very different lines of business under different country-specific conditions. Austrian production company Hafner and Spanish social service organisation Coomundi demonstrate this point. Hafner's management argues that a reconciliation policy helps to realise the company's goals. Even in times of social cutbacks, a win-win situation is to some extent good for the company because it helps to achieve common goals.

Company-internal research on work satisfaction would be a good first step in improving an organisation's culture. It should focus on professions rather than gender, but analyse the data in a way that is gender-aware. It would be beneficial to use items like career options, availability limits, work-life balance, and stress.

The relevance of the management role seems to confirm the top-down principle of gender mainstreaming. This makes the training of managers and decision-makers urgent: gender training in companies that leads to differentiated perspectives on men and masculinities has to start here. It is equally important that gender awareness be present at different levels in the organisations' hierarchies, as will be outlined in the following.

The Company-institutional Level

There are no existing contact persons for men nor any collective representations of their interests within companies. Due to this, problems and solutions become particularised, precarious, difficult and insecure. This mainly obstructs ways towards changes in gendered role models definitions and a collective social embodiment of these changes.

A basic precondition for improvement is to cast aside the traditional position of reducing men to "obstacles" to or "supporters" of gender equality. Men should be regarded as part of the company's gendered system and should be recognised as a group within the process, which has its own equality interests. Thus, all gender-relevant processes within the company and representatives steering these have to learn about the diversity of men in terms of living circumstances or models of masculinity and, through this, question their own stereotypes of masculinity and men. By doing this, the long-term reproduction of one-dimensional masculinity might be interrupted, enabling a wider spread recognition of different kinds of men and inviting men to be more a part of gender equality issues.

On a concrete level, men and equality have to become not only a "boss' matter," but also include work councils, human resources representatives, and department managers. Equality representative bodies should be composed of men and women to avoid a "women only" policy and atmosphere.

To support this process, further education in companies (or on an inter-organisational level) should focus on work-life balance, emphasising the relation between masculinity, work and health, which seems to be a topic worthy of specific treatment.

Public childcare should be complemented or supported by company kin-dergartens, and working time accounts give employees more flexibility.

The reconciliation of work and life is not seldom seen as an expense fac-tor, but it might be a win-win deal for employees and for companies. The German-Suisse economy research institute Prognos (2003) has revealed a number positive findings. Drawing upon "realistic" and rather "conservative" assumptions and exploring 10 German companies, the authors conclude: "All in all, the total costs of an inadequate reconciliation of job and family in 'Family Ltd.' could be decreased by 55% in the realistic scenario, and by 78% in the optimal scenario" (ibid.: 30, translation by M.G.).

Five central effects of family friendly policies:

- Reduction of staff turnover and a rise in the parental leave returnee quota,
- Shortened absence periods directly following the end of maternity bene-fits,
- Reduction of missed work and sick leave,
- Improved personnel marketing,
- Improved company image.

Research evidence like this should be received by politicians as well as deci-sion-makers in companies. Here it is of particular importance not to restrict "family friendliness" to women and mothers, but to include caring men.

6.2.3   The Area of Research and Education

Educational Policy

Individual attitudes and habitudes concerning labour, profession and life per-spectives can be described as a product of a gendered socialisation. Boys and girls have traditionally been (and are still) taught to behave and act socially according to the aforementioned gendered division of social spheres and work. Here, institutional education – most of all in schools – plays a major role. There are already some institutions and networks – e.g., the Network for Education Berlin/Brandenburg in Germany – that are becoming aware of the problem of gendered stereotypes in career choices and professional orientations, which are strongly connected to gender inequality.

First attempts have been undertaken in Germany to establish "boys' days":[49] projects that aim at giving boys the opportunity to act in "female" professional fields like health care, education and chemist shops (cf. Bentheim 2004). This might be a useful model to be implemented in other places.

According to UN-recommendations, more programmes should be developed "in schools and community contexts to provide boys and male youth with skills required for caring roles and domestic work." (United 2003)

It is also important to develop flexible programmes that are not too normative in a negative way. A starting point could be a gender-related reflection in kindergartens, schools and vocational institutions on three levels:

– The structural and interactional biases within the institution: the gender of the leader, board and staff, gendered ways of interaction and career courses stereotypes. Institutional role models are of particular importance for children and youngsters.
– Stereotypes and preoccupations in the minds of teaching and caring staff.
– Stereotypes and gendered models in educational and training media like books, programmes, comics, puppets, etc.

The aim would be to provide gender-sensible educational institutions, which work as a "companionship" for children and youngsters in preparing for their future. This may widen the range of life options towards a multitude of life and labour models.

Gender Research

Research can yield further contributions in the construction of a social world marked by gender equality. Scientific research should especially focus on dismantling the static image of men and deconstructively demonstrate the cultural involvement and historical differentiation within formations of masculinity (cf. Holter 2003a: 197). Through this process, further and also purposive change will become conceivable, feasible and implementable. This also frees up gender research from the traditional feminist discourse about men, which is by and large static and in which men are designated as the problem. This traditional discourse – although a historically important impetus – opens up too few possibilities of change and does not offer enough movement and mobilisation potential (cf. ibid: 93-101).

---

49   These are derived from already established "Girls' Days".

In the triangle of research, human resources development and gender policy, the cultural involvement and production of gender has to be understood more clearly, which calls for a transfer of knowledge of cultural studies and sociological evidence into practice. Within this process, an understanding of masculinity which is historical, changeable, dependent from socio-structure and gender relations has to be broadened and deepened.

Without supporting anti-feminist backlash, investigations should be carried out focusing on the price of dominant masculinity concepts for men: Masculine socialisation should also be perceived as a process of separation and repression; the theme of men as victims of violence should be taken up.[50]

Based on the development of survey methods, a new approach is necessary. Only a fraction of men and women live in a traditional nuclear family. Both families as well as employment have become differentiated. Unfortunately, a large part of empirical sociological research is still working with survey methods that presuppose a "normal family." Critical modernisation theories in gender research (e.g. Böhnisch 2003) can make visible the discontinuities in the work lives of men and women.

6.3 Closing Remarks

Regarding labour market changes, new perspectives on the diverse forms of work will be important. A multitude of work forms for men is already normal and will increase in the future. The gendered implications of this process are slowly becoming visible to the public. Having been established as "the human standard" in general, men have become the "forgotten" or "hidden" subject in terms of gender issues. This is most of all perceivable at the workplace. Organisations should evaluate and challenge their own demands and perspectives on men and women and not only continue to look at women's side.

This report cannot offer an instant remedy for social problems and challenges. But the authors think that urgent problems arising from the restructuring of labour and the changes in life patterns require a recognition of the particular problems and perspectives of men.

Although the sample is somewhat unique and does not represent the vast majority of men, it still presents the diversity of intrinsic change motives amidst different cultures and social conditions. Moreover, it offers first models for what we originally called "a life-enhancing time culture" for men inte-

---

50   Here, in particular, the Northern European men's research projects that are connected to NORFA (Nordic Research Academy) can serve as point of attachment and point of reference. The men's research in these countries out shows just how political practice is characterised by a strong orientation toward equality.

grating different spheres of life. Gender equality may not be a necessary implication of this model, but vice versa, the promoting of female professional options, reconciling partnership, care and work and changing cultural patterns towards equality require this change of and for men. Above all, gender equality policy and especially European policy of gender mainstreaming can only be successful when these problems and perspectives are included.

Our results, however, demonstrate how much is still to be done, even just in the field of research. As shown above, with the diversity among men, studies on change patterns of men by class and social settings continue to be necessary.

We are convinced that change processes can be advantageous to men. Their life expectancy in 1996 was 6.2 years less than women's. Although this relation has slightly improved, "the life expectancy increase of men still leaves them with a lower life expectancy than that of women 20 years ago." (White and Cash 2003: 29)

This appears, for instance, on the level of over-performing managers, who show particular ailments like fighting stigmata: "Diseases show, how important you are" (Höyng and Puchert 1998: 269). Climbing up the career ladder and exhausting ones physical basis corresponds as much with the unwritten laws of masculinity as perception or communication of a crisis don't. The connection between these risks and male life patterns may be closer than assumed. Beginning to take hold is the notion that sustainability and resource orientation are both individually and economically a very promising approach, or as Berlin Interbank lawyer Georg H. puts it:

Yes, work and free time. When work and free time are proportioned in a healthy way – I can recommend that to anyone. Nothing is worse than when the people come here in the morning and are grumpy. They say: 'Ugh, I'm here again already...' If you say however: 'I'm here for three weeks and after that I have two weeks to live my own life,' that, that's so much more satisfying. It's because the end of this period of work is foreseeable. It's not just endless. People count: 'Ugh, my next vacation is in six or seven months! Until then I have to come here everyday, ugh, only some kind of illness can save me.' That's a really shitty perspective on life.

References

Abril, P. (2002): Country Report Spain for Work Changes Gender. Labour Market, Flexibility and Family-Work Reconciliation (unpublished paper).

Acker, J. (1991): Hierarchies, Jobs, Bodies: A Theory of Gendered Organisations, in: Lorber J. and Farrell, S.A. (1991): The Social Construction of Gender, London, 162-179.

Acker, J. (1992): Gendering Organisational Theory, in: Mills, A.J. and Tancred, P. (Ed.) Gendering Organisational Analysis, London (248-260).

Adam, B. D. (2004): Care, Intimacy and Same-Sex Partnership in the 21st Century. Current Sociology, 52, 265-279.

Allafi, S. (1999): Erste Ergebnisse des Mikrozensus 1998. In: Wirtschaft und Statistik, H. 3, 163-170.

Amichai-Hamburger, Y. (2003): Country Report Israel for Work Changes Gender. Gender Issues in the Israeli Workforce (unpublished paper).

Antonovsky, A. (1987): Unraveling the Mystery of Health – How People Manage Stress and Stay Well, San Francisco.

Atanassova, M. and Dulevski, L. (2003): Country Report Bulgaria for Work Changes Gender (unpublished paper).

Beauvoir, S. de (1972): The Second Sex, New York.

Beck, U. (1986): Riskogesellschaft. Auf dem Weg in eine andere Moderne (Risk Society towards a New Moderity), Frankfurt am Main.

Beck-Gernsheim, E. (1994): Auf dem Weg in die postfamiliale Familie – Von der Notgemeinschaft zur Wahlverwandtschaft (Towards a postfamilial family), in: Beck, U. and Beck-Gernsheim, E. (Ed.): Riskante Freiheiten (Risky liberties), Frankfurt/Main, 115-138.

Behnke, C. (2000): „Und es war immer, immer der Mann". Deutungsmuster von Mannsein und Männlichkeit im Milieuvergleich ("And Always, Always it has been the Man"), in: Bosse, H. and King, V. (Ed.): Männlichkeitsentwürfe. Wandlungen und Widerstände im Geschlechterverhältnis (Outlines of Masculinity), Frankfurt/Main, 124-138.

Berger, P.A. (1996): Individualisierung. Statusunsicherheit und Erfahrungsvielfalt (Individualisation). Opladen.

Biddulph, S. (2003): Männer auf der Suche. Sieben Schritte zur Befreiung (Translation of: Biddulph 1998: Manhood), München.

Bischoff, J. and Detje, R. (1989): Massengesellschaft und Individualität – Krise des "Fordismus" und die Strategie der Linken (Mass Society and Individuality), Hamburg.

Bly , R. (1993) Eisenhanns. Ein Buch über Männer (Iron John), München.

Böheim, R. and M.P. Taylor (2000b): The Search for Success: Do the Unemployed Find Stable Employment?, ISER WP 2000-5, University of Essex.

Böhnisch, L. (2003): Die Entgrenzung der Männlichkeit. Verstörungen und Formierungen des Mannseins im gesellschaftlichen Übergang (Removing the Borders of Masculinity), Opladen.

Bosch, G. (2001): Konturen eines neuen Normalarbeitszeitverhältnisses (Outlines of a New Standard Working Time). WSI-Mitteilungen, Vol. 4, 219-41.

Bosch, G., and Wagner, A. (2003): Dienstleistungsgesellschaften in Europa und Ursachen für das Wachstum der Dienstleistungsbeschäftigung (Service Societies in Europe and Reasons for the Growth of Employment in Services) . In: Kölner Zeitschrift für Soziologie und Sozialpsychologie, 3/2003, 475-499.

Bourdieu, P. (1984): Distinction. A Social Critique of the Judgement of Taste, Cambridge.

Bourdieu, P. (1990): The Logic of Practice, Stanford.

Bourdieu, P. (2000): Die männliche Herrschaft (The Male Domination), in: Dölling, I. and Krais, B. (Ed.) Ein alltägliches Spiel (An Everyday Game), Frankfurt/Main, 153-217.

Brandt, B. and Kvande, E. (2002): Reflexive Fathers: Negotiating Parental Leave and Working Life. In: Gender, Work and Organization, 9, (2), 186-203.

Brouwer, I. and Wierda, E. (1998): The Combination Model: Child Care and the Part Time Labour Supply of Men in the Dutch Welfare State, in: Schippers, J., Siegers, J. and Jong-Gierveld, J. de (Eds.) Child Care and Female Labour Supply in the Netherlands. Amsterdam: Thesis Publishers, 133-162.

Bruyn-Hundt, M. (1996): Scenarios for a Redistribution of Unpaid Work in the Netherlands, in: Feminist Economics, 2 (3), 129-133.

Buchmann, M., Kriesi and I.; Sacchi, S. 2004: Labor-Market Structures and Women's Paid Work: Opportunities and Constrains in the Swiss Labor Market. In: Zollinger Giele, J. and Holst, E. (Eds.): Changing Life Patterns in Western Societies. Amsterdam, 165-188.

Butler, J. (1990): Gender Trouble. Feminism and the Subversion of Identity, New York/London.

Carrigan T., Connell R. W. and Lee J. (1996): Ansätze zu einer neuen Soziologie der Männlichkeit (Approaches to a New Sociology of Masculinity), in: BauSteine-Männer (Ed.): Kritische Männerforschung. Neue Ansätze in der Geschlechtertheorie (Critical Men's Research), Berlin and Hamburg, 38-75.

Chancengleich (2003/2004): Aktionsprogramm des DGB und der Mitgliedsgewerkschaften. (Equal Opportunity Action Program of German Trade Unions).

Cockburn, C. (1985): Machinery of Dominance: Women, Men and Technological Know-how. London.

Cockburn, C. (1991): In the Way of Women. Men's Resistance to Sex Equality in Organisations, London.

Connell, R. W. (1987): Gender and Power: Society, the Person and Sexual Politics, Cambridge.

Connell, R. W. (1995): Masculinities, Berkeley and Los Angeles.

Connell, R. W. (1999): Der gemachte Mann. Konstruktion und Krise von Männlichkeiten (German edition of: Connell 1995: Masculinities), Opladen.

Deutsch, J. and Silber, J. (2003): Comparing Segregation by Gender in the Labor Force Across Ten European Countries in the 1990s. Ramat Gan (unpublished paper).

Döge, P. (2004): Vom Geschlecht zur Differenz – Politikwissenschaft im Zeichen von Diversity (From Gender to Difference), in: Döge, P., Kassner, K. and Schambach, G. (eds.): Schaustelle Gender. Aktuelle Beiträge sozialwissenschaftlicher Geschlechterforschung (Recent Contributions to Sociological Gender Research), Bielefeld, 61-83.

Dörr M. (1997), Helden der Arbeit. Transformation der Arbeitsgesellschaft und männliche Identität (Heroes of Labour), in: Psychosozial, 20, IV 2003, (Nr. 70), 71-93.

EC (2003): European Commission, Directorate-General for Employment and Social Affairs. Employment in Europe 2003 – Recent Trends and Prospects, Luxembourg.

Engelbrech G. and Reinberg A., 1997: Frauen und Männer in der Beschäftigungskrise der 90er Jahre – Entwicklung der Erwerbstätigkeit in West und Ost nach Branchen, Berufen und Qualifikationen (Women and Men in the 90ies Occupational Crisis). Eine Untersuchung auf Basis von Mikrozensus-Daten, IAB-Werkstattbericht Nr. 11, Nürnberg.

Engelbrech, G. (1998): Erziehungsurlaub im Ost-West-Vergleich (Parental Leave – A Comparison between East and West Germany), in: Arbeit und Arbeitsrecht, Jg. 53, H. 2., 57-58.

European Foundation for the Improvement of Living and Working Conditions (2003a): A New Organisation of Time Over Working Life (Summary) Loughlinstown.

European Foundation for the Improvement of Living and Working Conditions (2003b): A New Organisation of Time Over Working Life (Report), Loughlinstown.

European Foundation for the Improvement of Living and Working Conditions (2002): Working time preferences in sixteen European countries. Office for Official Publications of the European Communities, Luxembourg.

Falter, J.-M. (2002): Self-employment Choice of Men in Switzerland (unpublished paper).

Filipp, S.-H. (2000): Selbstkonzeptforschung in der Retrospektive und Prospektive (Researching concepts of the self in retrospetive and prospective), in: Greve, W. (Ed.): Psychologie des Selbst (Psychology of the Self), Weinheim, 7-14.

Finder, R. and Blaschke, S. (1999): Tendenzen im Dienstleistungssektor, Tendenzen der Frauenbeschäftigung (Tendecies in Service Sector, Tendencies in Women's Employment). Bericht des Forschungszentrums W.A.S. im Auftrag der Frauengrundsatzabteilung, BMAGS, Wien.

Fossestøl, K. et al. (2004): Relasjonsmestrere - om kunnskapsarbeid i det nye arbeidslivet (Relations Masters – Knowledge Work in the New Working Life), Oslo.

Fthenakis, W. E. and Minsel, B. (2001): Die Rolle des Vaters in der Familie. Zusammenfassung des Forschungsberichts (The Role of the Father in the Family), Berlin.

Gärtner, C. (2000): Männer zwischen Familie und Beruf. Biographische Konstruktionen einer Doppelorientierung (Men between Family and Profession), University of Bremen (unpublished diploma thesis).

Gärtner, M. and Riesenfeld, V. (2004): Geld oder Leben? Männliche Erwerbsorientierung und neue Lebensmodelle unter veränderten Arbeitsmarktbedingungen (Money or Life?) in: Boekle, B. and Ruf, M.: Eine Frage des Geschlechts. Ein Gender Reader (A Question of Gender), Wiesbaden, 87-104.

Gershuny, Jonathan (2003): Changing Times. Work and Leisure in Postindustrial Society. Oxford University Press, Oxford

Gilmore, D. D. (1990): Manhood in the Making: Cultural Concepts of Masculinity, New Haven.

Goldin, C. (1990): Understanding the Gender Gap: An Economic History of American Women, New York.

Gregoritsch, P., Kalmár, M. and Wagner-Pinter, M. (2000): Einkommen von Frauen und Männern in unselbständiger Beschäftigung (Earnings on Men and Women in Ocupations of Employment). Endbericht. Studie im Auftrag des Bundesministeriums für Wirtschaft und Arbeit, Abteilung für grundsätzliche Angelegenheiten der Frauen, Wien.

Greve, W. (2000): Die Psychologie des Selbst – Konturen eines Forschungsthemas (The Psychology of the Self), in: Greve, W. (Ed.): Psychologie des Selbst (The Psychology of the Self), Weinheim, 15-36.

Hagenkort, S. (Ed. 2003): German Labour Market Trends. Federal Statistical Office, The spotlight series, Wiesbaden.

Hallgren, A. et. al. (1999): Jämstalldhet och lönsamhet (Gender Equality and Profitability). Närings- och teknologiutvecklingsverket (NUTEK), Rapport 061, Stockholm.

Hanchane, S. (2002): The Socio-Demographic Determinants of the Professional Insertion of Youth on the Labor Market: A Longitudinal Analysis by Gender Based on French Data. Aix-en-Provence (unpublished paper).

Hausen, K. (Ed. 1993): Geschlechterhierarchie und Arbeitsteilung. Zur Geschichte ungleicher Erwerbschancen von Männern und Frauen (Gender Hierarchie and Division of Labour), Göttingen.

Hearn, J. et al. (Ed. 1998): The Sexuality of Organisation, London.

Hearn, J. et. al. (2002): Critical Studies of Men in Ten European Countries 1. Men and Masculinities, 4, 380-408.

Heintz, B., Nadai, E., Fischer, R. and Ummel, H. (1997): Ungleich unter Gleichen (Unequal among Equals). Studien zur geschlechtsspezifischen Segregation des Arbeitsmarktes, Frankfurt/New York.

Hentges, G., Meyer, M.-H., Flecker, J., Kirschenhofer, S., Thoft, E., Grinderslev, E. and Balazs, G. (2003): The Abandoned Worker. Socio-Economic Change and the Attraction of Right-Wing Populism. European Synthesis Report on Qualitative Findings. Deliverable 3 for the FP5-project SIREN. Vienna.

Higgins, E.T. (1987): Self-Discrepancy: A Theory Relating Self and Affect. Psychological Review, 94, 319-340.

Hipp, L. (2004): Teilzeitarbeit. Von einer Arbeitsmarktfalle für Frauen zu einer Arbeitsmarktbrücke für beide Geschlechter? (Part Time Work), in: Boekle, B. and Ruf, M. (2004): Eine Frage des Geschlechts. Ein Gender Reader, Wiesbaden, 73-85.

Hirdman, Y. (1988): Genussystemet – reflexioner kring kvinnors sociala underordning (The Gender System – Reflections on the Submission of Women). Kvinnovetenskapligt Tidsskrift, 3, 49-63.

Holter, Ø. G. (1981): Sjekking, kjærlighet og kjønnsmarked (Dating, Love and Gender Market). Pax, Oslo.

Holter, Ø. G. (1989): Menn, Oslo.

Holter, Ø. G. (1994): Likeverd 1994? Inntrykk fra en undersøkelse av familieforhold og holdninger til likestilling (Equality 1994?). Sosiologisk Tidsskrift, 4, 303-316.

Holter, Ø. G. (1997a): Work, Gender and the Future. Journal of Organisational Change Management, 10, 167-174.

Holter, Ø. G. (1997b): Gender, Patriarchy and Capitalism – A Social Forms Analysis. Dr. philos thesis sociology, Work Research Institute, Oslo.

Holter, Ø. G. (2003a): Can Men Do It? Men and gender equality – the Nordic experience. TemaNord: 510, Copenhagen.

Holter, Ø.G. (2003b): Country Report Norway for Work Changes Gender (unpublished paper).

Holter, Ø. G. (2004): Norway Work Changes Gender WP3 report, Oslo (unpublished).

Holter, Ø. G. and Aarseth, H. (1993): Menns livssammenheng (Men's Life Context), Oslo.

Holter, Ø. G., Karlsen B, and Salomon, R. (1998): Omstillinger i arbeidslivet (Restructuring in Working Life), Oslo.

Holter, Ø.G., Gärtner, M., Riesenfeld, V. and Scambor, E. (2003): Men's Work and Life. A Six Country European Study of Labour, Gender and Welfare. Report on Organisation Research in Work Changes Gender (unpublished paper).

Honnegger, C. (1991): Die Ordnung der Geschlechter. Die Wissenschaft vom Menschen und das Weib (The Organisation of Genders), Frankfurt.

Höyng, S. and Gärtner, M. (2003): Country Report Germany for Work Changes Gender (unpublished paper).

Höyng, S. and Puchert, R. (1998): Die Verhinderung der beruflichen Gleichstellung. Männliche Verhaltensweisen und männerbündische Kultur (The Frustration of Professional Equality), Bielefeld.

Jalmert, L. (1984): Den svenske mannen (The Swedish Man), Stockholm.

Jenkins, S.P. and O'Leary, N.C. (1997): Gender Differentials in Domestic Work, Market Work, and Total Work Time: UK Time Budget Survey Evidence for 1974/5 and 1987, Scottish Journal of Political Economy, 44(2), 153-164.

Kapeller, D., Kreimer, M. and Leitner, A. (1999): Hemmnisse der Frauenerwerbstätigkeit (Obstacles for Female Occupation). Forschungsberichte aus Sozial- und Arbeitsmarktpolitik, Nr. 62, Bundesministerium für Arbeit, Gesundheit und Soziales, Wien.

Keupp, H., Ahbe, T., Gmür, W., Höfer, R., Mitzscherlich, B., Kraus, W. and Straus, F. (1999): Identitätskonstruktionen. Das Patchwork der Identitäten in der Spätmoderne (Constructions of Identity), Reinbek bei Hamburg.

Kimmel, M. (2004a): The Gendered Society (2nd ed.). New York.

Kimmel, M. (2004b): Frauenforschung, Männerforschung, Geschlechterforschung: einige persönliche Überlegungen (Women's Studies, Men's Studies, Gender Studies), in: Meuser, M. and Neusüß, C.: Gender Mainstreaming. Konzepte – Handlungsfelder – Instrumente, Bonn, 337-355.

Kleber, M. (1988): Arbeitsmarktsegmentation nach dem Geschlecht. Eine kritische Analyse ökonomischer Theorien über Frauenarbeit und Frauenlöhne (Labor Market Segmentation by Gender), München.

Klenner, Geschlechtergleicheit in Deutschland? (Gender Fairness in Germany?), in: Aus Politik und Zeitgeschichte B 33-34, 2002, S.18

Klopp, Tina (2003): Kinder, Küche, Kurzzeitjobs (Children, Kitchen, Short-time Jobs), in: Konkret 09/2003.

Kohn, M. and Schooler, C. (1983): Work and Personality – an Inquiry into the Impact of Social Stratification, Norwood.

Kreckel, R. (1993): Doppelte Vergesellschaftung und geschlechtsspezifische Arbeits-marktstrukturierung (Double Socialisation and the Gender Specific Order of the Labour Market) , in: Petra Frerichs/ Margareta Steinrücke (Ed.): Soziale Un-gleichheit und Geschlechterverhältnis (Social Inequality and Gender Relations), Schriftenreihe "Sozialstrukturanalyse", Band 3, Opladen, 51-64.

Kreimer, M. (1998): Frauenarbeit und Flexibilisierung (Women's Work and Increa-sing Flexibility), in: Zilian, H.G. and Flecker, J. (Eds.): Flexibilisierung – Prob-lem oder Lösung? (Flexibilisation – Problem or Solution?) Berlin, 137-162.

Kreimer, M. (2003): (Un-)Vollkommene Konkurrenz auf Arbeitsmärkten? Zur Be-deutung der Arbeitsteilung für Frauen- und Männerkarrieren. (Im-)Perfect Com-petition on Labour Markets?), Graz.

Kreimer, M., Scambor, E., Scambor C., Obendrauf, W (2003): Country Report Aus-tria for Work Changes Gender (unpublished paper).

Kreimer, Margareta (1999): Arbeitsteilung als Diskriminierungsmechanismus (Divisi-on of Labour as a Mechanism of Discrimination). Theorie und Empirie ge-schlechtsspezifischer Arbeitsmarktsegregation, Frankfurt u.a.

Kroll, R. (2002): Metzler Lexikon Gender Studies, Stuttgart.

Kuhn, M. and McPartland, T.S. (1954): An Empirical Investigation of Self-Attitudes. American Sociological Review, 19, 68-76.

Lange, Ralf (1998): Männer, Macht, Management. Zur sozialen Konstruktion von hegemonialer Männlichkeit in Organisationen (Men, Power, Management) in: Widersprüche, Heft 67, 45-61.

Laustsen, M. and Sjørup, K. 2003 Hvad kvinder og mænd bruger tiden til – om tids-mæssig ligestilling i danske familier (How Women and Men spend Their Time). Socialforskningsinstituttet 03:08, Copenhagen.

Layte, R. (1999): Divided Time. Gender, Paid Employment and Domestic Labour, Aldershot.

Lehner, E. (1999): Arbeit, das Lebenselixier von Männern. Männliche Existenz im Spannungsfeld von Familie und Beruf (Work, the Men's Elixir). Organisations-beratung, Supervision, Coaching, 6, 101-116.

Lehner, E. (2003): Frauen-, Männer-, Geschlechterpolitik oder: Wer braucht Männer-politik? (Women Policy, Men Policy, Gender Policy or: Who Needs Men Pol-icy?), in: Zulehner, P. M. (Ed.): MannsBilder. Ein Jahrzehnt Männerentwicklung (Pictures of the Male), Ostfildern, 225-235.

Lenz, H.-J. (2001): Mann versus Opfer (Man versus Victim), in: BauSteineMänner (Ed.): Kritische Männerforschung (Critical Men's Studies), Hamburg, 359-396.

Linville, P.W. (1985): Self-Complexity and Affective Extremity: Don't Put All your Eggs in One Cognitive Basket. Social Cognition, 3, 94-120.

Linville, P.W. (1987): Self-Complexity as a Cognitive Buffer against Stress-Related Illness and Depression. Journal of Personality and Social Psychology, 52, 663-676.

Maier, F. (1991): Patriarchale Arbeitsmarktstrukturen. Das Phänomen geschlechts-spezifisch gespaltener Arbeitsmärkte in Ost und West (The Phenomenon of Gen-der Specific Divided Labour Markets), in: Feministische Studien, 9 (1), 107-116.

Maihofer, A.: Geschlecht als Existenzweise. Macht, Moral, Recht und Geschlechter-differenz (Gender as a Way of Existence). Frankfurt a.M. 1995.

Marcia, J.E., Waterman, A.S., Matteson, D.R., Archer, S.L. and Orlofsky, J.L. (1993): Ego Identity. A Handbook for Psychological Research, New York.

Meuser, M. (1998): Geschlecht und Männlichkeit. Soziologische Theorie und kulturelle Deutungsmuster (Gender and Masculinity), Opladen.

Meuser M. (2000): Perspektiven einer Soziologie der Männlichkeit (Perspectives of a Sociology of Masculinity), in: Janshen, D. (Ed.): Blickwechsel: Der neue Dialog zwischen Frauen- und Männerforschung (Changing views. The New Dialogue between Women's and Men's Studies), Frankfurt/Main, 47-79.

Meuser, M. and Behnke, C. (1998): Tausendundeine Männlichkeit? Männlichkeitsmuster und sozialstrukturelle Einbindungen (A Thousand and One Masculinities?), in: Widersprüche, Heft 67, 18.Jg., Bielefeld, 7-25.

Monee (1999): The Monee Project: Women in Transition. Unicef Regional Monitoring Report 6, Florence.

Moscovici, S. (1976): Social Influence and Social Change, London.

Mühlberger, U. (1998): Atypische Beschäftigung in Österreich. Sozial- und arbeitsmarktpolitische Implikationen atypischer Beschäftigungsverhältnisse (Atypical Occupation in Austria), in: WISO – Wirtschafts- und sozialpolitische Zeitschrift, 21 (4), 73-102.

Münz, R. and Neyer, G. (1986): Frauenarbeit und Mutterschutz in Österreich. Ein historischer Überblick (Female Labour and Maternity Protection in Austria), in: Münz, R., Neyer, G. and Pelz, M.: Frauenarbeit, Karenzurlaub und berufliche Wiedereingliederung (Female Labour, Parental Leave and Occupational Reahbilitation). Veröffentlichungen des österreichischen Instituts für Arbeitsmarktpolitik, Heft XXX, Linz, 13-76.

Nef, R. (2001): Vorwort: Der Lebensunternehmer, die Lebensunternehmerin – Leitbild für die Zukunft (Preface: The Life Businessmen, the Life Businesswoman – Mission Statement for the Future), in: Nef, R. and Steimer, G. (Ed.): Arbeits- und Lebensformen der Zukunft (Work and Life Forms of the Future), Zürich, 3-5.

Neuman, S. and Ziderman, A. (2002): Work Histories of Israeli Men and Women, 1983-1995, Ramat Gan (unpublished paper).

NUTEK (1999): Hallgren, A. et.al, Jämstalldhet och lönsamhet (Gender Equality and Profitability). Närings- och teknologiutvecklingsverket (NUTEK), Rapport 061-1999, Stockholm

Ohlendieck, L. (2003): Gender Trouble in Organisationen und Netzwerken (Gender Trouble in Organisations and Networks), in: Pasero, U. and Weinbach C. (Ed.): Frauen, Männer, Gender Trouble. Systemtheoretische Essays (Women, Men, Gender Trouble), Frankfurt/Main, 171-185.

Oschmiansky, H. and Schmid, G. (2000): Wandel der Erwerbsformen. Berlin und die Bundesrepublik im Vergleich (Changes of Labour Forms), Berlin.

Pateman, C. (1988): The Sexual Contract, Oxford.

Peinelt-Jordan, K. (1996): Männer zwischen Familie und Beruf – ein Anwendungsfall für die Individualisierung der Personalpolitik (Men Between Family and Occupation), München.

Pfau-Effinger, B. 1998: Arbeitsmarkt- und Familiendynamik in Europa – Theoretischen Grundlagen der vergleichenden Analyse (Labour Market and Family Dynamics), in: Geisler, B., Maier, F. and Pfau-Effinger, B. (Eds.), FrauenArbeitsMarkt – Der Beitrag der Frauenforschung zur sozio-ökonomischen Theorieentwicklung (WomenLabourMarket), Berlin, 177-194.

Puchert, R., Raschke, C. and Höyng, S. (1995): Probleme der innerbetrieblichen Gleichstellungspolitik unter spezieller Berücksichtigung der Reaktionen von

Männern auf Frauenfördermaßnahmen (Problems of Company-Internal Equality Policy, with Special Regards to Men's Reactions on Women's Affirmative Action). Abschlussbericht zum Forschungsprojekt), Berlin.

Rabe-Kleberg U. (1987): Frauenberufe – Zur Segmentierung der Berufswelt (Women's Jobs), Bielefeld.

Ramos, X. (2002): Labour Market Flexibility Temporary Jobs and Unemployment Duration (unpublished paper).

Ramos, X. (2003): Domestic Work Time and Gender Differentials in Great Britain 1992-1998: How Do 'New' Men Look Like? (unpublished paper).

Reskin, B. and Padavic, I. (1994): Women and Men at Work, London, New Dehli.

Rubery, J. (1978): Structured Labour Markets, Worker Organization and Low Pay, in: Cambridge Journal of Economics, 2 (1), 17-36.

Rüling A., Kassner, K. and Grottian, P. (2004): Geschlechterdemokratie leben. Junge Eltern zwischen Familienpolitik und Alltagserfahrungen (Living Gender Democracy). In: Aus Politik und Zeitgeschichte 19, 11-18.

Scambor, Ch. and Scambor, E. (2004): „Bist ein Mann, gehst arbeiten..." Männer zwischen Produktions- und Reproduktionsarbeit und die Rolle der Unternehmen ("Go and work, if you are a man...") (in print).

Spitzley, H. (2003): Kurze Vollzeit für alle. Plädoyer für eine andere Arbeitskultur (Short Full Time for Everybody. Pleading for a Different Working Culture), in: Frankfurter Rundschau, 10 September 2003, 9.

Straus, F. (2001a): Qualitative Netzwerkanalyse (Qualitative Network Analysis), IPP Munich, (unpublished paper).

Straus, F. (2001b): Netzwerkanalyse (Network Analysis), in: Keupp, H. and Weber, K. (Ed.): Psychologie. Ein Grundkurs (Psychology. A Basic Course), Reinbek bei Hamburg (276-302).

Strauss, A. and Corbin, J. (1998): Basics of Qualitative Research, Thousand Oaks, London, New Delhi.

Tálos, E. (1999): Atypische Beschäftigung in Österreich (Atypical Occupation in Austria), in: Tálos, E. (Ed.): Atpypische Beschäftigung. Internationale Trends und sozialstaatliche Regelungen (Atypical Occupation). Wien, 252-284.

Taylor, F. W. (1913): Die Grundsätze wissenschaftlicher Betriebsführung (The Principles of Scientific Management), München.

Thorsrud, E. (1973): Strategi for forandring i arbeidslivet (Strategy for Change in Working Life), in: Holter, H. and Hem, L. (Ed.): Sosialpsykologi, Oslo.

UN Statistics Division (2002): The World's Women 2000: Trends and Statistics (Table 5.B) "Part-Time Employment". Data for 1996-1998.

UN (2003): United Nations Economic and Social Council, Commission on the Status of Women. Thematic Issue before the Commission: The Role of Men and Boys in Achieving Gender Equality. Report of the Secretary-General, New York.

Vester, M. and Gardemin, G. (2001): Milieu und Klassenstruktur. Auflösung, Kontinuität oder Wandel der Klassengesellschaft? (Social Backgrounds and Class Structure), in: Rademacher, C. and Wiechens, P. (Ed.): Geschlecht – Ethnizität – Klasse (Gender – Ethnicity – Class), Opladen, 219-274.

Vester, M., von Oertzen, P., Geiling, H., Hermann, T. and Müller, D. (2001): Soziales Milieu im gesellschaftlichen Strukturwandel. Zwischen Integration und Ausgrenzung (Social Ambience in Societal Structural Change), Frankfurt/Main.

Völger, G. and von Welck, K. (Ed.; 1990): Männerbande und Männerbünde. Zur Rolle des Mannes im Kulturvergleich (Men's Alliances and Men's Lots), Colone.

Wagner, A.; Lehndorff, S. 2003: Zur Entwicklung der Arbeitszeiten von Männern und Frauen in Ost- und Westdeutschland – Eine Analyse mit Daten des Mikrozensus (On the Development of Male and Female Working Hours in East and West Germany). Dokumentation der Auftaktveranstaltung am 25. Juni 2003 in Berlin zur tarifpolitischen Initiative von ver.di.

Walby, S. (2002): Reducing Gendered Violence, in: Eriksson, M., Nenol, A. and Nilsen, M. M. (Ed): Køn och våld i Norden (Gender and violence in the Nordic countries). Report from a conference in Køge, Denmark, 23-24 November 2001. TemaNord 545.

Weber, M. (1980): Wirtschaft und Gesellschaft (Economy and Society), Köln.

Werneck, H. (1998): Übergang zur Vaterschaft. Auf der Suche nach den „Neuen Vätern" (Transition into Fatherhood), Vienna.

West, C. and Fenstermaker, S. (1995): Doing Difference. in: Gender and Society 9, 8-37.

Wetterer, A. (1993): Professionalisierung und Geschlechterhierarchie. Vom kollektiven Frauenausschluss zur Integration mit beschränkten Möglichkeiten (Professionalisation and Gender Hierarchy), Kassel.

White, A. and Cash, K. (2003): A Report on the State of Men's Health across 17 European Countries. The European Men's Health Forum, Brussels.

Wilthagen, T. (1998): Flexicurity: A New Paradigm for Labour Market Policy Reform? Discussion Paper FS-I 98-202, Berlin.

Wilz, S. M. (2002): Organisation und Geschlecht. Strukturelle Bindungen und kontingente Kopplungen (Organisation and Gender), Opladen.

Winker, G. (1998): Neue Lebensentwürfe von Frauen durch flexible Arbeit in der Informationsgesellschaft (New Life Concepts of Women by Flexible Work in the Information Society), in: Bundesministerin für Frauenangelegenheiten und Verbraucherschutz (Ed.): Arbeit 2002, Zukunft der Frauen. Arbeitsmarkt – Chancengleichheit – Informations- und Kommunikationstechnologien (Women's Future). Dokumentation der EU-Konferenz vom 3.-4. September 1998 in Linz. Wien, 142-167.

Witz, A. and Savage, M. (Ed.; 1992): Gender and Bureaucracy, Oxford, Cambrigde.

Zulehner, P. M. (Ed.; 2003): MannsBilder. Ein Jahrzehnt Männerentwicklung (Pictures of the Male. A Decade of Men's Development), Ostfildern.

Zulehner, P. M. and Volz, R. (1998): Männer im Aufbruch. Wie Deutschlands Männer sich selbst und wie Frauen sie sehen (Men in Transition. How German Men See themselves and how they are Seen by their Wives), Ostfildern.

Zulehner, P.M. and Slama, A. (1994): Österreichs Männer unterwegs zum neuen Mann? Wie Österreichs Männer sich selbst sehen und wie die Frauen sie einschätzen (Austrian Men on their Way to the New Man?), Vienna.

Internet References (December 31, 2004)

Arbeitsamt (2000): Arbeitsmarkt in Deutschland, at: http://www.pub.arbeitsamt. de/hst/services/anba/jg_2000/heft042000_frauen/beschaeftigung2.shtml.

Corral, A. and Isusi, I. (2003) at: Part Time Work in Europe, European Foundation for the Improvement of Living and Working Conditions, at: www. eurofound.eu.int/publications/files/EF0441EN.pdf.

CROME reports at: http://www.cromenet.org.

Galinsky, E. et. al. (2003): Leaders in a Global Economy – A Study of Executive Women and Men, at: http://www.catalystwomen.org/ bookstore/files/exe/Global LeadersExecSumm.pdf.

Gräfinger, E. (2001): Väter im Erziehungsurlaub: Reaktionen, Erfahrungen, Erkenntnisse (Men in Parental Leave), at: http://www.familienhandbuch.de/cmain/ f_Aktuelles/a_Elternschaft/s_905.html .

Kimmel, M. (1997): Integrating Men into the Curriculum, at: http://www.law.duke. edu/journals/djglp/articles/gen4p181.htm.

Krauss, A.N. (2002): Women in the Economy and the Labor Force in Israel, in: Women in Israel - Compendium of Data and Information, Part 4 at: http://www. iwn.org.il/pdf%5Cch4sub1eng.pdf.

Kreimer, M. (2002): Väterkarenz (Fathers' Leave). Work-Changes-Gender working paper, at: www.maennerberatung.at/download/research_vaeterkarenz.pdf.

LIS 2004: The Luxemburg Income Study. at: http://www.lisproject.org/keyfigures/ ineqtable.htm.

Prognos (2003): Betriebswirtschaftliche Effekte familienfreundlicher Maßnahmen (Operation al Effects of Family Friedly Actions), on behalf the German Federal Ministry of Family, Seniors, Women and Youth, at: http://www.bmfsfj.de/ RedaktionBMFSFJ/Broschuerenstelle/Pdf-Anlagen/PRM-24912-Broschure-Betriebswirtschaftli,property=pdf.pdf.

Scambor, Ch., Scambor, E. and Voitle, J. (2003): Men in Caring Situations. Report Pre-Study Austria WP3., at: www.maennerberatung.at/download/research_ menincaringsituations.pdf

Sørensen, B. A. (2003): Journalister i arbeid - en reise i tre tiårs redaksjonsmiljøer (Journalists at Work). Norsk Journalistlag, Oslo, at: http://www.nj.no/ Arbeidsforhold/Arbeidsmiljo/?module=Articles;action=Article.publicShow;ID=1523.

Venable, D. (2002): The Wage Gap Myth, Brief Analysis 392, National Center for Policy Analysis, at: http://www.ncpa.org/pub/ba/ba392.